Cinema Wars

Cinema Wars

Hollywood Film and Politics in the Bush-Cheney Era

Douglas Kellner

A John Wiley & Sons, Ltd., Publication

This edition first published 2010
© 2010 Douglas Kellner

Blackwell Publishing was acquired by John Wiley & Sons in February 2007. Blackwell's publishing program has been merged with Wiley's global Scientific, Technical, and Medical business to form Wiley-Blackwell.

Registered Office
John Wiley & Sons Ltd, The Atrium, Southern Gate, Chichester, West Sussex, PO19 8SQ, United Kingdom

Editorial Offices
350 Main Street, Malden, MA 02148–5020, USA
9600 Garsington Road, Oxford, OX4 2DQ, UK
The Atrium, Southern Gate, Chichester, West Sussex, PO19 8SQ, UK

For details of our global editorial offices, for customer services, and for information about how to apply for permission to reuse the copyright material in this book please see our website at www.wiley.com/wiley-blackwell.

The right of Douglas Kellner to be identified as the author of this work has been asserted in accordance with the Copyright, Designs and Patents Act 1988.

Library of Congress Cataloging-in-Publication Data

Kellner, Douglas, 1943–
    Cinema wars : Hollywood film and politics in the Bush-Cheney era / Douglas Kellner.
        p.   cm.
    Includes bibliographical references and index.
    ISBN 978-1-4051-9823-3 (hardcover : alk. paper) – ISBN 978-1-4051-9824-0 (pbk. : alk. paper) 1. Motion pictures–Political aspects–United States. 2. Motion pictures–United States–History–21st century. 3. Documentary films–United States–History and criticism. 4. Documentary films–Political aspects–History and criticism. 5. Environmental films–United states–History and criticism. 6. United States–Politics and government–2001–2009. 7. Politics in motion pictures. 8. Terrorism in motion pictures. 9. Iraq War, 2003—Motion pictures and the war. I. Title.
    PN1995.9.P6K45 2010
    791.43′658–dc22
                                                                    2009036207

A catalogue record for this book is available from the British Library.

Set in 10/13 Sabon by SPi Publisher Services, Pondicherry, India
Printed and bound in Malaysia by Vivar Printing Sdn Bhd

001   2010

Contents

Acknowledgments

I would like to acknowledge the influence of Susan Sontag and Andrew Sarris, whose work on film in the 1960s when I was a philosophy student at Columbia University made me aware that cinema was emerging as an art form of special relevance. The film programs at my neighborhood Thalia and New Yorker cinemas, and film series at the Museum of Modern Art, Bleeker Street Cinema, and other movie scenes in New York at the time enabled me to see major works of the great European auteurs and a wide range of contemporary cinema. A year in Paris, with frequent visits to the Cinémathèque Française and my neighborhood Cinéma Olympique, gave me a sense of the aesthetic and thematic value of American cinema, as well as history lessons in global cinema.

My film education continued during years of teaching at the University of Texas where the Cinema Texas program, Rick Linklater's Austin Film Society, and a vibrant cinematic culture enabled me to see the best of classic and contemporary cinema and meet many involved in production and film criticism. While my early film study focused on auteurs, at Texas I grasped the importance of genre and the system of Hollywood film production and aesthetics. I should especially note the influence of Thomas Schatz, Horace Newcomb, and Janet Staiger on my understanding of the significance of production, the audience, and a dominant Hollywood aesthetic. Since the 1970s, I have subscribed to *Cineaste* and *Jump Cut*, which I have often read cover to cover and intensely read and reread during this project. I should also acknowledge reading the Calendar section of the *Los Angeles Times* daily since arriving in Southern California in the mid-1990s.

At the University of Texas in the mid-1980s I began work with Michael Ryan on *Camera Politica* and am indebted to this collaboration for aspects of the approach to Hollywood film used in this book. I also began engaging British cultural studies in the 1980s and am indebted to students in my classes at the University of Texas and UCLA for passionate discussion of Hollywood film and other aspects of media culture. Further, I would like to thank Loran Marsan and Heather Collette-VanDeraa for expert editing and to Heather for providing illustrations for the book. Former students at Texas and UCLA, now engaged in university teaching and publishing, provided helpful comments and critique, including Daniel Cho, Richard Kahn, Randy Lewis, Tyson Lewis, Clayton Pierce, and Richard von Heertum. I am also grateful to commissioning editor Jayne Fargnoli for helping me get the text through the production process, for invaluable editorial suggestions, and support of my work over the years. Thanks also to her assistant Margot Morse and to Jack Messenger for expert copy-editing.

I am most indebted to Rhonda Hammer, who sat with me through so many of the films analyzed in this book, offering profuse critical insights and providing a sharp critique of the text, which helped with revising it.

List of Plates

Introduction
Film, Politics, and Society

From the 1960s to the present, US culture, society, and politics have been the site of intense political struggles. In this context, film and media culture in the United States has been a battleground between competing social groups, with some films advancing liberal or radical positions and others reproducing conservative ones. Many films, however, are politically ambiguous, exhibiting a contradictory mixture of political motifs or attempts to be apolitical.

During the past decade, the United States suffered through some of the most compelling drama in its history since what many consider to be the stolen election of 2000 (Kellner 2001), an event that inaugurated an eight-year nightmare, the consequences of which we are still suffering. The Bush-Cheney administration began by pushing a hard-right agenda.[1] After the September 11, 2001 terror attacks on New York and Washington, it rammed through harsh restrictions on civil liberties in the so-called USA Patriot Act and began a disastrous war in Iraq in the name of protecting the US from terrorism and weapons of mass destruction. In a meeting with Karl Rove in Hollywood, film producers were called upon to serve the country in the "war on terror" and make patriotic films.[2] However, the credibility of the Bush-Cheney-Rove era eroded as the costly failure in Iraq became evident, the administration showed utter incompetence in the Hurricane Katrina catastrophe, and divisive conflict emerged over Iraq, civil rights, energy policy, the environment, the economy, and a wealth of other issues. The extent of the disaster of the Republican regime was capped by the meltdown of the US and global financial markets in Fall 2008, during a hard-fought US presidential race won by Barack Obama.

Cinema Wars will attempt to show that the turbulence of the era is reproduced in the Hollywood films of the 2000s.[3] While during the

Vietnam War the Hollywood film industry generally avoided presenting films engaging the conflict, waiting until years after the US had pulled out, a whole series of films has emerged on the Iraq and Afghanistan wars, as have cycles of films on terrorism, war and militarism, environmental crisis, and the conflicts of the 2000s over gender, race, class, sexuality, religion, and other hot button issues.

Hollywood Film as a Contested Terrain

From this viewpoint, contemporary Hollywood cinema can be read as a contest of representations and a contested terrain that reproduces existing social struggles and transcodes the political discourses of the era.[4] I use the term *transcode* to describe how specific political discourses like Reaganism or liberalism are translated, or encoded, into media texts. For example, *Easy Rider* (1969) and *Woodstock* (1970) transcode the discourses of the 1960s counterculture into cinematic texts in image, sound, dialogue, scene, and narrative. Films like *Red Dawn* (1984) and *Rambo* (1984) transcode the conservative discourses of Reaganism (see Kellner and Ryan 1988), while *Syriana* (2005) transcodes mistrust in the Bush-Cheney era of government, big oil corporations, and corporate power, and *Michael Clayton* transcodes fears of corporate corruption and wrong-doing. As we will see, many conservative films transcode Bush-Cheney discourses on foreign policy and militarism, while films like *Lions for Lambs* (2007) and *Rendition* (2007) transcode liberal discourses critical of Bush-Cheney administration politics in cinema wars over US foreign policy (see discussion of these films in the Conclusion).

Further, while some Hollywood films articulate in aggressive fashion contemporary liberal, conservative, or radical ideologies, and thus intersect with current public controversies,[5] other films are complex, multilayered, and open to multiple readings, like *No Country For Old Men* (see below), or the *Star Wars* films (see chapter 4), while many are simply incoherent.[6] Sometimes the political ideologies of films are implicit, while at other times they are quite explicit,[7] as in the liberalism of certain films by Robert Redford, George Clooney, and Michael Moore, or the conservativism of Chuck Norris, Mel Gibson, and the *Rambo* films.

Since the 1960s, culture wars in the US have tended to be between liberals and conservatives with radicals on the left and right articulating more extreme and oppositional positions.[8] Traditionally, conservativism in Western democracies affirmed the market and capitalism over the state, advocated individualism and freedom over equality and justice, and supported traditional values like the heterosexual patriarchial family, religion, and conservative cultural values. During the 2000s, "conservativism" was represented by the Republican Party, although many claim that Bush, Cheney, and many of their followers are better labeled "right-wing extremists" as they pushed militarism and an aggressive unilateralist foreign policy, discarded civil liberties in their USA Patriot Act, and broke with international law in its advocacy of torture, "extraordinary rendition," and "preemptive war." "Liberalism," in turn, since the New Deal in the 1930s, has been associated in the US with a regulatory state, civil liberties and rights for minorities, equality, and secularism, although liberals also largely champion a so-called free market economy. We will see that over the 2000s a hegemonic rightwing conservativism advocated by the Bush-Cheney administration was defeated by a social liberalism represented by the Obama campaign and that the battle was played out in Hollywood film of the era.

Hence, I will attempt to show that cinematic wars over issues like terrorism, war and militarism, the environment, rights, and other issues have been intensely fought in the 2000s on the terrain of Hollywood cinema. Although I use the term *Hollywood* to refer to a specific style and type of what has become a globally dominant cinema, contemporary US cinema also exhibits a wider range of styles and aesthetics, types of film, and critical-oppositional works than the more mainstream genre films usually categorized as Hollywood cinema. Indeed, as we shall see, film itself is highly contested in the United States and globally, with alternative and oppositional cinematic works emerging even within the mainstream, as with Spike Lee and Michael Moore, as well as from the independent film movement. Moreover, global film production has often absorbed Hollywood techniques and personnel, just as Hollywood film has drawn on global financing and production teams, as well as talent. Likewise, independent cinema has passed into the mainstream, as the number of Academy Awards for low-budget and independent films in 2005 and 2008 testifies, generating a symbiosis of Hollywood and independent film production sometimes labeled "Indiewood."[9]

There has also been a growing overlap between film and television production as the quality of TV improves, especially on pay TV channels like HBO and Showtime (see Johnson 2007). Further, Hollywood films increasingly use digital cameras and equipment associated with

George W. Bush was satirized in many entertainment films and documentaries of the era.

video. Computerized special effects and editing have also undercut the divide between film and video. Actors, directors, and other talent have long crossed over between US film and television, and differences in viewing are also eroding as more people watch TV and films at home on large-screen entertainment systems. Hence, I will occasionally deal with television movies or series that articulate with the themes under investigation.

Films are an especially illuminating social indicator of the realities of a historical era, as a tremendous amount of capital is invested in researching, producing, and marketing the product. Film creators tap into the events, fears, fantasies, and hopes of an era and give cinematic expression to social experiences and realities. Sometimes the narratives are contrived to represent political figures and events of the era, as when *Primary Colors* (1998) provides an explicit satirical take on Bill Clinton, or *W.* (2008) presents a biopic of George W. Bush. Sometimes, however, films provide indirect commentary and critique of their social and political context, as do many of the films discussed in this book.

The cinema wars over religion in the United States, for instance, were evident in the success of Mel Gibson's *The Passion of the Christ* and the popularity of Dan Brown's novel *The Da Vinci Code* and a blockbuster film modeled on the novel.[10] Deployment of violence and fear to promote an ultraconservative Christian agenda is evident in Gibson's *The Passion of the Christ* (2004). Almost completely ignoring Christ's social gospel and teaching, the film focuses on the last hours of Jesus's life and especially his arrest, torture, and crucifixion. Wasting little time in getting into torture and violence, the film begins with the temple guards arresting Jesus in the Garden of Gethsemane, where they savagely beat him and take him to the Jewish high priest, Caiaphas. On the way, they suspend Jesus from a bridge, choking him and dangling him over the water, incidents for which there is no gospel basis.[11]

Gibson's version of Christianity is exceptionally violent and bloodthirsty, and evokes horror at the magnitude of Christ's suffering, as well as hatred for his tormentors and torturers. Gibson conveys his messages through images and spectacle, not words, thus undercutting a key aspect of Christianity as a religion of the book and the word. Gibson's film purposely uses the archaic Aramaic language and is very sparing in its use of subtitles; hence, it is the spectacle that most engages viewers. This follows a contemporary trend to promote a culture of image and spectacle, but goes against a more traditional Christianity that is suspicious and critical of graven images and relies on "the word" for its teaching. Gibson, however, is clearly a purveyor of graven images, and highly problematic ones at that.

Like the Bush-Cheney administration, Gibson's *Passion* employs tactics of shock and awe to overpower its audience. It overwhelms rational faculties with its intense and horrific images, unrelenting violence, and seductive music. Like every great work of propaganda, it manipulates its audience into its traps, in this case a fundamentalist Manicheanism which divides the world into a battle between absolute Good and Evil.[12] It is significant that Gibson's *Passion* works on a visceral level of emotion rather than thought, which seems highly foreign to Gibson's mindset. Gibson, like George W. Bush, is disdainful of intellectuals and critical thinking, privileging emotion and faith over reason, operating at a "gut" level.

Indeed, there is a series of interesting similarities between George W. Bush and Mel Gibson. Bush has famously declared that Jesus is his favorite philosopher, and part of Gibson's highly effective publicity for *The Passion* stressed his allegedly deep Christian beliefs, which drove him to produce and market the film. Both Gibson and Bush Junior are born-again Christians who claim they have overcome struggles with drugs and alcohol to embrace a highly fundamentalist Christianity.

Both are Manichean to the core, see themselves on the side of good, and view their enemies and adversaries as evil. For both, you're either with us or against us; Gibson and his followers attacked critics of *The Passion* as anti-Christian and even minions of Satan. Both Bush and Gibson are morally self-righteous and champion redemptive violence in the struggle for good. Both are extremely megalomaniac, seeing themselves as chosen vehicles of God, yet often appear addled and inarticulate when confronted with difficult questions (possibly due to years of excessive drug and alcohol abuse that impaired their cognitive faculties). Each deploys his political or cultural power to advance the ends of his conservative version of Christianity, arguably with highly controversial effects. And both have been accused of mendacity and a purely instrumental relation to truth, using language to justify themselves, whatever the veracity of their claims.[13] And as a popular joke has it, the similarities between Jesus Christ and George W. Bush are evident in that both believe they are appendages of God and both owe their job to their father.

Gibson's *Passion* was one of a series of popular films that feature graphic violence which were a mark of the second Bush-Cheney administration. As the violence in Iraq accelerated in 2006–2007, a spate of powerful films emerged that interrogated violence in US society and culture, such as *American Gangster, No Country for Old Men, Before the Devil Knows You're Dead, Zodiac, The Assassination of Jesse James by the Coward Robert Ford, The Dark Knight*, and *There Will Be Blood*. In addition, a wave of marginal violent films of the era, often highly successful at the box office, like *Saw I–V, Halloween, Hostel I* and *II, The Girl Next Door, Shooter, Street Kings, War, Shoot 'em Up!, You Kill Me, We Own the Night, Lakeview Terrace, Torture*, and countless others, put on display the violence and brutality in contemporary US culture.

While the most popular and awarded films often put on display key insights into current sociopolitical dynamics, sometimes less mainstream films present ideological problematics and are socially revealing, portraying phenomena not acceptable in mainstream cinema, such as extreme violence and sexuality, or torture. One can also practice "reading against the grain" – finding progressive insights in putatively reactionary films and conservative moments in relatively liberal films. While I focus on major filmmakers, blockbusters, and some of the most popular and discussed films of the era, marginal films can also be socially revealing and articulate key experiences and critical visions.

For example, the violence and brutality of the era is on display in a cycle of horror films that feature torture, such as the *Saw* and *Hostel* film series. The *Saw* franchise, which unveiled a five installment torture and gorefest series between 2004 and 2008, puts on display the demented illusions, grotesque hypocrisy, obscene violence, and utter lunacy of the Bush-Cheney era, which finds its true face in the sick and twisted killer-ex-machina Jigsaw (Tobin Bell). The premise of the series is that Jigsaw evolves complex "tests" and torture devices to punish miscreants of various sorts. *Saw IV* (2007) provides the back-story that indicates Jigsaw became crazed when his pregnant wife was accosted by a junkie in a violent encounter and lost their child. Thereafter, Jigsaw turned his energies as engineer and builder to construct elaborate torture mechanisms and tests to punish "Evil" of various sorts, just as the Bush-Cheney administration was constructing apparatuses of torture in Afghanistan, Iraq, Guantanamo, and other sites throughout the world to punish its alleged enemies and "evil doers."

In *Saw II* (2006), Jigsaw kidnaps seven convicted drug users or dealers and submits them to torture and survival tests, leaving rules for "games" on a cassette tape *à la Mission: Impossible* that usually pits the "players" against each other, so it is either kill or be killed – a brutal Darwinian vision that informs the series, as well as the political unconscious of contemporary conservativism and, especially, Dick Cheney and his minions. While the 1980s stalk-and-slash films punished teenagers who had sex by having them slashed by a faceless killer, Jigsaw pursues a rigorous anti-drug morality, torturing and killing individuals who dealt or used hard drugs, just as the Bush-Cheney administration imprisoned a record number of inmates – often poor and of color – for drug possession, and a record number of terror suspects held without trial and proper legal procedure. And just as Jigsaw legitimates his monstrous activities through demented appeals to a higher morality, so too did the Bush-Cheney administration.

Yet *Saw II* also attacks corrupt police, as it turns out that every one of the dealers/users kidnapped in his survival game had evidence falsely planted on them that led to their imprisonment, leading Jigsaw to capture and torture the wayward cop Eric Matthews (Danny Wahlberg), who framed the victims. Jigsaw has also imprisoned Eric's son, who would be in great danger if his identity was discovered by the drug dealers. The incarceration of an innocent young man transcodes fears of kidnappers and sexual abuse of children; this is especially ironic, given that Bush and

Cheney did, in a sense, kidnap the sons (and daughters) of many American people, whose children were faced with tortures, brutality and harm in far more graphic and realistic manners than in Jigsaw's games, losing limbs, being ambushed and blown apart with improvised explosive devices (IEDs), and suffering from post-traumatic syndrome.

Ironically, the policeman Matthews was pursuing the same Vengeance-Outside-the-Law morality as Jigsaw, planting evidence to punish wrong-doers and thus carrying out his own form of vigilante justice – just like the Bush-Cheney administration, which became like its most "evil" enemies when it resorted to constructing false evidence, rendition, torture, and murder. Another feature of Jigsaw's "games" involves complex torture devices that test one's will to survive by forcing victims to dismember vital organs in order to free themselves. *Saw IV* exhibits a pedagogical device that attempts to justify Jigsaw's machinations and recruit followers to his twisted philosophy and deeds. A SWAT team cop, Rigg (Lyriq Bent), who is obsessed with finding the tormentors and killers of his police colleagues, is recruited to play Jigsaw's games. The plot mechanisms attempt to get Rigg to see and feel what Jigsaw feels; to see that society's scum and enemies require the fiercer retribution of Jigsaw's machinations, providing an allegory of how the Bush-Cheney administration attempted to get the public to accept its doctrines of torture, preemptive war, and savage military intervention ("shock and awe" to flush out and destroy evil doers).

In the contemporary context, the lunatic killer Jigsaw can therefore be read as a metaphor for Dick Cheney and his subordinates, a group of fanatical, warped, and vicious advocates of torture and murder, believing that their torturing and murdering is in the cause of good because it is punishing evil. The motif of vengeance that runs through the *Saw* franchise articulates the conservative and Old Testament "eye for an eye" mentality that brutally punishes and eliminates wrongdoers and enemies. This Manichean mentality projects evil onto its "other," denying its own violent and aggressive tendencies.

The *Saw* franchise thus puts on display the brutality involved in US policies of torture and retribution, showing individuals who defend and practice such atrocities – at odds with traditional American political morality – to be ill, depraved, and extremely dangerous. Thus the *Saw* franchise can be read as an acute diagnosis of US society's most heinous features, and to demonstrate the noxiousness and lunacy of the rightwing extremists running the country. On the other hand, that these films have

The villain Jigsaw in the *Saw* franchise can be seen as a metaphor for Dick Cheney and his subordinates, who believed that torture and murder could be in the cause of good because it is punishing evil.

been extremely popular is a cause for worry that there are more potential recruits to take over from disillusioned Pentagon, CIA, and other potential torturers and killers. Many viewers may identify with the torture sequences and obtain sadomasochistic pleasure from watching them, pointing to a propensity to take pleasure in others' misfortunes and suffering. The *Saw* films may also convince viewers that guilty individuals are worthy of punishment and torture. The *Saw* franchise's popularity and continuation is thus an index of a pathological society riven with unmastered aggression and violence.

The Dark Knight, the highest grossing film of 2008,[14] also can be read as a critical allegory about the corruption, violence, and nihilism of the Bush-Cheney era. *Superman I* and *II* (1978 and 1980) and other superhero films of the late 1970s and 1980s showed the yearning in the American popular imagination for a Savior/Redeemer who would save the country from the morass of confusion coming out of the 1960s and 1970s and restore an older America, helping to fuel Reaganite conservatism (see Kellner and Ryan 1988: 217ff). Some of the superhero films of the last years of the Bush-Cheney administration, by contrast, can be read as a critique of the failed conservative regime. The Batman films of the late Bush-Cheney era show the polity to be utterly corrupt and the economic, political, and legal system in paralysis, approximately the case by the end of the failed era.

The theme of police, military, and government corruption and failure to solve social problems is on display throughout Christopher Nolan's *Batman Begins* (2004). His Batman (Christian Bale) is a human-all-too-human figure who must overpower his fears (of bats) and remorse over the murder of his parents after Bat-figures in an opera frightened the young lad and he maneuvered his parents to leave early, leading them to a mugging and murder. Grown up, he is devastated with remorse and guilt, but learns the martial arts disciplines and gains the technology necessary to be a crusader against evil.

The evil in *Batman Begins* involves the deranged scientist Dr. Jonathan Crane, a.k.a. Scarecrow, plotting to poison Gotham's water supply – a barely disguised figure for weapons of mass destruction (WMDs). Other villains involve the League of Shadows and its sinister and mysterious leader Ra's al Ghul, a figure for the threat of China as a potential strategic enemy. These villains possess a gas extracted from a rare flower that can decimate the populace – another WMD figure, evoking fears of biological weapons.

Evil also dwells within Batman's family corporation, as it is Earle (Rutger Hauer), the ruthless CEO of Wayne Enterprises, who is producing, among other things, WMDs, and who aids the villains. Further, the film presents an almost totally corrupt legal system, dominated by corporate and criminal powers, an analogue to the Bush-Cheney partisan evisceration of the political and legal system, just as the malfeasance of corporate criminals in the film is an analogue to corporate corruption and crime in the contemporary era.

In Nolan's follow-up Batman saga, *The Dark Knight* (2008), the vision is darker, the corruption and chaos more pervasive. The film overlaps with recent social apocalypse films that portray the system under crisis and careening toward collapse (see chapter 1). Crime is on the rise again in Gotham, but tabloid newspapers are questioning Batman's vigilante tactics with headlines screaming: "Batman: Crusader or Menace?" Bruce Wayne/Batman's longtime love, Rachel (Maggie Gyllenhaal), is involved with Gotham's charismatic and committed DA Harvey Dent (Aaron Eckhart), who is presented as the squeaky-clean Good Knight. Despite Dent's involvement with his beloved Rachel, Batman, questioning his own tactics and outside-the-law vigilante status, comes to believe that Gotham needs a completely honest and competent DA to clean up crime and replace Batman as the center of law enforcement, and thus strongly supports Dent.

It appears that the Joker (Heath Ledger) is behind the recent crime outbreak in Gotham, which includes hits on a mob bank, unleashing retaliatory crime by the town's criminal elements. The Joker is presented as the spirit of anarchy and chaos of a particularly destructive and nihilistic nature. In the contemporary context, the Joker represents the spirit of terrorism and the film is full of iconography related to 9/11, with dark whirling clouds of smoke and explosions of sound in the opening frame suggesting a city under attack. As the convoluted plot unfolds, the cinematic spectacle portrays a series of assaults on the inner city, targeting corporations, banks, the police, and the legal system. In this desperate situation, Batman goes after the Joker, employing surveillance of the telephone system, putting civil rights and the constitution aside, and torturing the Joker once he is caught. This appears to legitimate Bush-Cheney politics against terrorism: if our enemy, the logic runs, is absolutely evil, anything we do to destroy him is good, including going over to the Dark Side.[15] In fact, a columnist for Rupert Murdoch's *Wall Street Journal* claimed that Batman was a figure for George W. Bush himself, who went over to the Dark Side to fight terror and took criticisms from liberals for pursuing his unpopular but supposedly necessary policies of torture and surveillance.[16]

The film, however, sharply puts in question the tactics of the Dark Side, as it appears that the Joker has manipulated Batman, Dent, and the police to get them to carry out his evil agenda. Surveillance helps capture the Joker who, when submitted to torture, lies, leading Rachel to be kidnapped and murdered. The previously upright Dent is drawn into the abyss by the Joker, killing one person a day to keep Rachel alive. When she is killed he goes over the edge and into the Dark Side himself, symbolized by his disfigurement and transformation into Two-Face. Like the villain Chirgyh in *No Country for Old Men*, Dent sacrifices morality and choice for a flip of the coin, deciding people's fates through a plunge into a completely meaningless existence of pure contingency and nihilism.

Thus, *The Dark Knight* portrays the morass and abyss of the Bush-Cheney era. Together, the Batman films of the 2000s articulate the dark, deep pessimism of people plagued by their own economic and political elites and deadly enemies who want to destroy them. The murky political allegory suggests that going over to the Dark Side twists and corrupts individuals and society. To paraphrase Nietzsche, if you look into the face of a monster long enough you become the monster.

In this book, I argue that there are a number of recurring themes in many of the major and minor Hollywood films of the past decades, which articulate some of the key events and sociopolitical and economic conflicts of the time. Many of these films resonate with and can be read within the history of the social and political struggles and context of their period. In this way, film can help interpret the social and political history of an era, and contexualizing films in their matrix of production, distribution, and reception can help illuminate the multiple and sometimes contradictory meanings and effects of specific films, genres, and filmmakers. *Cinema Wars* engages a broad array of films, genres, directors, and cinematic spectacle, ranging from some of the most popular films and acclaimed directors to more marginal fare. Often, Oscar-winning films reflect the mood and zeitgeist of an era, as when during the relatively peaceful and prosperous 1990s feel-good years affirmative films like *Forrest Gump* (1994), *Titanic* (1997), and *Shakespeare in Love* (1998) won Oscars. By contrast, films like the Academy Award winning productions of the last three years of the Bush-Cheney administration – *Crash* (2005), *The Departed* (2006), and *No Country for Old Men* (2007) – reflect a more anxiety ridden era, when events appear out of control, violence is rampant, and socioeconomic insecurities and crises are intensifying.[17] Although films dealing with Iraq and terrorism did not do well at the box office, suggesting audience fatigue with Bush-Cheney politics, in 2005 "message movies" dominated the Best Picture nominations, including *Brokeback Mountain, Capote, Crash, Munich,* and *Good Night, and Good Luck.* While the masses did not turn to these movies for escapism, serious members of the production community, critics, and audiences turned to these cinematic visions for insight into the contemporary morass.

The 2009 Academy Awards could be read as a fierce repudiation of the Bush-Cheney years and an embrace of the Obama vision of diversity, progressivism, and hope. The number of awards won by non-Americans attests again to the increasingly global nature of film and cinematic culture, but also constitutes a rejection of the narrow nationalism and chauvinism of the Bush-Cheney years. The eight awards for *Slumdog Millionaire* in particular exhibit a yearning for diversity, complexity, critical vision, and sympathy for the marginalized and oppressed after eight years of one-dimensional conservative ideology and an administration and culture attuned to wealth and power. *Slumdog* obviously resonated for a global audience distraught by the crisis of capitalism that exploded around the time of its release.

Sean Penn's upset win as Best Actor for *Milk* over Mickey Rourke's performance in *The Wrestler* attests to recognition that Penn is one of the greatest actors of his generation, but also provides a nod to the individual who was probably the fiercest critic in Hollywood of the Bush-Cheney regime. Penn played heroic gay activist Harvey Milk in *Milk*, the first openly gay elected representative in US politics, who was assassinated by a deranged homophobe. Bestowing Oscars on Penn and *Milk*'s scriptwriter Dustin Lance Black, who won acclaim for Best Adapted Script, represents a strong repudiation of the homophobia that continues to fester in the US. In particular it represents Hollywood's rejection of the Proposition 8 California ballot initiative that denies gays and lesbians marriage rights previously granted. Black and Penn got some of the most rousing ovations of the evening and both made well-received political speeches accepting of gays and lesbians. Black stated that as a 13-year-old gay moving to California, hearing about Harvey Milk's activism gave him hope that he could live an open life and be accepted and respected. Penn's expression of genuine surprise in winning led him to open with an exclamation: "You Commie, homo-loving sons of guns." His denunciation of homophobes demonstrating outside was well received and attests to the liberalism of the Hollywood community.

However, the ceremonies and speeches also put on display the limitations of Hollywood liberalism in confronting grave crisis. Although the format was based on Depression era spectacle and Hollywood as a dream machine and mode of escape, no one really mentioned the economic crisis or the ongoing wars in Iraq and Afghanistan (protested in earlier Oscar ceremonies), nor were there references to the ecological crisis and need for immediate and serious action, topics that Hollywood films of the era dealt with and that will be engaged in the following chapters.

Cinema, Politics, and Social History: From Cinematic Realism to Allegory

In general, cinema is a form of vision that provides ways of seeing, either reproducing conventional modes of seeing and experiencing the world, or enabling one to perceive things one has not viewed or experienced. There is also an important aural dimension to films, so that audiences can sometimes see, hear, and experience things differently, from another perspective, thus enlarging their range of vision and experience. Cinema frames the world, offering "a world viewed" (Cavell 1971), proliferating motion pictures ("movies") that depict action and movement and thus provide panoramas of time and vistas of history. Cinema may focus vision on external, surface appearances, or provide deeper and more critical visions of human beings, social relations, or historical processes, as do many of the best contemporary films.

Films can display social realities of the time in documentary and realist fashion, directly representing the events and phenomena of an epoch. But films can also provide allegorical representations that interpret, comment on, and indirectly portray aspects of an era. Further, there is an aesthetic, philosophical, and anticipatory dimension to films, in which they provide artistic visions of the world that might transcend the social context of the moment and articulate future possibilities, positive and negative, and provide insights into the nature of human beings, social relations, institutions, and conflicts of a given era, or the human condition itself.

Films marked by the conventions and style of cinematic realism attempt to present actual events and persons. They include critical documentaries and films like Oliver Stone's historical dramas, which try to provide a representation of events like the Kennedy assassination (*J.F.K.*, 1991), the Vietnam War (*Platoon*, 1986; *Born on the Fourth of July*, 1989), *Nixon* (1995), or countercultural figures like *The Doors* (1991), as well as Stone's post-9/11 film *World Trade Center* (2006). Stone's cinema combines epic historical scope with depictions of constructions of the everyday life of figures like Richard Nixon, the firefighters of *World Trade Center*, or George W. Bush in *W.* (2008). Using the classical techniques of Hollywood cinema, Stone attempts in these films to create highly realistic characters, plots, and narratives to capture the historical actualities of the moment.

These cinematic mappings attempt to represent historical events, individuals, character types, cultural norms, and other defining features of a specific society.[18] Of course, documentary films, however rigorous, and cinematic realism are both constructs. As the Oliver Stone examples easily suggest, films are interpretations whose critical visions of social and historical realities have their own ideological and idiosyncratic biases and perspectives.[19] Properly interpreted and contextualized, films can provide key insights into specific historical persons, events, or eras.

Allegorical films include fantasy and horror genres that require informed interpretations concerning what social realities, or fantasies, specific films represent.[20] Critical allegorical interpretation requires searching for the social conditions and experiences behind their cinematic representation. The series of haunted and collapsing house films of the late 1970s to the present (e.g., *The Amityville Horror* films and the *Poltergeist* trilogy), for example, can be interpreted as projecting the fears of middle-class families losing their homes or having their families torn apart during the Reagan era (see Kellner 1995), when the middle class was indeed downwardly mobile, divorce was up, and families were losing homes (as happened again in accelerating fashion in the 2000s, when a mortgage crisis exploded in the Bush-Cheney era).

Historical dramas or contemporary thrillers can also provide allegories of the contemporary era. Paul Thomas Anderson's *There Will Be Blood* enacts a scathing denunciation of a hypermasculine American will-to-power and the destructive effects of greed and predatory capitalism. While *No Country for Old Men* grounds evil and violence in a remorseless nature and fallen human beings, *There Will Be Blood* roots greed, violence, and madness in an unrestrained capitalism and patriarchy, uneasily bolstered – and sometimes undermined – by the pillars of religion and family. Anderson's epic historical drama thus attempts to get at the roots of America's malaise and madness and shows its problems deeply rooted in its core institutions and values, ultimately providing a critical commentary on the contemporary moment.

This family saga of oil wealth and its bloody consequences can also be read as an allegory about the Bush family and its vicious quest for money and power, culminating in George W. Bush and Dick Cheney's invasion of Iraq – in part for oil – and resulting in blood.[21] The story centers on the rise to wealth and power of oilman Daniel Plainview (Daniel Day Lewis), whose son is nicknamed H. W., precisely the initials of George H. W. Bush. In Bush family history, H. W. refers to Herbert Walker, one of the pioneering buccaneers of the Bush-Walker family dynasty who was the business partner of Prescott Bush and father of Dorothy Walker, who Prescott Bush married. Prescott Bush and Herbert Walker made their fortunes, among other ventures, by managing the American interests of German businesses and the Nazis, including industrialists like Krupp, who helped initially finance German fascism and built sectors of its military infrastructure. Dorothy and Prescott Bush's son George H. W. Bush in turn was infamously to go into the oil business, as was his wayward son George W. Young George W., known in the family as Junior, spectacularly flopped in all his oil ventures, but managed to identify with the interests of the industry throughout his presidency, no doubt contributing to, first, record oil prices and, then, economic crisis by the summer and fall of 2008.[22]

In the context of the present era, one could also read *There Will Be Blood* as an allegory about the Bush-Cheney Iraq invasion. Like Plainview, the key members of the administration, connected to the oil and energy industries, sought new sources of oil and there was blood and hellish fires and explosions following the "shock and awe" invasion. Like Plainview, Bush-Cheney are stubborn and unyielding, failing to see the errors of their ways, and driven by dark forces of power and domination. Like Plainview, Bush-Cheney have arguably taken leave of their senses and no good end for their violent ventures was in sight during their Reign of Error.

I suggested allegorical readings of *There Will Be Blood* and the *Batman* films of the 2000s, so that they can be read as providing commentary on the Bush-Cheney administration, as well as embodying other themes. Likewise, a series of political thrillers during the waning of the Bush-Cheney regime can be read as allegories articulating liberal fears of rightwing oppression, including *The Manchurian Candidate* (2004), *Syriana* (2004), and *V for Vendetta* (2006), which I engage in chapter 4.

Films thus provide illumination into the contemporary moment through their images, scenes, and narratives. As Walter Benjamin and T. W. Adorno argued, cultural forms like films can provide "dialectical images" that illuminate their social environments.[23] Films may be a less sublime mode of culture, although they have their aesthetic moments of beauty and transcendence, and modernist moments of style, innovation, contestation, or resistance.

Readings of films thus can engage themselves with the aesthetic dimension that ranges from analysis of cinematic form and style to philosophical visions of life.[24] The Coen brothers' *No Country for Old Men*, which won Academy Awards for Best Picture and Best Director in 2007, is based on a novel of the same title by Cormac McCarthy, and both take a pessimistic look at violent masculinity run amok in their story of a working-class man who finds a stash of money from a drug deal gone awry and is pursued by both the criminals and the sheriff. Thematically, *No Country* transcodes bleak existentialist philosophy that God is Dead, existence is without meaning or redemption, life is always haunted by the abyss of nothingness, destructive fate can strike at any time, Evil prevails over Good, the Good are punished or impotent, and the Evil Ones get away with it. Indeed, the film is pervaded by an existential ethos of anxiety, dread, treachery, and the always imminent possibility of violent death. This is clearly the most grim vision of an existentialism without the heroism of authentic action, self-creativity, or self-overcoming advanced by Nietzsche, Heidegger, Sartre, and others.[25] Yet, as Daniel Cho has suggested, one can also read the film as an anti-Bush-Cheney allegory where the Law and Patriarchy are impotent to deal with Terror. In fact, *No Country* is a multilayered film that can give rise to multiple readings.[26]

By virtue of their style and form, innovative films can present visions of a better life, as well as provide critical insight into the present moment, or philosophical illumination of human existence. Films potentially have a utopian dimension which enables audiences to transcend the limitations of their current life and times to envisage new ways of seeing, living, and being. They can also project idealized views of a better world that can provide ideological halos, which when critically decoded can generate insights into the ideological problematics and struggles of their era. As Fredric Jameson (1981) pointed out, even popular films like *The Godfather* (1972) and *Jaws* (1975) can have utopian moments, such as the opening scenes of communal family life in *The Godfather*, and in *Jaws* the New England community before the shark attack, and the bonding and heroism of the men seeking to protect the community. Further, films can provide dystopic warnings about coming catastrophes, as my discussion of eco-disaster films in chapter 1 will illustrate.

In sum, films are a crucial part of contemporary cultures and are embedded in fundamental economic, political, social, and cultural dimensions of the present age. Films raise issues and can provoke debates over salient concerns of the present moment, as when Andrew Light (2003) claims contemporary films raise important debates concerning surveillance technology, identity politics, or environmentalism, generating arguments that can contribute to political enlightenment or philosophical understanding. Throughout this book, I attempt to show how critical interpretations of film can help provide understanding of contemporary US culture and society, and thus contribute to important debates over politics and the state, corporations and the economy, economic and environmental crisis, terrorism, war and militarism, and threats to democracy.

In general, I use history and social theory to analyze Hollywood films from 2000 to 2008, and use the films in turn to illuminate historical trends, conflicts, possibilities, crises, and anxieties of the era. Reading film contextually thus involves situating films within their sociohistorical environment and showing how they articulate sociopolitical events and struggles of the time. Political discourses are often relational, opposing contrasting positions in a specific historical situation over war or militarism, gender or sexuality, religion or the state. There may, of course, be more than two opposing political positions, but in mainstream corporate media and entertainment it is roughly a contrast between liberal and conservative discourses, although more radical discourses may emerge and there are frequently levels of contradiction and ambiguity. From this diagnostic perspective, Hollywood films provide important cinematic visions concerning the psychological, sociopolitical, and ideological make-up of US society at a given point in history. Reading films contextually allows one to gain insights into social problems and conflicts, and to appraise the dominant ideologies and emergent oppositional forces.

Hollywood Film and the Contemporary Moment: Signs of the Times

Representations of the present era and its sometimes hidden histories are evident in key films of the 2000s. The transition from the Clinton-Gore era of relative peace and prosperity to the militarist interventionism and multiple crises of the Bush-Cheney administration was anticipated in a series of war films and political thrillers released before and just after 9/11. Films have an anticipatory dimension and can predict and anticipate events of the era. Before the 9/11 terrorist attacks on the World Trade Center in New York and the Pentagon in Washington, DC, Hollywood films presented domestic terrorist attacks on US soil and threats of attacks from a variety of terrorist groups. Edward Zwick's *The Siege* (1998) contains astonishing anticipations of the domestic terrorism that would emerge in the US and globally in the 2000s. Playing out debates, still heated and ongoing, about how to deal with terrorist threats, *The Siege* anticipates the extreme positions the Bush-Cheney administration would take and lays out counterarguments.

The film opens with footage of a bombing of Khobar Towers holding US troops stationed in Saudi Arabia and reflecting a 1996 bombing of US barracks. News footage shows a suspected Arab terrorist behind the plot, Sheik Ahmed Bin Talal, uncannily resembling Osama Bin Laden. Clips from Bill Clinton threatening retaliation are followed by the sheik driving through the desert and tracked by US satellite technology, leading to his capture. Shortly thereafter, a sinister looking American eyes him, whom we later learn is Major General Devereaux (Bruce Willis), who holds the sheik in a secret location. The scene cuts to New York City where the FBI is informed that hostages are being held aboard a bus containing a bomb. Agent Anthony (Hub) Hubbard (Denzel Washington) and his Arab-American partner Frank Haddad (Tony Shalhoub) of the FBI counterterrorism unit take charge of the operation and learn that the explosive was a giant paint-bomb. But the FBI team receives a phone call stating that there will be real bombs and demands following the incident and a fax arrives stating "release him."

Learning that an agent who appears to be working for the CIA is investigating the crime scene, Hub and Frank confront the mysterious woman (played by Annette Bening), but she refuses to disclose her identity. There is a report concerning another bomb aboard a bus, and although Hubbard is able to persuade the terrorists to release children and older people, the bomb explodes, killing scores of innocents. The woman CIA agent identifies herself as Elise Kraft and becomes involved with the investigation. Soon after, one of her own agents, Samir Nazhde (Sami Bouajila), is identified as a signatory to a visa application of one of the suicide bombers in his capacity as a teacher of Arab studies, and she becomes intimately involved in the investigation.

Terrorist threats intensify as the FBI locates a sleeper cell in Brooklyn and kills them all in a shootout. But another cell bombs a Broadway theater, killing many, including members of the city's cultural elite. There is talk of bringing in federal troops as incidents escalate with Hubbard storming a school and killing a lone terrorist to prevent another slaughter. But, soon after, the bombing of the offices of the FBI Counterterrorism Division at One Federal Plaza creates demands to declare a state of emergency and to bring in the military.[27]

Although Major General Devereaux had earlier insisted that the Army was not the right "tool" for this job, being a "broadsword not a scalpel," he is put in charge of a military operation with the president declaring martial law and rounding up young Arab-American men as suspects in detention camps, including Frank Haddad's son. Devereaux seals off Brooklyn and angry New Yorkers stage protests against the military occupation, detention camps, and the singling out of Arabs for detainment. Frank resigns in anger over his son's detention, and Hub is now paired up with CIA agent Sharon Bridger, who tells him that "Elise Kraft" was a cover name and that she was in charge of an operation in Iraq that organized Islamic Iraqis to overthrow Saddam Hussein. That operation was abandoned, however, leading many of her operatives to be killed, although she was able to extract Samir, whom she hopes will lead her to the final terrorist cell.[28]

Hubbard and Kraft track down a suspect, Tariq Husseini, who they arrest, but Devereaux takes custody of him and eventually tortures and kills him in an interrogation. A powerful scene features a debate over the morality of torture that anticipates the arguments of Barack Obama against Dick Cheney, with the Denzel Washington character making the arguments against torture and the Bruce Willis character the case for illegal detention and torture.

As a peaceful march unfolds, involving all ethnic groups in New York demonstrating against the occupation of Brooklyn and detention of Arabs and Muslims, agent Bridger learns that Samir himself is the final cell and plans to act as a suicide bomber within the peace march. Bridger is horrified, noting that the march features Christians and Moslems, black and white, and young and older, all protesting the incarceration of Arab-Americans and chanting "No Fear! No Fear!" as they march through the streets. Since it was precisely the motif of fear that the Bush-Cheney administration exploited to push through their rightwing agenda, the images of masses of Americans opposing detention camps and protesting against military occupation is a rare display of protest and mass demonstrations in a Hollywood film.

To disrupt the peace march, Samir has strapped a bomb to his body and intends to detonate it among the marchers, but Hubbard and Haddad arrive in time to prevent the carnage. In a dramatic showdown, Samir fatally shoots Bridger as she struggles to stop him, but Frank and Hubbard shoot and kill Samir. In a stunning aftermath, Hubbard, accompanied by other FBI agents, places Devereaux under arrest for the torture and murder of Tariq Husseini, the illegal detention of the sheik, and violation of a range of international laws. Anticipating Dick Cheney, Devereaux declares himself to be above the law, claiming he is the protector of the nation, and commands his soldiers to aim their guns at the FBI agents who are trying to arrest him. Hubbard, however, makes a powerful speech telling Devereaux and the armed FBI and military forces that the civil liberties and human rights which the general took from Arab suspects who were illegally detained, tortured, and even murdered, are what our forefathers fought and died for. The armed troops apparently accept Hubbard's passionate arguments, and Devereaux submits to arrest. Martial law ends, and the detainees are freed, including Haddad's son.

While *The Siege* appears in retrospect as a liberal critique in advance of the Bush-Cheney post-9/11 policies, its legitimation of torture, and its "extraordinary renditions" and secret prisons, the film was quite controversial when it was released. The Arab-American Anti-Discrimination Committee came out fiercely against the film on its release in 1998 with its spokesperson Hussein Ibish asserting: "*The Siege* is extremely offensive [in its representations of Arabs as terrorists]. It's beyond offensive. We're used to offensive, that's become a daily thing. This is actually dangerous."[29] Critic Jack Shaheen agreed: "When I read the screenplay, what immediately caught my attention was the fact that Arab-Muslims were blowing up New York City, killing hundreds of innocent people. That's an image that we see over and over again."[30]

Yet the screenplay by director Ed Zwick, Menno Meyjes, and Lawrence Wright, who later wrote an important book on Bin Laden and Al Qaeda titled *The Looming Tower* (2006), is highly intelligent and well informed, with a sharp critique of the US policies in advance of the 9/11 terrorist attacks and inadequate responses. While the large number of Arab-American sleeper cells portrayed in the film were in retrospect exaggerated, and although the association of Muslims and Arabs with terrorism was excessive, the film anticipated in uncanny fashion both the dangers of Islamic terrorism on American soil and the dangers of an ultra-rightwing reaction by the US government. *The Siege* also showed the lack of coordination and tensions between the CIA and FBI which experts agree were a contributing factor to 9/11. The film indicated as well how US policy in the Middle East produced enemies who became committed terrorists. It portrayed the sort of illegal "rendition" of alleged political enemies and torture and murder of political prisoners that has created tremendous controversy that is still boiling in the Obama era. And *The Siege* depicted rogue elements of the military carrying out their own policies of torture and murder, driven by what they saw as a higher calling to protect the nation and eliminate evil, outside the bounds of political constraints and international law.

In addition, *The Siege* broke with the white male hero tradition of action adventure films and portrayed a multicultural group of Americans protecting the polity, led by a dynamic African American with a highly competent Arab-American partner, and strong women and other ethnic associates. The Denzel Washington character, Hubbard, is intelligent, charismatic, competent, and highly articulate in defending the constitution and American values, anticipating Barack Obama. His Arab-American partner Frank is similarly highly intelligent and competent, and the audience is forced to view the indiscriminate arrests of Arab-American men from his point of view, as he goes to a detention camp to try to find his son who was incarcerated. By contrast, the Bruce Willis figure, performed by an actor who often portrays the white superhero in action and adventure films, plays a power-mad military villain, uncannily anticipating the arguments and policies of Dick Cheney and his band of villains. Finally, the happy ending of the film is the restitution of the US constitutional order and not the slaughter of villains of color, as usually happens in Hollywood rightwing action adventure films.

The Siege can thus be read retrospectively as both a cautionary warning against the dangers of domestic terrorism and overreaction on the part of the state. Its frightening depictions of the setting up of military detention centers and mass arrests of groups based on ethnic profiling, evokes memories of arrest and mass detention of Japanese Americans during World War II – actions now deemed unnecessary, immoral, and unconstitutional. Since the Bush-Cheney administration had on its books such detention centers in an extension of the so-called USA Patriot Act, *The Siege*'s warning was prescient. Against rightwing extremism, the film takes a strong civil liberties position, with one character asserting during the mass detention of Arab Americans: "What if it was black people? Huh? What if it was Italians? Puerto Ricans?" The film shows how terrorism can be used to justify racism against Arabs and Muslims and warns about how fear can be manipulated by opportunistic rightwing politicians to violate American rights and traditions.

William Friedkin's *Rules of Engagement* (2000) also anticipated the wave of anti-American hatred in the Middle East and how US military power would be deployed against it. Based on a story and earlier script by Senator James Webb (D-Va), and written by Stephen Gaghan, the action opens in the jungles of Vietnam, where two young officers are caught in a firefight. Terry Childers (Samuel L. Jackson) assassinates a captured Vietnamese prisoner and threatens their commander with death unless he calls off the attack that has Hayes Hodges (Tommy Lee Jones) and his platoon pinned down. The Vietnamese officer assents, and Childers thus saves Hodges' life, while the rest of Hodges' troops are killed. The film cuts to Hodges' retirement, some 28 years later, where he reunites with Childers, who complains that military life has "become a whole new ball game: no enemies, no front, no victories, no defeats, no mama, no papa. We're orphans out there."[31] Childers is soon sent to Yemen to extract an ambassador and his family whose embassy is surrounded by angry Arab demonstrators. Snipers fire on the embassy, Marines are killed, and Childers, believing there to be armed terrorists in the crowd shooting at them, tells his men to "waste the motherfuckers."

Childers is accused of violating rules of engagement and killing 83 innocent civilians. He is forced into a high-profile trial, after we have seen the national security adviser (Bruce Greenwood) destroy a tape which we discover has pictures of angry Arabs firing a multitude of weapons from the crowd at the embassy, which presumably would have exculpated Childers. Both the national security adviser and the ambassador are revealed to be lying villains who pursue their own self-interest and political expediency, and scapegoat the "warriors' warrior" Childers. The result is that the film makes military warriors heroes, and transcodes Bush-Cheney claims concerning the virulence of Islamicist terrorist threats to the US and the need for an unrestrained military response. *Rules of Engagement* implies that liberal rules and hesitations can obstruct necessary military action, thus legitimating in advance the administration's willful breaking of the law and the Geneva conventions in the Iraq War and "war on terror." Furthermore, Arabs are shown as a faceless, anti-American rabble, while US anti-military demonstrators who mobilize to protest Childers' actions are shown to be an ignorant and uninformed mob – typical corporate media representations of anti-war demonstrators.[32]

Another pre-9/11 film dealing with terrorism, *Swordfish* (2001), put on display a growing obsession with terrorism and allegorically presents the lengths to which sectors of the US government would go to deal with the threat. The highly improbable plot has a rogue intelligence agent amassing millions to carry out "black ops" (i.e., covert off the book operations) against terrorist groups who threaten the US. Produced by Joel Silver (*The Matrix*) and Jonathan D. Krane (*Face/Off*) and directed by Dominic Sena, the film uses the action adventure formula to pull off an elaborate political conspiracy drama. *Swordfish* opens during a bank heist where an apparently criminal mastermind, Gabriel Shear (John Travolta), has rigged hostages with explosives to get access to bank computers and a get-away helicopter. The scene flashes back to the recruitment by the mastermind some months earlier of a computer hacker, Stanley Jobson (Hugh Jackman). Gabriel eventually tells the hacker that there are nine and a half billion dollars in 1980s DEA accounts that were used to launder money and catch drug gangs, but the money has been sitting idle and accruing interest. The rogue superpatriot tells how during the 1950s J. Edgar Hoover and the FBI set up a black ops operation to fight enemies of the state. Gabriel explains that his robbery scheme is intended to get the DEA money to procure resources to violently assault with high-tech nuclear and other advanced weapons any terrorist group or country that attacks the US in a black ops attack. After the rogue "patriot" bribes, threatens, and eventually kidnaps the hacker's daughter, Stanley breaks the code and appears to transfer the money to Gabriel's bank accounts.

In a side plot, Halle Berry plays Ginger, a seductive femme fatale girlfriend of Gabriel who is used to procure the reluctant hacker and who, when he discovers her with a recording wire-piece, claims she is a DEA agent. Stanley thus bonds with Ginger, but it turns out she is really Gabriel's accomplice, helping to manipulate Stanley. But the hacker has some twists of his own, leading to the dilemma of multiple endings on the DVD of the film. In the theater ending, to save his daughter, Stanley transfers money to Gabriel's Monte Carlo back account which Ginger disperses to multiple accounts; shortly afterwards, news reports of dead terrorists mysteriously attacked begin to appear, suggesting that Gabriel has successfully gotten the funds and is manipulating the black ops. In an alternative DVD ending, Ginger finds out that there is only $500 in the account and she and Gabriel cheerfully sail off to their next adventure.

Obviously, the original ending is more faithful to the film noir and cyberpunk fiction roots of the story. In his DVD commentary, Dominic Sena notes how the hacker Stanley was modeled after a William Gibson character in a cyperpunk novel and the aesthetic has the speed, violence, complex high-tech subtext, political conspiracy motifs, low-life crime mileux, ambiguity, and narrative complexity of a cyberpunk novel.[33] Pre 9/11, the film, however, takes terrorism as a game and its cynicism made it marginal and in bad taste in the subsequent post-9/11 situation (see chapter 2).

After 9/11, Hollywood heavily promoted conservative political thrillers. John Moore's *Behind Enemy Lines* (2002) puts on display the extreme militarism and conservativism that followed the 9/11 attacks. While it is narratively incoherent, it is straight-up reactionary in its political discourse. It was the first movie dealing with war released after 9/11, and its gung-ho patriotism led the Fox studio to move up its release a couple of months to late November 2001. The plot features a fighter pilot, Lt. Chris Barnett (Owen Wilson), disgruntled because he is sent to Bosnia to police a situation that is unclear. Barnett is depicted as ready to resign because he hasn't seen any exciting action. His commander (Gene Hackman) sends Barnett on a spy mission during which he veers off to photograph suspicious Serb activity, is shot down, and miraculously survives despite having a sharp-shooter assassin and the Serb army after him. However, the French-led NATO command refuses the US general's demands to rescue him because of the delicate political situation (previewing later French-US tensions over Iraq).

Behind Enemy Lines was supported by the US Navy, and early images of the planes taking off from a battleship look suspiciously like those from *Top Gun* that became a major recruiting tool in the 1980s (see Kellner 1995: 75ff). Not surprisingly, *Behind Enemy Lines* footage was incorporated into a popular Navy recruitment ad shown in theaters and on TV for months. John Moore, the director of the film, was best known at the time as the creator of a Sega video game ad, and his improbable narrative, jerky camera, and comic-book vibe reflect his inexperience and origins.

The specific political context of *Behind Enemy Lines* is muddled and it is not clear in what time or place the action unfolds.[34] TV news footage shown is from Sky TV News, owned by Rupert Murdoch, who also owns the film company 20th Century Fox that produced the film, so the militarist and conservative propaganda dimension is obvious and on the surface. Many critics were harsh about the utterly unrealistic escape through Serb territory and the blundering actions of the main hero, who makes himself an easy target throughout. Ironically, the story was based on the exploits of USAF Captain Scott O'Grady, who was shot down over Bosnia and escaped capture. He sued 20th Century Fox for misrepresentation, as he claimed he did not swear constantly, did not hotdog while in flight, and never disobeyed orders.

Hack action film director Andrew Davis's *Collateral Damage* (2002) anticipates terrorist attacks on the US and legitimates the use of extreme violence to exterminate the evil doers, intersecting with the Bush-Cheney Manichean discourse that divided the world into absolute good and evil. The film was ready for release on October 5, 2001, but sensitivity concerning audience response after 9/11 led to its postponement. On a DVD featurette recounting the film's history, Davis noted that it was tested on audiences in November 2001 and that positive audience response indicated that the public was ready and even eager for action adventure political thrillers about terrorism. The movie was officially released on

February 8, 2002 in over 2,000 theaters and took in a worldwide gross of $78,382,433.[35]

Starring Arnold Schwarzenegger as fireman Gordy Brewer, *Collateral Damage* opens with Gordy entering a dangerous fire in a building, breaking down a door with a fire-ax, and rescuing individuals, evoking memories of the heroic firefighters in the World Trade Center. The film cuts to his wife's waking up in the morning. After a domestic interlude which presents Gordy as a loving husband and father, the family drops off the son at the doctor's for a check-up. As Gordy arrives to pick them up at a café, a bomb explodes, killing his wife and son and triggering a rightwing revenge fantasy narrative.

The café was situated next to the Colombian embassy and Colombian terrorists set the bomb to send the message that the US should not interfere in Colombia's affairs. Although the terrorists responsible for the blast use leftwing and anti-imperialist rhetoric, they are really venal killers who operate a cocaine factory in Colombia and ruthlessly kill all opponents. The highly clichéd and moralistic scenario establishes the terrorists as absolutely evil and the US as absolutely good, legitimating the sort of extreme actions against terrorism that the Bush-Cheney administration was concocting.[36]

While *Rules of Engagement* and *Collateral Damage* both transcode the emerging Bush-Cheney administration rightwing rhetoric against terrorism, Ridley Scott's *Black Hawk Down* (2001) anticipated the fierce radical Islamic anti-Americanism that exploded on 9/11. *Black Hawk Down* also provides a preview of the violent urban warfare that would erupt in Iraq after the US invasion and occupation. Begun months before 9/11, *Black Hawk Down* was held back from release for some weeks after the terror attack, but was given a broad national release in late December 2001 and into 2002, when it became a popular hit.[37]

Based on Mark Bowden's novel, the film deals with the fierce 18-hour firefight and shooting down of two Black Hawk helicopters in Somalia in October 1993, and the bloody attempts to rescue their crews and other troops pinned down in violent urban warfare. *Black Hawk Down* opens with titles stating that 300,000 people had died in Somalia during a drought and bitter civil war. The UN intervened in 1992 to deliver humanitarian food aid and provide police forces, but a Somali militia killed and skinned 25 Pakistani UN peace-keeping personnel, requiring a US/UN response. The narrative focuses on Army Ranger and Delta Force units going into Somalia in order to extract Somali militants centered

Ridley Scott's *Black Hawk Down* shows US troops pinned down by hostile Islamic radical forces in Somalia that in retrospect provides a preview of the US intervention in Iraq.

around clan-militia leader Muhammad Aidid. As in Iraq, the US forces do not have good ground intelligence in Somalia and face a violent, well-armed and organized insurgency as they begin their extraction mission. The mission quickly descends into chaos as hordes of insurgent troops surround the US troops, picking them off with sniper fire, shooting down two of the Black Hawk helicopters with hand-held missiles, pinning down the soldiers in dangerous urban conditions, and overwhelming one of the shot-down copters, anticipating the horrors of urban warfare that US troops would face in Iraq.

Critics of *Black Hawk Down* have disparaged the non-stop barrage of military spectacle which overwhelms the spectator with the sights and sounds of war without allowing the audience sufficient distance to think or analyze the actions (McCrisken and Pepper 2005). The Pentagon supplied the filmmakers of *Black Hawk Down* with the helicopters needed to make the film and Delta Force soldiers to help supply authenticity, and the film privileges US military humanism and heroics. Although it is strongly militarist, *Black Hawk Down* can be read as a cautionary tale about the dangers of interventionism in countries that have hostile forces, copious arms supplies, and urban battlegrounds where the US loses its technological advantage. As with Iraq, Somalia was "Mission: Impossible" for the US troops, who were thrown into a hornet's nest of violent insurgency. While there were criticisms that Scott's film was racist in showing hordes of Africans assaulting the white US troop,[38] in fact, the film shows the insurgency as very well organized, motivated, and competent, killing 19 US troops and wounding many more. Titles at the end, however, indicate that over 1,000 Somalis were killed in the intervention.

Sometimes contemporary films set in earlier historical eras can provide commentary and critical visions of the present moment. While no films explicitly about Vietnam appeared in the 1960s and 1970s during the fateful intervention – with the exception of the John Wayne propaganda film *The Green Berets* (1967) – many saw Robert Altman's *M.A.S.H.* (1970), a black comedy about a medical team in Korea, as largely about Vietnam, while critics saw some of the violent Westerns of Sam Peckinpah, Robert Aldrich, and others as anti-Vietnam allegories (see Wood 1986; Kellner and Ryan 1988). Hence, George Clooney's *Good Night, and Good Luck* (2005), which portrays Edward R. Murrow's fight against Joe McCarthy and the extreme right in the 1950s, captures, on one hand, the horrors of McCarthyism and the paranoia it injected into institutions ranging from the media to the military, which were targets of his witch-hunts. Yet it also provides critical reflections on the Bush-Cheney right-wing extremist regime that had attempted to politicize government agencies from the Justice Department to the Environmental Protection Agency (EPA), and which imprisoned without trial those it deemed enemies under the so-called USA Patriot Act. For instance, the Bush-Cheney administration unleashed the largest wire-tapping operation in US history, while fiercely attacking its critics in the media, often trying to destroy their lives.

Some films explicitly articulate the ethos of the day. *The Deal* (2005), written and co-produced by a Goldman-Sachs employee, Ruth Epstein, directed by Harvey Kahn, and co-produced and starring Christian Slater, captures the corporate greed and willingness to break rules for short-term profit that contributed to the Wall Street and global financial meltdown of 2008. Slater plays Tom Hanson, a Wall Street litigator, who is asked to give "due diligence" on a merger between a US oil corporation named Condor and a Russian oil corporation named Black Star, even though he is not an expert in oil drilling. Set in a future a few years ahead, there is a war between the US and a Confederation of Arab States, producing a major energy crisis. The oil company merger would bring much needed oil from Russia, but it turns out that the deal is a scam in which the Russian Mafia would deliver Arab oil to Russia that could then be sent to the US to circumscribe the embargo. Although Hanson's career rests on putting through the deal, he does not want to risk getting caught up in a major scandal and goes to the US government to report the scam. It first appears that the government is the White Knight that will solve the problem, but Hanson learns that it is in on the scam, disclosing a corrupt corporate and political culture.

Syriana, released the same year and which I discuss in chapter 4, provides a much better sense of the complexity of oil geopolitics than the corporate conspiracy potboiler *The Deal*, although in retrospect it looks like it was no secret Wall Street and US corporations were involved in shady activities that would lead to a meltdown. Tony Gilroy's *Michael Clayton* (2007), in turn, portrays how the corporate, legal, and political systems were all caught up in economic corruption. Featuring George Clooney as an ethically challenged legal fixer assigned to protect an agro-chemical company from damaging revelations concerning the harmful environmental impact of its products, the film presents the destructive effects of a corrupt corporate and conservative culture (I discuss *Michael Clayton* in more detail in the conclusion). The pharmaceutical industry is sharply criticized in the film *The Constant Gardener* (2005), which portrays a global conglomerate, with government complicity, testing dangerous drugs in Africa and killing the wife of a British diplomat and a co-investigator when they begin to uncover the dangerous truth.

Mike Judge's *Idiocracy* (2006), by contrast, satirizes corporate and consumer culture and the dumbing down of America, while Hal Hartley's *The Girl From Monday* (2005) presents its critique of consumer capitalism in the form of a fake science fiction film. Austin Chick's *August* (2008) uses Indie-style cool to portray a dot.com meltdown and the downfall of a twenty-something portraying himself and his company as the newest cutting-edge of the technological revolution. The film puts on display the hype and lack of substance behind the brazen self-promotion in some start-up companies, providing, in retrospect, a startling allegory for how the major US banks and investment firms were based on castles of sand and went belly-up when the bills became due.

Obviously, documentary films often make it their business to engage contemporary events and problems, and, as I argue in chapter 1, the 2000s have exhibited a "golden age of documentary" with a large number of docs that have dealt with the history and horrors of the Bush-Cheney administration, the intensified environmental crisis, the nightmare of Iraq, and a "war on terrorism" that has compromised American ideals and interests. During the 2000s, documentaries have broken box office records for the form and produced highly acclaimed and controversial products and directors, as chapter 3 on Michael Moore and discussions of critical documentaries throughout this book will attest.

While *Cinema Wars* will deal with major films that capture the ethos, fantasies, hopes, fears, and catastrophes of the era, offbeat genre films can also provide insights into contemporary society and culture. M. Night Shyamalan's *The Village* (2004) can be read as an allegory about Americans who submitted to conservative authoritarian leadership after 9/11 and were manipulated by a politics of fear to submit to the mythologies of their leaders to conform to a conservative regime. The clever plotline presents what appears to be a nineteenth-century utopian community, cut off from civilization, that cultivates fears of Those Who We Do Not Mention in the woods beyond the community, anxieties fueled by staged attacks by creatures in red outfits. It turns out that the community is living in the present on a land preserve purchased by one of its founders. Like the Bush-Cheney regime, the leaders are manufacturing fears of outside others to create homogeneity in the community and submission to the dominant values and leadership.

M. Night Shyamalan's *The Happening* (2008) articulates the inchoate dread and paranoia in post-9/11 America with its tale of inexplicable mass suicides infecting first urban and then small town areas. Rumors at first accuse terrorism for the horrors, but then government, nuclear power, and even nature are blamed in the narrative. In its eco-horror genre ambience, it is as if nature itself were rebelling against humans and setting off toxic forces.

Hence, creepy horror films can articulate deeply rooted fears that all is not well in the land of the brave and the home of the (once) free. Likewise, even a musical drama like Tim Burton's *Sweeney Todd* (2007) can be read as articulating both the violence and the deep cultural pessimism of the Bush-Cheney era. Its story recounts how a barber is driven to insane rage and vengeance when a corrupt aristocratic judge sends him to prison and exile in Australia so he can prey on the poor fellow's wife, who he drives to insanity and then adopts the couple's daughter as his ward. The film presents a highly Expressionist, grotesque, and violent version of the Stephen Sondheim opera about the "demon barber of Fleet Street" who becomes a serial murderer as he seeks vengeance on those who wronged him. The initial Sondheim drama opened on Broadway in 1979 and became a theatrical hit of the 1980s, articulating with the Reagan years. Its tale of how Sweeney Todd's victims were chopped up and ground into meat pies by his smitten landlady Mrs. Lovett to create a lucrative business allegorically presents how in the ultraconservative Reagan-Thatcher era everything can be turned into a commodity and people will do anything for money. Hal Prince's Broadway stage setting showed an industrial-era London where everything could be mass produced, even dead bodies, which were converted into food, a joke on the fast-food craze of the era.

Tim Burton's 2007 film, however, and the stage play launched in the 2000s by director-designer John Doyle, plays up the violent, macabre, and vicious aspects of the story, a perfect allegory of the ultraviolence of the Bush-Cheney era. The biting lyrics of the play capture the era's bleak cultural nihilism, as when Sweeney Todd exclaims: "There's a hole in the world like a great black pit / and it's filled with people who are filled with shit / And the vermin of the world inhabit it." The relentless intensification of violence that leads Sweeney Todd to kill his tormentors and unknowingly murder his daughter, followed by his own murder by a young boy devoted to the landlady, captures the sense of helplessness and deep pessimism of a world forced to watch Bush-Cheney machinations inexorably lead to violence and catastrophe without anyone able to stop the insanity. Further, Sweeney Todd is ultimately destroyed by his quest for extra-legal vengeance, a lesson that the Bush-Cheney Gang failed to learn.[39]

If *Sweeney Todd* articulates the brutality and despair of the era, *V for Vendetta* (2006) articulates allegorically hopes for the overthrow of the conservative regime (see chapter 4). As I will show, a wide variety of films express fierce resistance to the oppression of the Bush-Cheney era, using modes ranging from documentary and realist fiction to allegory and satire. Yet other films, as documented, transcode conservative discourses or satirize all politics and ideologies.

While "torture porn" and other brutal films capture the violent and demented aspects of the Bush-Cheney era, *Rambo* (2008) transcodes in comic-book fashion its crusading militarism. In *Rambo III* the good-natured but dimwitted killing machine John Rambo sides with the Afghan mujahideen in one of the last battles of the Cold War.[40] Although the Soviet Union was to collapse, Rambo ultimately found himself on the wrong side, as the mujahideen became the forces that constituted al Qaeda and the Taliban. Making sure that he picked the "right side" this time, Sylvester Stallone (who wrote, produced, and starred in *Rambo IV*) researched the film, allegedly asking people from *Soldiers of Fortune* and the UN where the most appalling violation of human rights was taking place, and supposedly there was a consensus on Myanmar (formerly Burma, which is the name of the Evil Place Stallone chose to use in the film).[41]

During the last year of the Bush-Cheney administration, as its popularity regularly reached new lows and US prestige in the world continued to plummet, US conservativism needed a boost and a hero, and *Rambo* tries to provide them with one. This time, John Rambo is a snake trainer and metal forger near the Thailand-Myanmar border and some Christian humanitarians want to rent his boat to take medical supplies to the Karen people. The Karen are suppressed by the Myanmar government, as an opening montage of political newsreels informs us. Rambo hesitates to help them, but an attractive and idealistic woman (Julie Benz) persuades him, so Rambo and the humanitarians go up river to deliver supplies, providing him the opportunity to kill Burmese bandits who try to rob them and threaten to rape the woman.

A later trip up river to deliver the supplies reveals that the government has slaughtered scores of natives, destroyed their villages, and left heads on a pole as a warning. While exposing the repression of the Myanmar government would have been salutary, the film *Rambo IV* is intensely racist, following the "heart of darkness" formula whereby civilized white people go into barbarian sites of savagery. While the Myanmar government is no doubt repressive and totalitarian, the film *Rambo* shows the Myanmar army as vicious savages engaging in orgies of rape, pillage, and murder, with drunken scenes of debauchery punctuating brutal ethnic cleansing. The Great White God Rambo mobilizes some scraggly mercenaries to fight the hordes of Yellow Barbarians, slaughtering scores and saving the heroine, another sexist scenario where Woman-in-Danger requires salvation by the superhuman hero.

Yet the John Rambo figure appears dimmer than ever, reduced to Zen-like utterances such as "Live for nothing, or die for something" (his exhortation to the mercenaries to slaughter Myanmar troops rather than flee), or more characteristically "Fuck the world" (his response to the male humanitarian aid worker). The images of Rambo, however, are the same iconic representations of the White Male Warrior in the previous films. *Rambo IV* recycles these defining images, providing a sense of déjà vu all over again. Images of violence in the *Rambo* films have incrementally climbed, with one critic counting in the 2008 *Rambo* 83 "bad guys" killed by Rambo, 40 bad guys killed by accomplices of Rambo, and 113 good guys killed by villains, for a total of 236 people killed – almost double the 132 people killed in *Rambo III* (1988) and more than triple the amount killed in *Rambo II* (1985).[42]

Militarism, superheroes, and Hollywood film production are themselves satirized in Ben Stiller's *Tropic Thunder* (2008), which provides a multidimensional satire of the war film, the movie industry, and cinematic heroes like Rambo. Yet it walks the fine line with *Crash* between putting on display and satirizing, or deconstructing, racial stereotypes and reproducing them. *Tropic Thunder* opens with what appears to be a Vietnam War movie, but it is quickly apparent that the story depicts a movie about the making of movies and dissecting Hollywood character types. By juxtaposing images from the various characters' films, TV reports on their lives, and narrative scenes that often play against the cinematic stereotypes and public images of stars, it puts on display the social construction of masculinity and cinematic heroes, showing that actors who play ultra-macho roles in Hollywood action genre films are often insecure, narcissistic, wimpy, and pathetic. The film provides a particularly devastating satire of Hollywood and the culture industry, taking on studio producers, directors, agents, stars, and the whole media/publicity apparatus, showing that Hollywood film is aware of its construction of ideology and its stars, genres, and hype, and can provide material aiding in critically interpreting US cinema in the contemporary moment.

Cinema Wars presents Hollywood film and US culture and society as a contested terrain and attempts to elucidate the political conflicts of the era. As well as discussing films that articulate Bush-Cheney conservatism and militarism, I will engage films that present critique and opposition to the regnant Bush-Cheney administration, and highlight political battles over the polity and society, including war, terrorism, the environment, corporations and the state, and the politics of race, gender, and sexuality.[43] Since the 1960s, intense clashes over all of these issues have erupted in the United States, and became increasingly consequential as Bush-Cheney administration policies increased differences between the haves and have nots, and cut back on environmental programs, social welfare programs, and the rights of women, people of color, and gays and lesbians, while unleashing militarism and breaking international law in the name of fighting terrorism. As the Bush-Cheney administration pushed through an aggressively rightwing and militarist agenda that deeply divided US society, there was increased contestation for and against the ultraconservative policies, struggles evident in the Hollywood films of the period.

There exists a traditional rightwing attack on liberal Hollywood, so this book will probably produce froth and ravings among the anti-Hollywood right who sees the industry as a left-liberal conspiracy.[44] I would counter that Hollywood is largely a business. When there is dissatisfaction in society with a political regime, Hollywood is quick to exploit it with films transcoding the disaffection or anger with the ruling group, whatever its politics. However, it probably should be admitted that many in the Hollywood film community are liberals, so there will be liberal and socially critical films no matter who is in power and even during a conservative regime (Kellner and Ryan 1988).

Further, it is likely that there were so many anti-Bush and Cheney films because the regime was arguably the worst and certifiably the most unpopular in US history.[45] While critical images or discourse concerning George W. Bush in the period when he was popular immediately after 9/11 were taboo, and it was considered unpatriotic to attack the president and the administration, creators of media culture began articulating critical perspectives on the administration when its failures were becoming apparent. Eventually, it was easy, and perhaps in some quarters obligatory, to take shots at the Bush-Cheney regime after the catastrophe of Iraq, the inept administration performance over Hurricane Katrina, revelations of copious scandals, cronyism, and corruption, and, of course, the collapse of the US and global economy which topped the reign of error and infamy and helped propel Barack Obama into the presidency in the 2008 election.

Reading Film Diagnostically: Imagining Obama

I will engage in a *diagnostic critique* that uses films to analyze and interpret the events, hopes, fears, discourses, ideologies, and sociopolitical conflicts of the era.[46] This approach involves a dialectic of text and context, using texts to read social realities and events, and using social and historical context to help situate and interpret key films. Much as Walter Benjamin used the poetry of Charles Baudelaire to illuminate the scene of Paris in the mid-nineteenth century, we can use films to provide critical insight and knowledge about the present historical era. For diagnostic critique, film is an important source of knowledge, if used judiciously with the tools of history, social theory, and a critical media/cultural studies.[47] Critical study of film, many have argued, may provide privileged insight into how people behave, look, and act in a particular era, as well as their dreams, nightmares, fantasies, and hopes. Diagnostic critique may illuminate past and present historical situations and anticipate future ones.

In *Camera Politica* (1988), Michael Ryan and I claimed that popular Hollywood film of the late 1970s anticipated the election of Ronald Reagan, with a plethora of conservative hero films and yearning for deliverance from evil forces (like communism, statism, and liberal malaise). There were, moreover, many anticipations of the yearning and acceptance of a Barack Obama in television and Hollywood films of the 2000s. The country was arguably made ready to think about a president of color and became accustomed to black presidents through a variety of sources within Hollywood film and television. As early as 1972, James Earl Jones played a black president in *The Man*, although posters for the film read: "The first black president of the United States. First they swore him in. Then they swore to get him."[48] More recently, Morgan Freeman played a calm and competent president in the 1998 disaster movie *Deep Impact*, Tommy Lister played president in *The Fifth Element* (1997), and Chris Rock took on the role of hip hop president in the comedy *Head of State* (2003). Perhaps, however, it is Dennis Haysbert's popular David Palmer on the TV thriller *24* who is the best-known black president in media culture. Playing a competent and charismatic leader for over five seasons, Haysbert himself believes: "Frankly and honestly, what my role did and the way I was able to play it and the way the writers wrote it opened the eyes of the American public that a black president was viable and could happen…. It always made perfect sense to me. I never played it like it was fake."[49] To Haysbert's dismay, his character was assassinated and his younger, more inexperienced brother, Wayne Palmer, ascended to the presidency. His reign was marked by insecurity (not surprising on *24*) and uncertainty.[50]

The most astonishing anticipation of Obama's election can be found in the popular TV series *The West Wing* that featured Martin Sheen as president and dramatized adventures with his White House staff. A *New*

The election of African-American president Barack Obama was anticipated in films and TV series of the era.

York Times article indicated that one of the *West Wing* scriptwriters, Eli Attie, called David Axelrod, one of Obama's key advisers in 2004, and asked him to tell him about Barack Obama. After Obama's address to the 2004 Democratic National Convention, Axelrod and Attie had discussions about Obama's refusal to be defined by his race and his desire to bridge partisan and racial divides. As *The West Wing* unfolded during its final 2004–2006 seasons, there were anticipations of Obama in a Latino Democratic Party presidential candidate, Matthew Santos (Jimmy Smits). As Santos pursued the race for the presidency, the parallels between the fictional TV candidate and Obama were startling: both were coalition-building newcomers who had not served long in Congress; both were liberal and sought a new politics; both were very attractive and had very photogenic families; both were fans of Bob Dylan and, of course, both were candidates of color.

Even more striking, the Republican candidate in the fictional *West Wing* election campaign during the 2005–2006 season was modeled on John McCain, circa 2000. The fictional Republican Arnold Vinick (Alan Alda) played a maverick California senator who broke with his party on the environment, had strong foreign policy credentials but was more liberal than his party on social issues, and chose a conservative governor to serve as vice-president to shore up the base. Santos talked of hope and change in his election campaign and declared: "I don't want to just be the brown candidate. I want to be the American candidate."[51]

Morgan Freeman's film trajectory in the 2000s shows how the American public is able to perceive individuals in a multiracial mode and accept powerful black men in positions of authority. After playing president in *Deep Impact*, Freeman played God in *Bruce Almighty* (2003) and *Evan Almighty* (2007), and was a Voice of God narrator in films like *War of the Worlds* (2005), *March of the Penguins* (2005), and *Feast of Love* (2007). In Rob Reiner's *The Bucket List* (2007) Freeman's character finds himself in a hospital cancer ward with an irascible billionaire played by Jack Nicholson. When they discover that they have six months to live, Freeman proposes that they make a "bucket list" of what they would like to do before they die (i.e., kick the bucket), and since the Nicholson character is super-rich there is no limit to their possibilities. The Freeman character is once again the moral center of the film, and calmly, intelligently, and with good humor allows the unlikely pair to achieve their goals, at the end helping the Nicholson character unite with his estranged daughter.

All of these films present the Freeman persona bonding with people of different races, ages, and classes, showing a propensity in contemporary US culture to accept African Americans in a variety of roles, and to respect and accept people of color in terms of their personalities and admirable qualities. Furthermore, according to the Internet Movie Database, Freeman acted in at least 36 films in the years 2000 to 2008, incarnating the moral center of wisdom in the films just mentioned, and playing the narrator and key moral figure in Clint Eastwood's *Million Dollar Baby* (2004). Freeman has also played detectives, criminals, assassins, and assorted characters in a wide variety of films and genres, as well as serving as a popular narrator for a large number of films.

Denzel Washington has emerged as well as a major player in Hollywood, acting and directing films and playing starring roles on

Broadway. In the 2004 remake of *The Manchurian Candidate* (see chapter 4) the Washington character rescues the polity from corporate and political conspiracies, as he did earlier in Alan J. Pakula's *The Pelican Brief* (1993) and Edward Zwick's *The Siege* (1998) (Coyne 2008: 195). Receiving three Golden Globe awards and two Academy Awards for his work, Washington is recognized as one of the most acclaimed and popular actors of our time.

The recent trajectory of Will Smith also shows how a man of color can play roles previously reserved for white actors. As Jan Stuart points out, in recent films Smith has erected "a gallery of Olympian everymen," playing an off-beat superhero in *Hancock* (2008) and a homeless overachiever in *The Pursuit of Happyness* (2006). In Stuart's words, these are "canny exemplars of the divinity next door with warts and all." *Seven Pounds* (2008) "rounds out with those two films a kind of trilogy of self-deification," with Smith playing a character who, like the star of the 1950s TV series *The Millionaire*, randomly chooses individuals to "dramatically change [their] circumstances," exactly as Obama advertised he would try to do and which many people fantasize he would do.[52] In a recent poll of theater owners in the annual survey run by Quigley Publishing, Smith was named the number one box office attraction of 2008, and as of January 2009 had grossed an astonishing $2,511,011,862 globally in his 19 films.[53]

I am not arguing that Hollywood film or any TV series directly helped elect Barack Obama; rather, it was his highly effective campaign that was decisive, as well as the major economic crisis which drove people to question Republican laissez-faire market economics.[54] I am arguing, however, that film and television anticipated having a person of color as president and may have helped make the possibility thinkable.

In addition to black superstars, there are many people of color in contemporary US film and television presented in a manner in which their race does not play a significant narrative role and is often unacknowledged. This is not to say that racial oppression and racism have disappeared in US film, culture, and society – this book will cite many examples of continued racial stereotypes and blatant racism. It does suggest, however, that the culture at large is ready to accept and even affirm people of color in high-starring and real-life executive positions, even the president of the United States.

Creators of popular culture often anticipate political and social changes, presenting certain forms of behavior, ideas, or figures like black presidents before they have actually appeared. Serious amounts of money are invested in the production of films and television, so they must resonate with audiences and often anticipate what people are thinking about, fantasizing, or yearning for. German writer Siegfried Kracauer, once close to Benjamin and Adorno, laid bare the historical-political allegorical dimension of film and provided one of the first systematic studies of how films articulate social, political, and psychological content. His classic book *From Caligari to Hitler: A Psychological History of the German Film* (1947) argues that German interwar films reveal a highly authoritarian disposition to submit to social authority and a fear of emerging chaos. For Kracauer, German films reflected and fostered anti-democratic and passive attitudes of the sort that anticipated the rise of Hitler and paved the way for Nazism.

Building on these traditions, Barbara Deming demonstrated in *Running Away From Myself* (1969) how 1940s Hollywood films provided insights into the social psychology and reality of the period. Deming argued: "It is not as mirrors reflect us but, rather, as our dreams do that movies most truly reveal the times" (p. 1). She claimed that 1940s Hollywood films provided a collective dream portrait of the era and proposed deciphering "the dream that all of us have been buying at the box office, to cut through to the real nature of the identification we have experienced there" (pp. 5–6). Her work anticipated later, more sophisticated and university based film criticism of the post-1960s era by showing how films both reproduce dominant ideologies and also contain critical elements that cut across the grain of the ideology they promote. Deming also undertook a gender reading of Hollywood film that would eventually become a key part of film criticism.

Academic film studies that emerged in the 1960s and 1970s provided more historically grounded sociological approaches, theoretically informed film criticism, and aesthetic analysis of cinematic form and style. During the 1970s, film criticism emerging from France and Great Britain in journals like *Cahiers du cinéma* and *Screen* combined Marxian ideology critique, structuralist and poststructuralist analysis of cinematic form, psychoanalytic probing of latent content and meanings, and feminist, gay and lesbian, and other critical perspectives to develop robust film criticism that we are still drawing upon today.[55]

In addition to laying bare the sociopolitical fantasies and personal dreams and nightmares of an era, critical analysis of film can help dissect and deconstruct dominant ideologies, as well as show key ideological resistance and struggle in a given society at a specific moment. The groundbreaking work of critical media theorists like the Frankfurt School and French structuralism and poststructuralism revealed that culture is a social construct that reproduces dominant ideology and its contestations, intrinsically linked to the vicissitudes of the socially and historically specific milieu in which it is conceived. Poststructuralism stressed the openness and heterogeneity of the text, its embeddedness in history and desire, its political and ideological dimensions, and its contradictions and excess of meaning. This led critical theory to more intricate, multilevel interpretive methods and more radical political readings and critique.

I combine discourses and methods from these traditions of critical theory, cultural studies, and film theory to provide diagnostic critique of the politics and social struggles of the 2000s. My model of a multiperspectivist cultural and film studies includes study of production, texts, and audiences in their sociohistorical context, drawing on a wealth of perspectives and theories to interpret, in this case, key films of the era, as well as some marginal ones.

In This Book

In the chapters that follow, I draw upon a multiplicity of different film theories and approaches to Hollywood cinema, some signaled in this introduction, to help develop a multiperspectivist film criticism that presents the intersection of film, politics, and the vicissitudes of US culture and society. Chapter 1 opens with exploration of the "golden age of documentary," in which a large number of films capture key political issues and struggles of the contemporary era, ranging from the stolen election of 2000 to the Iraq war and environmental crisis, intensified by decades of neglect by conservative regimes such as the Reagan administration and both Bush administrations. After examining a series of documentaries that dissect the Bush-Cheney regime and corporations that largely supported them, I discuss environmental crisis documentaries and some fictional entertainment films that use animation and narrative to depict the dangers of global warming and climate change. Hollywood films in the new millennium include a series of allegories of disaster that I engage and relate to current fears and dangers of societal and eco-catastrophe. In an uncanny fashion, social apocalypse films anticipate not only intensifying environmental crisis, but also the financial meltdown of Fall 2008, which was deemed the greatest economic crisis since the Great Depression of the 1930s.

Chapter 2 opens with analysis of 9/11 as a spectacle of terror akin to a disaster film, an event which enabled the Bush-Cheney regime to carry through its hard-right and militarist agenda. I engage the first films to represent events of 9/11 in the Hollywood films *United 93* and *World Trade Center*. Next, I turn to a major "television event," *The Path to 9/11*, that I interpret as "Disney Television Republican Propaganda." I conclude with a discussion of how some Hollywood films articulated the fears and paranoia of the post-9/11 era, including *Mission:Impossible III* (2006), *War of the Worlds* (2005), and some more marginal thrillers dealing with terrorism.

Chapter 3 discusses Michael Moore's work, exploring the specific style, politics, and filmmaking strategies employed in his major documentaries, which have been among the most successful and controversial of all time. In engaging Michael Moore's "provocations," I discuss his relation to Emile de Antonio and a leftwing partisan documentary film tradition, and then read *Roger and Me* as a documentary of personal witnessing that engages issues of capitalism and class. *Bowling For Columbine* is interpreted as an exploratory documentary montage that takes on guns, US history, the military, and societal violence in the United States, and that provides a complex vision that offers no easy answers. *Fahrenheit 9/11* is read as an example of a partisan political intervention that takes on the Bush-Cheney administration, 9/11, and Iraq, aiming at no less than the defeat of a sitting president in the 2004 election. *Sicko* (2006) is presented as Moore's most radical critique of the crisis of American values, worldview, and its institutions.

Chapter 4 takes on a wide range of anti-Bush-Cheney Hollywood films, ranging from realist critique to allegory and satire, capturing the turmoil and chaos of the era. I show how many political thrillers were mobilized to critique Bush-Cheney policies and major figures in the administration, while other conservative and militarist films can be read as legitimating the Republican administration. Certain Hollywood political thrillers offer barely disguised allegorical critiques of the Bush-Cheney regime, ranging from Jonathan Demme's 2004 remake of *The Manchurian Candidate* to *The Bourne Conspiracy* trilogy. A wide range of thrillers offer conflicting political visions of the Middle East and threats of terrorism, with some criticizing Bush-Cheney administration interventions, or more broadly imperialism, to others legitimating militarist and imperialist policies. I also present a reading of the *Star Wars* prequels as anti-Bush-Cheney allegory. Finally, I discuss a number of satires and dystopic allegories that can be read as critical of the Republican administration.

Chapter 5 takes on the cinematic Iraq War, first examining a series of documentaries that depict the invasion of Iraq, the occupation and insurgency, and impacts on the Iraqi people and US soldiers. Then I examine some documentaries that attempt interpretation of the Iraq fiasco, before engaging Iraq and its aftermath in Hollywood fiction films, including a series of films released in 2007–2008 which cumulatively explore the magnitude of the Iraq disaster for Iraqis, Americans, and people of the region.

The conclusion assesses "Hollywood Cinema Wars in the 2000s," discussing relations between film and politics in the contemporary moment. I conclude with discussion of how certain films exemplify key aspects of the politics and struggles of the era, moving from the conservative hegemony of the Bush-Cheney regime to a new era marked by the Obama presidency. I then offer final reflections upon what Hollywood film reveals as the limitations and failures of the Bush-Cheney administration.

Notes

1   I use the term *Bush-Cheney administration* to call attention to the extraordinary role of Dick Cheney and his associates during the Bush Junior years. A series in the *Washington Post* under the rubric "Angler" documented the unprecedented role Dick Cheney played in the Bush presidency. See www. blog.washingtonpost.com/cheney/ and the book *Angler* based on this series by Gellman (2008). For more critical analysis of Cheney, see Nichols (2004) and Mayer (2008).

2   "Hollywood considers role in war effort," *CNN*, November 12, 2001 at www.archives.cnn.com/2001/US/11/11/rec.hollywood.terror/index. html (accessed September 18, 2008). Following a meeting between Bush adviser Karl Rove and Hollywood executives, a White House spokesperson announced: "The administration will share with studio executives the themes we're communicating at home and abroad of patriotism, tolerance and courage." See Robert Reno, "Harrumph for Bush's Hollywood," *Common Dreams News Center*, November 13, 2001 at www.commondreams.org/views01/1113-06.htm (accessed September 18, 2008). Jack Valenti, Hollywood insider and president of the Motion Picture Association of America, claimed afterwards that the talk resulted in increased distribution of first-run US films to troops and the making of

public service films, and not mandating specific themes or films (see McCrisken and Pepper 2005: 204f).

3   I will use "Hollywood film" and "cinema" interchangeably to describe contemporary cinema in the United States. "Hollywood" has traditionally been used to describe the specific form of film production, genres, and distribution and reception in the US. In a global era of cultural production, the geography of US film obviously transcends Hollywood as a site, but to stress continuities, I use the still widely shared phrase "Hollywood film" to describe films largely financed and produced by companies in the US which follow the conventions associated with classical Hollywood cinema. The term "cinema" has richer connotations than "film," referring to the system of production, distribution, and reception, as well as the genres, styles, and aesthetics of a given national cinema. On the classical Hollywood cinema, see Bordwell, Staiger, and Thomson (1985); on continuities between the classical and contemporary Hollywood cinema, see Bordwell (2006); for an overview of Hollywood film and its relation to cinema/film history and US society, see Thomson (2004).

4   Throughout, I employ concepts and models developed in Kellner and Ryan (1988) and Kellner (1995).

5   *Ideology* refers to the dominant ideas in a society that legitimate the ruling institutions, groups, and social relations. Following Marx's critique of ideology as the dominant ideas of the ruling class, Antonio Gramsci (1971) expanded ideology to refer to the ideas of major groups struggling for hegemony, such as liberals and conservatives in the US context, and socialists and communists vs. conservatives in certain European contexts. British cultural studies expanded the concept of ideology to include how such ideas reproduce domination and subordination in the realms of gender, sexuality, race, ethnicity, religion, and other domains of social life. While some Hollywood films are pure ideological propaganda, others are highly contradictory, ambiguous, and even incoherent and difficult to read, which can also generate multiple readings. For more on the concept of ideology, see Durham and Kellner (2006); for the debates over ideology and its use in analyzing media culture, see Kellner (1978, 1979); Centre for Contemporary Cultural Studies (1980); Kellner and Ryan (1988); Thomson (1990).

6   As Robin Wood (1986) suggests, while the "incoherent text" can be extremely revealing about the ideological and socio-psychological problematics of the contemporary moment, it can also be simply muddled and incoherent, and merely reflect ideological confusion and ambiguity. For example, Wood argues that William Friedkin's *Cruising* (1980) was largely seen as homophobic, reproducing stereotypes of gay male culture, although there are other dimensions of the film sympathetic to gay culture and that deconstruct oppositions between hetero- and homosexuality. I will offer examples

of incoherent texts from contemporary Hollywood films that put forth conflicting political and ideological positions.

7   The term *politics of representation* comes from Stuart Hall and British cultural studies (see Kellner 1995). It refers to the specific political coding of representations in film and other artifacts of media culture, as to whether, for instance, narratives transcode liberal, conservative, radical, or ambiguous positions, or whether representations of women are sexist, progressive, or contradictory. For more on the politics of representation, see Durham and Kellner (2006) and Hammer and Kellner (2009a).

8   On culture wars between liberals, conservatives, and radicals in US society from the 1960s into the present, see Hunter (1991) and Jensen (1995). "Conservativism" and "liberalism" have had different and contested meanings in varying cultures and historical periods, and I am focusing on the cultural wars in US society in the 2000s as represented in contemporary US film.

9   On independent cinema and its relation to mainstream Hollywood cinema, see Pierson (1995), Biskind (2004), and Tzioumakis (2006).

10 For a contrast between Gibson's *The Passion* and *The Da Vinci Code*, see Hammer and Kellner (2009b).

11 For an extended discussion of how Gibson's film departs from the gospels and depends on problematic versions of Jesus's arrest and death, see Hammer and Kellner (2009b).

12 On how a fundamentalist Manicheanism that divided the world into a battle between Good and Evil constructed the mindset of the Bush-Cheney administration, see Kellner (2003b) and Greenwald (2007).

13 On the Bush-Cheney administration's systematic use of a politics of lying, see Kellner (2007b). In interviews, Mel Gibson falsely claimed he was basing *Passion* on the gospels and vehemently denied anti-Semitic motives in producing the film. He also claimed that the Holy Ghost was directing the film, as if Gibson were the vessel of God. Many scholars have noted how the *Passion* departs from standard gospel accounts. There has been sharp criticism of the film's anti-Semitism, a reading enhanced by Gibson's outburst of anti-Semitic ravings during an incident of driving under the influence in 2006; see Hammer and Kellner (2009b).

14 As of January 19, 2009, *The Dark Knight* had grossed $997,033,655 worldwide (see www.boxofficemojo.com/movies/?id=darkknight.htm).

15 Ron Suskind (2006) quotes Dick Cheney as saying that even if there was a 2 percent chance that a specific group or individual was going to launch a terrorist attack, their arrest, violation of legal rights, and even torture were totally justified. Later, journalist Jane Mayer titled her book on the lawless and vicious nature of Bush-Cheney administration policy *The Dark Side* (2008), describing, again in Dick Cheney's own terms, where the administration went in order to fight terror.

16 See Andrew Klavans, "What Bush and Batman have in common," *Wall Street Journal*, July 25, 2008: A15.

17 The contrast in Oscars reflecting different eras was made by Patrick Goldstein, "A dark view on dark times," *Los Angeles Times*, February 25, 2008: E1, 12.

18 My notion of cinematic mapping is influenced by Fredric Jameson's (1981, 1992) notion of cognitive mapping, whereby film, literature, or cultural texts contribute to a process by which an individual subject situates her/himself within a larger social context, including one's place in society, or even the global world. Such mappings contain for Jameson a mixture of ideology and utopia, constructing individuals in many instances in terms of dominant ideologies, but they may also project utopian possibilities for another way of life. Cinematic mapping shows some of the ways that cinema constructs visions of social, political, and individual life that provides access – often distorted by ideology and bias – to contemporary social life, politics, and history.

19 For critical film theorists, *realism* is a dominant ideology and cinematic style of Hollywood film that attempts to provide an imitation of life and uses conventions like the reflection of life and character in a given society, continuity editing that creates a reality effect, and "realistic" characters, settings, and narratives to construct a picture of the real. For a more detailed analysis of the dominant Hollywood aesthetic, see Bordwell, Staiger, and Thompson (1985). Against arguments that there is a new post-classical or postmodern Hollywood aesthetic and style that represents a discontinuity with earlier Hollywood cinema, David Bordwell (2006) argues that despite new aesthetic and technological developments in Hollywood film, there is an "intensified continuity" that allows novel stylistic developments and cinematic effects, with important continuities with classical Hollywood cinema, a position with which I agree.

20 An allegory is a form of fantasy or storytelling that can be interpreted to provide insight into contemporary historical events; it is a figurative mode of representation which conveys meanings other than literal ones. On allegory as a form of articulation of sociohistorical reality, see Jameson (1981); on contemporary Hollywood film and allegory, see Kellner and Ryan (1988) and Kellner (1995).

21 As of January 5, 2009, the "Iraqi Deaths due to US Invasion" stood at 1,307,319 according to statistics at www.justforeignpolicy.org/iraq/iraqdeaths.html; the confirmed deaths of US military personnel (officially acknowledged) stood at 4,221 (www.icasualties.org/oif/). The war and occupation of Iraq had cost $585,692,590,217 (www.nationalpriorities.org/costofwar_home) (all accessed January 5, 2009).

22 On the Bush dynasty, see Phillips (2004) and Kelley (2004).

23   For dicussion of the work of Benjamin and Adorno, see Buck-Morss (1977) and Kellner (1989). Benjamin had a more optimistic and activist view than Horkheimer and Adorno of the potential of media such as film to promote progressive political ends. Benjamin (1969) argued that film, sports, and other forms of mass entertainment were creating a new kind of spectator, able to critically dissect cultural forms and to render intelligent judgment on them. For Benjamin, the decline of the *aura* of the work of art – the sense of originality, uniqueness, and authenticity – under the pressures of mechanical reproduction helped produce a public able to more actively engage a wide range of cultural phenomena. He argued, for instance, that spectators of sports events were discriminating judges of athletic activity, able to criticize and analyze plays, athletes, strategies, and so on. Likewise, Benjamin postulated that film audiences can become experts of criticism and ably discuss and evaluate film.

24   The concept of the aesthetic dimension that I am using derives from Herbert Marcuse (1979). See also Kellner (2007a).

25   On existentialism, see Robert C. Solomon, *From Hegel to Existentialism* (New York: Oxford, 1987), and my doctoral dissertation on *Heidegger's Concept of Authenticity*, of which *No Country* provides cinematic realization, available online at www.gseis.ucla.edu/faculty/kellner/Heidegger.pdf.

26   Daniel Cho, email, August 2, 2008.

27   The bombing of an FBI counterterrorism headquarters was similar to al Qaeda connected terrorist groups' targets of the time. For a useful account of how *The Siege* replicates real terrorist events depicted in the US government annual report *Patterns of Global Terrorism*, see Helena Vanhala, "Civil society under siege; terrorism and government response to terrorism in *The Siege*," *Jump Cut*, 50 (Spring 2008) at www.ejumpcut.org/currentissue/Seige/index.html (accessed June 2, 2009).

28   The fictional story of US forces training anti-Hussein Iraq troops and then abandoning them mirrors actual events, as well as the US training radical Islamic forces, including groups associated with Osama Bin Laden, in Afghanistan to fight the Russians in the 1980s; see Vanhala, "Civil society under siege" and Cooley (2002).

29   "Muslims feel under siege from Hollywood. Arab groups decry a sinister depiction in 'The Siege.'" November 5, 1998 at www.ccat.sas.upenn.edu/~haroldfs/popcult/handouts/demoniz/TERR05.htm (accessed May 31, 2009).

30   Willow Bay, "Director Ed Zwick defends 'The Siege,'" *NewsStand: CNN and Entertainment Weekly Report*, November 10, 1998 at www.cnn.com/SHOWBIZ/Movies/9811/10/siege/index.html (accessed May 31, 2009). In his entry on *The Siege* in his encyclopedic text *Reel Bad Arabs*, Shaheen (2001: 430f) lists the negative representations of Arab Americans, but does

not list the themes critical of their scapegoating in the movie, the protests against their detention, the critiques of US policy, or the fact that a rightwing general who represents the positions of Dick Cheney is the villain of the film.

31 For an excellent analysis of how *Rules of Engagement* portrayed a conflict between the old conservative values of military honor and truth, compared to a more multicultural, relativist, and opportunistic "new" politics, and how the film constitutes an attack on liberalism, see Semmerling (2006: 163ff).

32 Shaheen (2001: 404) describes *Rules of Engagement* as "one of the most blatantly anti-Arab scenarios of all time," attacking its utterly fictional portrayal of events in Yemen in an incident that did not happen and presenting the people as uniformly supporting Jihadist terrorism while covering up the fact that the crowd was armed and firing on the Americans. Boggs and Pollard (2006: 186) describe the film as blatant propaganda for the US military, and its portrayal of an Arab mob, including women and children, armed to the teeth and shooting at the embassy as highly improbable, as was the extent of the US response, with troops firing wildly into the crowd and massacring them.

33 For my own take on cyberpunk as a subculture and mode of literary fiction, focusing on William Gibson, see chapter 8 of Kellner (1995).

34 See a viewer's complaint on the Internet Movie Database (www.imdb.com/title/tt0159273/): "What's fundamentally wrong with this movie is summed up by the opening voice-over about 'The Cincinnati peace accord.' I jumped out of my seat screaming 'The whaaaat? It's the Dayton peace accord you bloody fool!' I might be accused of nit picking but I wish to say that I think it's absolutely obscene that Hollywood has made a movie set against the backdrop of a conflict that killed 278,000 human beings and not once do I get the impression that the production team know what they're talking about." For a coherent analysis of *Behind Enemy Lines'* political context and sharp critique of the film, see Boggs and Pollard (2007: 181ff).

35 See the Internet Movie Database website that confirms the production history recounted on the DVD at www.imdb.com/title/tt0233469/ (accessed December 19, 2008). For its worldwide gross, see www.boxofficemojo.com/movies/?id=collateraldamage.htm (accessed June 5, 2009).

36 In a penetrating study of the context and ideological problematics of *Collateral Damage*, Russell Meeuf notes how the film complexifies the issue of terrorism by pointing to acknowledged misdeeds of the US in Latin America, only to recuperate the Manichean conservative discourse that represents the US as incarnating good and its enemies evil, a reading of the film with which I agree; see "*Collateral Damage*: terrorism, melodrama, and the action film on the eve of 9/11," *Jump Cut* 48 (Winter 2006) at www.ejumpcut.org/archive/

jc48.2006/CollatDamage/index.html (accessed December 19, 2008). Meeuf goes on to indicate how Schwarzenegger provides a kinder, gentler superhero and revenge figure, a reading also offered in the DVD featurettes that present the Gordy character as an ordinary man, drawing on his firefighting training to achieve great heroics. There is truth in these readings that present Schwarzenegger as a more paternalistic hero, as opposed to his earlier roles as mechanistic killing machines, but the narrative plot of *Collateral Damage* closely follows the model of the American monomyth, which constructs its redemptive heroes as having a mission to protect civilization against barbarism, incarnate good to fight evil, be subject to punishments and torture during this quest, and ultimately use redemptive violence to restore community (see Jewett and Lawrence 2002). Schwarzenegger's incarnation of the superhero myth in *Collateral Damage* is more domesticated than the typical loner American hero, showing Gordy throughout in fatherly roles with his own family and then with the Colombian woman and her boy. In fact, following the mother's treacherous attempts to wreak havoc on US government buildings and her death at Gordy's hands, it appears that Gordy will adopt the boy, as he cradles him in a fatherly manner at the conclusion of the film. The Colombian terrorist couple's readiness to sacrifice their own son again highlights their absolute evil, which legitimates extreme US tactics as a response.

37   As of January 5, 2009, *Black Hawk Down* grossed worldwide $172,989,651 (see www.boxofficemojo.com/movies/?id=blackhawkdown.htm).

38   See Elvis Mitchell, "Mission of mercy goes bad in Africa," *New York Times*, December 28, 2001 at www.query.nytimes.com/gst/fullpage.html?res=9903 E3D61031F93BA15751C1A9679C8B63&sec=&spon=&pagewanted= print (accessed September 18, 2008), where he writes: "The lack of characterization converts the Somalis into a pack of snarling dark-skinned beasts, gleefully pulling the Americans from their downed aircraft and stripping them. Intended or not, it reeks of glumly staged racism. The only African-American with lines, Specialist Kurth (Gabriel Casseus), is one of the American soldiers who want to get into the middle of the action; his lines communicate his simplistic gung-ho spirit. His presence in this military action raises questions of racial imbalance that *Black Hawk Down* couldn't even be bothered to acknowledge, let alone answer."

39   Thanks to Randy Lewis for this point in a January 6, 2009 email. I will frequently use the term *Bush-Cheney Gang* to describe the dynamics of the Bush administration. While Mark Miller's (2004) "Bush and Co." captures the quasi-fascist corporate nature of the clique, I choose to use the gang metaphor since the Bush-Cheney administration systematically robbed the federal treasury to benefit the super-rich, to provide favors for its big corporate contributors, and to dismantle programs that largely benefit working people. In addition, the Bush-Cheney Gang systematically violated

international law and is generally seen in the world as a rogue regime that regularly subverted diplomacy, global treaties and organizations, as well as throwing aside the national security policies of the post-World War II period in favor of "preemptive war," aggressive unilateralism, and unrestrained militarism (see Kellner 2005).

40 Curiously, Mike Nichols' *Charlie Wilson's War* (2008) celebrates the hard-living Texas congressman who did more than anyone to provide US/CIA support for the Afghan mujahideen who defeated the Soviets and then went on to become the key players in the Taliban and al Qaeda. Although the end of the movie signals that "the crazies are pouring into Kandahar" (i.e., extreme Islamicist militants) and that the US intervention might not turn out to have the desired consequences, nonetheless, the film and DVD featurettes celebrate Wilson as a great American patriot. For a critique of the politics of the film by the author of *Blowback* (2000), see Chalmers Johnson, "Tom Hanks' Charlie Wilson movie: An imperialist comedy," *Alternet*, January 8, 2008 at www.alternet.org/story/73010/ (accessed January 4, 2009).

41 Stephanie Zacharek reports that according to the *Rambo* press releases Stallone was searching for a real-life zone in which to anchor his hero's exploits; *Salon*, January 25, 2008 at www.salon.com/ent/movies/review/2008/01/25/rambo/index.html?CP=IMD&&DN=110.

42 See John Mueller, "Dead and deader," *Los Angeles Times*, January 29, 2008: M7.

43 In a succeeding volume, tentatively titled *Contested Terrain: Struggles over Gender, Sexuality, Race, Class, and Religion in Contemporary Hollywood Cinema*, I will document the culture wars in US cinema during the 2000s on these and other topics.

44 For symptomatic rightwing attacks on Hollywood as a hotbed of liberalism and subversion, see Medved (1993).

45 In one of the last polls taken on the Bush-Cheney presidency, Bush's favorability ratings kicked in at an all-time low of 22 percent, while Cheney's favorability ratings came in at another record low of 13 percent. See the discussion of the *New York Times*/CBS News poll in Michael Duffy, "As Dick Cheney prepares to depart, his mystery lingers," *Time*, January 19, 2009 at www.time.com/time/printout/0,8816,1872531,00.html (accessed January 21, 2009). For an analysis of the dramatic decline of Bush's popularity following his highpoint after 9/11, see Greenwald (2007: 1ff).

46 On diagnostic critique, see Kellner and Ryan (1988) and Kellner (1995: 116–17; 2003b).

47 On the concept of media/cultural studies, see Durham and Kellner (2006) and Hammer and Kellner (2009a).

48 John Harlow, "Hollywood's warm-up act for Barack Obama: Fictional portrayals of black presidents helped America accept the idea of the real thing,"

TimesOnLine, November 8, 2008 at www.timesonline.co.uk/tol/news/world/us_and_americas/us_elections/article5114838.ece (accessed November 25, 2008).

49   Greg Braxton, "Black like them," *Los Angeles Times*, June 22, 2008: E1, 20. In another interview, Haysbert noted: "My role helped prepare the way for Obama, opening the eyes of the American people [so] that they felt they could vote for a black president without triggering the apocalypse." In Harlow, "Hollywood's warm-up."

50   As an aside, I might note that the sinister and treacherous president on *24* who succeeded Palmer, Charles Logan (Gregory Itzin), can be read as an amalgam of George W. Bush, Dick Cheney, Donald Rumsfeld, and others in the Bush-Cheney administration, although he also appears to be modeled after Richard Nixon.

51   Brian Selter, "Following the Script: Obama, McCain and 'The West Wing,'" *New York Times*, October 30, 2008 at www.nytimes.com/2008/10/30/arts/television/30wing.html?em (accessed December 28, 2008). Another article claims Obama's new chief of staff Rahm Emmanuel was anticipated by the *West Wing* fictional deputy of staff Josh Lyman (Bradley Whitford); see Hannah Strange, "Life imitates West Wing for Obama's attack dog Rahm Emmanuel," *TimesOnLine*, November 27, 2008 at www.timesonline.co.uk/tol/news/world/us_and_americas/us_elections/article5106463.ece (accessed December 28, 2008).

52   See Jan Stuart, "At 'Seven Pounds,' a bit of a load," *Los Angeles Times*, December 19, 2008: E1, 14. On Obama's Hollywoodesque info-mercial, see Douglas Kellner, "Barack Obama and Celebrity Spectacle in the 2008 US Presidential Election," *International Journal of Communications* (2009, 3: 715–41).

53   "Will Smith tops box-office poll," *Los Angeles Times*, January 3, 2009: E2. For Smith's cumulative box office, see www.boxofficemojo.com/people/chart/?id=willsmith.htm (accessed January 5, 2009).

54   For my preliminary analysis of the 2008 presidential election, see Kellner, "Barack Obama and Celebrity Spectacle."

55   Influential examples of film theory of the period include Cavell (1971), Metz (1974), Heath (1981), Kuhn (1982), and Bordwell, Staiger, and Thompson (1985).

1

Confronting the Horrors of the Bush-Cheney Era
From Documentary to Allegory

It is hardly an exaggeration to claim that the administrations of George W. Bush and Dick Cheney have been the most rightwing, extremist, ultra-conservative, and contested in recent history.[1] In retrospect, the 2000 election that pitted Bush against Al Gore was one of the most fateful in history and its outcome shocking and consequential. In particular, the presidential campaign of November 2000 displayed an astonishing conclusion, as on election night, it appeared that Al Gore was on his way to triumph as the big Eastern states of New York, Pennsylvania, New Jersey, and Florida were called for him. However, suddenly, Florida flipped over to Bush, who had swept the South and was accumulating enough electoral votes in the Middle West and West to be named the winner when Florida was called for Bush. Yet, in another reversal that a Hollywood drama writer would be hard pressed to imagine, Florida was deemed too close to call, and a recount was ordered, a process that would go on for 36 days and generate a media spectacle that would seriously divide the country (see Kellner 2001).

Following a series of Florida court decisions that more recounts were necessary, the Bush team, led by family consigliore James Baker, fought to stop the recount and freeze a Bush lead by a few hundred votes. The US Supreme Court then jumped in and ruled by a slim 5 to 4 margin that the state-wide recount of Florida's votes, ordered by the Florida Supreme Court, should stop and Bush should be declared the victor. The obviously partisan vote was certainly the most controversial in US history and was damned by its critics as a misuse of the Supreme Court that violated the Constitution (see Bugliosi 2001; Dershowitz 2001), generating what I call "Grand Theft 2000" (Kellner 2001).

After taking a hard-right course for the first nine months of 2001, and losing a Senate majority when a Republican senator jumped ship to caucus with the Democrats, Bush regained the initiative after the terrorist attacks of 9/11, discussed in the next chapter. He continued to push through an extreme rightwing agenda and to rush to war, first against Afghanistan and then Iraq – with momentous consequences.

In this chapter, I first highlight how documentary cinema portrayed the Bush-Cheney years, beginning with discussion of some provocative works that dealt with the 2000 election and the first years of the Bush-Cheney presidency. Then I examine how documentary and Hollywood fictional films portrayed environmental crisis and dealt with the issue of global warming and climate change, which had been initially denied and suppressed by the Bush-Cheney administration. I discuss how Davis Guggenheim's 2006 Academy Award winning documentary about Al Gore's crusade against global warming, *An Inconvenient Truth*, and a steady flow of environmental documentaries address these issues. I next show how a series of fiction and animated films allegorically present environmental crisis, and conclude with a discussion of how Hollywood genre films can be read as commentaries on the socioeconomic crises and fears of the present moment.

This chapter combines analysis of documentary and fiction film because both together provide critical insight into events and problems of the present age. For instance, allegories like *The Day After Tomorrow* (2004) warn about environmental catastrophe, while mutant monster and various horror, fantasy, and science fiction films point to the dangers of social horrors and even apocalypse. Documentaries at their best provide cogent contextualization and advance knowledge. However, I want to question the line between fiction and non-fiction films, as the former can provide experience and access to issues that may penetrate deeper, or awaken individuals more dramatically, than documentary, and thus may help cultivate insight and vision into contemporary issues, as well as deal generally with the human condition. On the other hand, documentaries may also have resonant images and characters that impress themselves deeply on audiences and change their perceptions and perhaps even behavior, as well as providing historical-contextual understanding and factual information. Yet documentaries themselves are constructs and have their biases and entertainment and fictive components, as I will emphasize.

The Golden Age of Documentary

The contours of the key events of the Bush-Cheney years and the struggles over their policies are visible in the US cinematic visions of the era. Enabled by the revolution in documentary production and distribution during the early 2000s (discussed below), and due to the number of fictional films that chose to allegorically criticize the Bush-Cheney administration, the regime of Bush-Cheney and their Republican Party allies was one of the most documented and critically portrayed in US cinematic history.

The Golden Age of Documentary was fueled in part by the bankruptcy of corporate news and information in the United States, in which a small number of corporations controlled the major television networks, as well as important newspapers and Internet sites, and failed to be adequately critical of the state and major corporations.[2] Corporate news media never adequately informed the country concerning the right-wing radicalism of George W. Bush and Dick Cheney in the 2000 election, treated Bush as a savior after 9/11 (see chapter 2), and served as propaganda machines for Bush-Cheney disinformation concerning alleged Iraqi "weapons of mass destruction" and ties to al Qaeda that provided legitimation for the invasion and occupation of Iraq (see chapter 5). The corporate media failed as well to cover the magnitude of environmental crisis intensified by Bush-Cheney policies, the dangers to the economy of a growing federal deficit and consumer debt, and the deregulation of financial institutions and other sectors of the economy. The magnitude of social problems generated by the Bush-Cheney administration propelled documentary filmmakers to fill the gap provided by the conformity and complicity of corporate news media and to take advantage of new digital technologies and modes of distribution which helped fuel the documentary explosion.

Hence, a variety of documentaries present critical visions of the Bush-Cheney administration, ranging from the films of Michael Moore to a series of docs produced and organized by Robert Greenwald which criticized various aspects of Bush-Cheney policy and dealt with the social problems that intensified during their reign of error. The proliferation of quality documentary films is due in part to a revolution in the production and distribution of documentary film in the last decade, resulting from the widespread use of inexpensive digital video cameras, computers, and other multimedia technologies that have made the production of films and videos more accessible and much cheaper. In addition, political groups on both the left and the right have created distribution networks to circulate material promoting their causes, and general audiences can buy documentaries and other films at a discounted price from a number of sources, including Amazon, or can rent them by mail from companies like Netflix or Blockbuster, or in video/DVD rental stores and websites. Finally, as we shall see in this and following chapters, the success of films by Michael Moore, Robert Greenwald, and other documentary filmmakers, in conjunction with pressing social problems and political scandals, inspired perhaps the most prolific and hard-hitting wave of documentaries in US, and perhaps world, cinema history.

Grand Theft 2000

Unprecedented (2001), directed by Richard Ray Perez and Joan Sekler,[3] presents a fast-moving and well-documented examination of the Florida fiasco, beginning with the efforts of Florida Governor Jeb Bush and his Secretary of State Katherine Harris to purge voting lists of so-called "felons" who turned out to be predominantly African-American and working-class voters, in largely Democratic Party strongholds, who were illicitly forbidden to vote because their names resembled those on the felon list. This dastardly deed perhaps blocked over 50,000 votes and is illustrative of the dirty tricks and illegal maneuvers whereby the Florida Bush machine allegedly stole the election with the complicity of the US Supreme Court (see Palast 2003; Kellner 2001).

Unprecedented unfolds the variety of dirty deeds whereby Al Gore lost votes in the Florida election. The film addresses the infamous "Butterfly Ballot" in which Gore supporters voted accidentally for Pat Buchanan, showing on screen the absurdly designed ballot that misled thousands of voters, mostly liberal senior citizens, in Palm County, Florida. Various other confusing ballots around the state, dysfunctional voting machines, irregular procedures, and obstacles to counting and recounting the vote, all of which tainted the Florida vote count and set the country into constitutional crisis, are critically interrogated in the film, which culminates in showing the Supreme Court pull off what many saw as a coup d'état for the Bush-Cheney Gang.

Narrated by Peter Coyote, *Unprecedented* is rich with documentary footage and insightful interviews with observers and experts like Allan Dershowitz and Vincent Bugliosi, who criticize the Supreme Court decision. The documentary footage shows that three of the Supreme Court Justices had conflicts of interest in that they had direct links to the Bush-Cheney administration, including Clarence Thomas's wife, who worked directly for the Bush campaign, and one of Justice Scalia's sons, who received a job in the legal division of the administration.

Unprecedented reveals how Republicans sent down operatives to attempt to stop the vote count through demonstrations and a sit-in in a Miami-Dade government office, where a vote recount was being attempted. Footage documented their attempts to disrupt the recounts, and photos identified that they worked for Republicans like Tom DeLay and were not local demonstrators. The film also shows how the media spectacle of the struggles around the recount was orchestrated for the television cameras and how the Bush team was able to manipulate the media, creating the impression that Bush had already won and that the Gore team were "sore losers" delaying the inevitable. Eventual counting of the votes of the entire state, as was occurring when the Supreme Court intervened, showed that Al Gore would have been elected had a fair recount been allowed, although the right wing circulated the mythology and Big Lie that the recount demonstrated Bush actually won.[4]

Both *Unprecedented* and Danny Schechter and Faye Anderson's *Counting on Democracy* (2001) examine the dangers of computerized voting, how Republican firms received most of the contracts, and how there was a clear racial and class gap in access to reliable voting machines that strongly benefited Republicans. *Counting on Democracy* uses the Florida example to make the case for reliable voting machines and accountable voting procedures, a problem that would continue to plague elections in the United States, as I suggest below.[5]

Another 2000 election film, *Journeys with George* (2001), made by Alexandra Pelosi, a former NBC News producer and Nancy Pelosi's daughter, puts on display the superficial, smug, and nasty side of George W. Bush while on the campaign trail, with his trademark smirk, simplistic slogans, and insulting comments to aides and the media. Yet while the film presents critical images for viewers inclined to view Bush negatively, the documentary also humanizes him, as he banters with the documentary crew and reporters, presenting his likeable and affable side as well. The fact that Bush allowed intimate access to his campaign to the daughter of a California congresswoman, Nancy Pelosi, who would eventually rise to be the first woman Speaker of the House, shows the interconnection between elite political families who often exaggerate differences and are part of the same "political club" (although political polarization would rise significantly during the Bush-Cheney era).

While *Journeys with George* focuses on the Bush campaign, *The Party's Over* (2001, released 2003 and originally titled *Last Party 2000*) provides documentary investigation of key issues and events on the 2000 campaign trail, examining both parties and focusing on youth and other protests against the two major political parties' conventions and platforms. *The Party's Over* is a follow-up to Marc Benjamin and Mark Levin's documentary *Last Party 1992*, which featured the inimitable Robert Downey on an excursion exploring the US political scene during the 1992 presidential election campaign. *The Party's Over* centers on Academy Award winning actor Philip Seymour Hoffman as a politically uninformed and alienated Gen-Xer who seeks to learn about American politics through filming the Republican and Democratic Party conventions and attempting to interview key figures. Hoffman questions why young people are so apathetic politically and are not more involved in the system. Discussing this with both famous and ordinary younger people, as well as politicians and pundits, the film documents widespread dissatisfaction with the current political system.

Much of *The Party's Over* appears to take the Ralph Nader line, endorsed by Michael Moore in 2000, that there is no real difference between the two political parties, both of which are dominated by corporations and money. Yet the interview footage (and subsequent results of the election) show clear differences. Moreover, in retrospect, the documentary makes Al Gore and the Democrats look very good, and, in view of their disastrous record, the Republicans and their figurehead Bush appear quite negatively, raising the question, how could this guy and this bunch ever capture the presidency?

Against party politics, *The Party's Over* champions social movements and struggles, opening with a montage of the civil rights, anti-war, gay and lesbian, and environmental movements. There is also sustained focus on contemporary youth movements like the Ruckus Society, as well as youth demonstrating at both the Republican and Democratic Party conventions. The message, highlighted in interviews with Eddie Vedder of Pearl Jam, John Sellers of the Ruckus Society, and other demonstrators, is that many young people are fed up with politics as usual, want to get involved, and are seeking to develop their own autonomous political movements and political culture – which dispels dominant media stereotypes of apathetic youth. There is also sustained focus on Cherie Homulka and the homeless movement, providing access to voices rarely heard in the mainstream media. The film reveals an amorphous range of activist groups in strong opposition to the conservative hegemony that would dominate during the Bush-Cheney years, and suggests that many individuals and groups were ready for activism and change, as in the 1960s and 1970s.

Just after the 2000 election, the Hollywood Director's Guild had a program honoring Michael Moore's television work. A highly upset Moore came out on stage and said he needed to talk about the 2000 election before anything else. Moore acknowledged that he had campaigned hard for Green Party presidential candidate Ralph Nader in 2000, but saw that the contest between Gore and Bush was a cliffhanger with the election probably going to whoever prevailed in Florida and New Hampshire. Moore claimed he went to Nader to discuss this problem and proposed that Nader tell voters in Florida and New Hampshire to accept the lesser evil so that the country would be spared the likely disaster of a Bush administration. According to Moore, Nader resisted the argument and Moore claims he himself went to Florida and New Hampshire to plead the case that Nader supporters should vote for Gore in this instance. Moore's arguments did not prevail and the election was close enough to allow the Bush-Cheney Gang to steal it (see Moore 2003). Ralph Nader thus appeared to be a spoiler and was viewed critically by many of his previous supporters.

The documentary *An Unreasonable Man* (2007) by Henriette Mantel and Steve Skrovan addresses Nader's entire life history. The film makes both the most positive and critical cases for and against Nader, documenting his unquestioned record of public service and achievements, as well as what now appears as his gross misjudgments in the 2000 and 2004 elections. Nader's refrain that there wasn't "a dime's bit of difference" between Bush and Gore now appears monumentally misguided, and the film makes clear that for many this blunder seals Nader's legacy. The film, however, is very fair, showing Nader's long list of anti-corporate campaigns and legislative achievements, ranging from car safety laws to OSHA and workers' safety regulations, the Clean Air Act, the Freedom of Information Act, and many other laudable achievements.

An Unreasonable Man probes Nader's personal life and finds no scandals, indicating that Nader is ascetic and almost monk-like in his dedication to causes, although many former associates find grounds to criticize him. The film suggests that Nader veered to the left during the Reagan years that undid much of the progressive legislation of the previous decades and was alienated during the Clinton years because he was not called upon to promote reform and found the Clinton administration too cozy with corporations. Yet the man and his motivations ultimately remain a mystery and his role in the 2000 and 2004 presidential elections continues to generate endless controversy, while his quixotic effort to run yet again for president in 2008 poses further questions about Nader's motivations (he appeared to have had little effect on this election).

The wave of progressive political documentaries during the Bush-Cheney era included homages to stalwarts of the left such as Noam Chomsky and Howard Zinn, and there is a fascinating documentary called *Senator Obama Goes to Africa* (2007) which made it appear to me that Barack Obama was the real deal, although the film could have been used against him to document that he's a flaming liberal and even radical. Another documentary, *Giuliani Time* (2006), takes on New York Senator Rudy Giuliani by exposing his family connections to organized crime, the covering up of his problematic family background while he was a New York and federal prosecutor, and the countless scandals and conflicts he was involved with in New York.

As the 2008 presidential primaries heated up, with Barack Obama engaged in a fierce competition with Hillary Clinton for the Democratic Party presidential nomination, and then facing Republican presidential candidate John McCain in the general election, once again the country faced the specter of a stolen election through the high-profile presentation of an HBO docudrama on the Florida election struggle titled *Recount*. Directed by Jay Roach of the *Austin Powers* movies and starring Kevin Spacey as Gore stalwart Ron Clain and Tom Wilkinson as Bush family consigliore James Baker, the docudrama focused on the two sides' behind-the-scenes maneuvering with the courts and media to push the election tally toward their candidate.

While *Recount* made it clear that it was a stolen election, with references to the erratic loss of Gore votes in certain precincts, the scrubbing of tens of thousands of "felons" from the voting account, and the unconscionable halting of vote tabulation by the US Supreme Court, it did not centrally focus on the mechanics of the election theft, barely scratching the surface of the greatest crime in US political history. To be sure, it put on display the hardball machinations of the Bush-Cheney team, the partisan antics of Katherine Harris (deliciously played by Laura Dern), and the failure of the Gore team to fight as fiercely as the Bush-Cheney Gang, signaling out video clips of Joe Lieberman, Gore's vice-presidential running mate, saying that suspicious votes coming from "military" voters should be counted, even if there was no postmark and they arrived days after the election. Yet *Recount* did not deal with how votes were systematically pilfered from all over the state, the statistical anomalies between previous voting records, polling, and the actual count in precincts where

Bush performed much better than he should have and Gore much worse. Nor did it dwell on the scandal of the Supreme Court intervening to stop the hand count of ballots throughout Florida, and the media consortium tabulation of hand-counted ballots that suggested that Gore really won if "intent of the voter" was used as a criterion.[6]

The Bush-Cheney Gang thus seized the presidency with the help of Jeb Bush and their Republican Party allies in Florida and five partisans on the Supreme Court. The result was the most scandalous, corrupt, and ultra-conservative regime in history, which provided payloads of fodder for documentary and other films on the reign of outrage.

Bush-Cheney and Co.: Scandals and Critique

A series of acclaimed and popular documentaries provided critical visions of the Bush-Cheney presidency, including hard-hitting films by Robert Greenwald and associates (discussed below) and Michael Moore (discussed in chapter 3). During this golden age of documentary an astounding number of filmmakers thoroughly dissected and critiqued the Bush-Cheney years. Documentary filmmakers became the muckrakers of the time, exposing multiple injustices and social problems and speaking truth to power.

Some documentary films focused on George W. Bush himself, such as Michael Galinsky and Suki Hawley's *Horns and Halos* (2002), an exposé of Bush's seedy personal life and business deals. Based on J. H. Hatfield's biography *Fortunate Son* (2000), it documents the initial blocking of the publication of this hard-hitting investigative biography. The narrative traces the book's publication by an independent press, Soft Skull, and harassment of the author and publisher Sander Hicks by members of the Bush entourage during the time Bush was running for president, and how Hatfield was eventually driven to commit suicide. The film focuses on Hatfield and Hicks' conflicted relations and their attempt to promote the book, killed by St. Martin's Press when it came out that Hatfield was an ex-con convicted of attempted murder. By focusing on the Hatfield-Hicks stories, however, and the sensationalized claim that Bush had been about to be convicted of cocaine use in 1974, but his family negotiated to get the charges dropped, attention was diverted from the book's detailed account of Bush's shady past, including business scams and failures bailed out by family friends, insider trading allegations, and years of drug and alcohol abuse.

Joseph Mealey and Michael Shoob's documentary *Bush's Brain* (2004), based on the book by James C. Moore and Wayne Slater (2003), tells the unsettling history of Bush's primary political adviser and alter ego, Karl Rove. The film exposes in detail the dirty tricks that were central to Rove's campaigns and his symbiotic relationship with George W. Bush. Rove's "ends justify the means" and "do anything to win" down and dirty politics go back to his days in college with Young Republicans and include tutelage with the legendary gutter politics adviser Lee Atwater, who ran Bush Senior's campaigns, and apologized on his death bed for his nasty tactics. The highlights of Rove's smears and dirty tricks in Texas state politics and the 2000 election are documented, and the film shows how once in office Rove continued to use hardball tactics to attempt to destroy enemies, including former ambassador Joe Wilson. Wilson's critique of the Bush-Cheney Gang's Iraq lies drove the White House crazy, leading Rove and Dick Cheney's assistant "Scooter" Libby to expose the CIA connections of Wilson's wife Valerie Plame, bringing up felony charges for Libby but allowing the sleazy Rove to slither away.[7]

In the same muckraker vein, *Bush Family Fortunes* (2004), based on Greg Palast's book *The Best Democracy Money Can Buy* (2003), explores the debacle of the 2000 Florida election. A British-based American journalist, Palast uncovered the story of the scrubbed "felon" list that deprived tens of thousands of citizens of their votes, as well as Bush family connections to the Bin Laden family and Saudis, and the hidden agendas of the Bush-Cheney Iraq invasion.

The revolution in documentary production and distribution which helped to produce a golden age of documentary is visible in the work of Robert Greenwald. Former network TV producer Greenwald assembled crews and financing for the production and distribution of a wide range of documentaries. This series includes one of the first widely seen documentaries on Iraq, *Uncovered: The War on Iraq* (2003 and 2004), that systematically exposed the lies and deceptions which the Bush-Cheney administration constructed to legitimate its failed invasion and occupation. Wanting to get out a quick documentary exposing the mendacity behind the Iraq invasion, Greenwald's first cut of his documentary, titled *Uncovered: The Whole Truth About the Iraq War*, was conceived in June 2003 and released in November 2003 in a 56-minute version.[8] It opened with 25 witnesses, mostly ex-CIA and government intelligence or diplomatic specialists, introducing themselves and their credentials. On trial were Bush-Cheney administration claims about Iraqi weapons of mass destruction (WMDs).[9] After a clip of a speech by Bush emphatically asserting "Saddam has weapons of mass destruction" and dramatizing the threat, Greenwald presents government experts who point-by-point criticize Bush's claims and related WMD assertions by other members of the administration. In a devastating segment, the film presents clips from Colin Powell's February 5, 2003 UN speech that claimed to present overwhelming evidence of Iraqi WMD programs, interspersed with critiques by a series of former CIA, State Department, and Iraq experts who took apart Powell's presentation, uncovering the utter mendacity behind the ill-fated Iraq incursion. Concluding segments contain Bush-Cheney administration spokesmen spin concerning why no Iraq WMDs had been found, followed by analyses of how the venture had strengthened terrorist recruitment and endangered the US. In retrospect, the administration spokesmen are totally discredited by the fact that no WMDs were ever found, nor were links between Iraq and al Qaeda. Watching Greenwald's rigorous display of mendacious claims by members of the Bush-Cheney administration and their critique by honorable experts in the field, makes clear how a clique of utterly dishonorable men and women seized control of the government and were opposed by individuals prepared to speak truth to power, demonstrating that US democracy had not yet been destroyed.

A later Greenwald-produced documentary, *Iraq for Sale: The War Profiteers* (2006), exposed how corporations allied to the Bush-Cheney administration were profiteering from the war, often with no-bid contracts, inflated prices, and services paid for but not delivered. Of course, one of the major war profiteers was Dick Cheney's former company Halliburton, which received lucrative no-bid contracts. The film opens by interviewing members of families of Halliburton employees killed in Iraq and who blame the company for inadequate protection and risking the lives of their loved ones.[10] Subsequent episodes document major corporations like Blackwater, closely tied to the Bush-Cheney administration, profiteering from the war, with scandalous examples of no-bid contracts and excessive charges for services. A three-minute sequence in voice-over and images over the closing credits documents Greenwald and his associates' attempts to telephone Halliburton and the other companies to get them to respond to their criticisms, but the calls went unanswered.

Greenwald helped assemble different teams to make these documentaries, worked with groups like Move-On to get financing and distribution,

A Robert Greenwald-produced documentary *Iraq for Sale: The War Profiteers* exposes corporate profiteering.

and established his own production and distribution company, Brave New Films, selling hundreds of thousands of politically enlightened documentaries that were quickly made, using existing TV and media footage, interviewing qualified spokespersons, and constructing narratives and an accessible structure for the documentaries that made them effective tools of political education and organization.[11]

Greenwald's strategy involved getting groups like Buzz-Flash, Bush-Watch, Move-On and other blogs, websites, and political groups to distribute his films. Move-On's impresario Eli Pariser came up with an idea that Greenwald and his associates enthusiastically promoted: having house parties to show their DVDs to provide collective discussion and attempt to organize viewers around the issues in the films. The strategy also involved partnering with groups concerned with the issues, churches, and other institutions that could help distribute the films, thus broadening documentary audiences significantly and helping to connect films and their audiences to ongoing struggles and movements.[12]

Greenwald's documentary teams also helped produce and distribute Nonny de la Pena's *Unconstitutional: The War on Civil Liberties* (2004), which dissected the Bush administration's so-called "USA Patriot Act" and its assault on civil liberties and the US Constitution. *The Big Buy: Tom DeLay's Stolen Congress* (2006) exposed the extent to which lobbies and rightwing corporations were shaping Bush administration policy (just as the Greenwald group was concluding the documentary, DeLay was accused of felonious crimes and forced to resign his House leadership position). In addition, Greenwald directed and produced *Outfoxed: Rupert Murdoch's War on Journalism* (2004), a powerful exposé of the Fox TV News network as a tool of the Bush-Cheney administration and Republican right. The film shows how talking points were circulated from the Republican Party to the Fox News network that dutifully reproduced the Bush-Cheney line of the day, a complicity confirmed in interviews with former Fox employees. *Outfoxed* helped disclose that Fox is basically a propaganda organization for the Republican Party and is in no way "fair and balanced" as they laughably claim.[13]

Greenwald's *Wal-Mart: The High Cost of Low Price* (2005) documented how the immensely wealthy corporation bought cheaply from China, denying US workers jobs in manufacturing, and paid their own workers a barely minimum wage, often without health benefits, as the corporate owners amassed multi-billion dollar profits. The documentary also showed growing opposition to Wal-Mart and the organization of efforts to preserve local communities from its intrusion.

Greenwald was not alone in documenting the abuses of the Bush-Cheney regime. In *Orwell Rolls in His Grave* (2004), Robert Kane Pappas presents a powerful critical vision that the United States under Bush-Cheney was becoming an Orwellian police state, with the rise to power of the radical rightwing of the Republican Party and compliant corporate media that advance its ultraconservative agenda. The documentary indicates how deregulation and privatization resulted in a few mega-corporations controlling broadcasting and serving as lapdogs for the Bush-Cheney administration and corporate elite, thus failing to perform their role as watchdogs essential to democracy.

A very powerful critique of US corporate broadcast media is found in Mark Achbar and Peter Wintonick's *Manufacturing Consent* (1992), which elaborates Edward Herman and Noam Chomsky's thesis of corporate media as propaganda instruments for the existing system. Achbar and Jennifer Abbott's documentary on *The Corporation* (2004) dissects the history and effects of the key capitalist institution of the corporation, which was systematically unleashed during the Bush-Cheney administration when it eliminated scores of important state regulations. Based on a book by Canadian law professor Joel Bakan, *The Corporation* explores the history of corporations being interpreted as legal persons with a range of constitutional rights and asks what kind of a person is the corporation anyway? Based on criteria delineated in the Diagnostic and Statistical Manual of Mental Disorders, the filmmakers suggest that the corporation is immoral, selfish, irresponsible, manipulative, unable to empathize or feel remorse, and even psychopathological. Using a diversity of voices ranging from CEOs and corporate flack to Noam Chomsky, the film dissects the history and institution of the corporation, as well as providing manifold examples of corporate malfeasance.

Another film in the muckraker documentary tradition, Alex Gibney's *The Smartest Guys in the Room: Enron* (2005), attacks one of the major corporations behind Bush-Cheney's rise to power, and a poster-child for corporate greed and corruption. The highly acclaimed film investigates the flim-flam whereby Enron sold "derivatives" and "futures," covering over its fraud with hype about how much money its investment scams were making, showing the media to be complicit in advancing Enron's shady business dealings as the latest in advanced corporate finance. The film highlights the corporate con games and Enron criminals who perpetuated them, but also the devastating consequences of their crimes on scores of workers and investors. The close connections between Enron's president Ken Lay and the Bush family are documented, exploding George W. Bush's lie that he really did not have personal or political connections with Lay. Lay himself comes off as a rah-rah salesman, while his associates Jeffrey Skilling and Andrew Fastow come off as the criminal masterminds.[14] A revealing segment shows how the Enron "traders" engineered the California energy crisis in the early 2000s, which led to skyrocketing prices and rolling blackouts, with chilling audiotapes featuring Skilling and other Enron executives joking about the scam.

Also pursuing corporate malfeascence, Chris Paine's *Who Killed the Electric Car?* (2006) tells the story of how after the California Air Resources Board (CARB) passed a law in 1990 mandating that automobiles sold in the state should conform to increasingly rigorous pollution laws aiming at zero-emission, the automobile industry failed to comply and fought efforts to produce more fuel-effective cars. To be sure, there were electric cars being produced and the narrative focuses on General Motor's EV1 vehicle. While scores of celebrities and ordinary people loved the electric car, it was pulled from the market in the Bush-Cheney era due to pressure from automobile and oil corporations. Committed to the electric car as a viable alternative, the filmmakers show how greedy corporations and corrupt political forces act against the public interest and even deny consumers products they would eagerly purchase.

Eugene Jarecki's *Why We Fight* (2006) explores the role of the military-industrial complex in US society and answers his question by suggesting that the military is one of America's biggest and most profitable businesses.[15] Starting with President Eisenhower's 1961 Farewell Address warning about the growth of the military-industrial complex, Jarecki mobilizes a variety of conservative and liberal voices to try to explain US militarism and the excessive growth of the military-industrial establishment. The film cuts from interviews to footage concerning military interventions like Vietnam and Iraq, and exposes the lies and mendacity used to sell these wars to the public. In one poignant sequence, a retired New York cop, Wilton Sekzer, describes his anger after 9/11 and how he successfully persuaded the government to put his son's name on one of the first bombs dropped in Iraq. When he is later confronted by TV images of Bush admitting that there is no connection between the al Qaeda terror attacks and Iraq, the cop is bitter, feeling that he was manipulated and lied to.

Hurricane Katrina is documented in three major films that put on display the Bush-Cheney administration's complete incompetence and failure to address sufferings of people of color and poor people. The event of Hurricane Katrina itself validated media critique of the regime and George W. Bush himself, which had been suppressed or muted in the mainstream media after 9/11 (see Kellner 2005). Spike Lee's political critique of the Bush-Cheney administration is displayed in a highly engaging HBO documentary on Hurricane Katrina, *When the Levees Broke: A Requiem in Four Acts* (2006), which is one of his major achievements. The film provides historical background and penetrating exploration of the episode, which is widely acknowledged as one of the major failures of the Bush-Cheney administration. Interviewing scores of survivors and experts on local geography and politics, Lee compiles a powerful tapestry of the many contributing causes to the hurricane disaster and how it impacted on ordinary lives.

Taking a different tack, *Trouble the Water* (2008) provides a first-person video account of Hurricane Katrina approaching the city and the failure of the city authorities and politicians to evacuate the citizens who did not have transportation to escape. Documentarians Tia Lessin and Carl Deal were interviewing people in a Red Cross shelter in Alexandria, Louisiana, when they encountered Kim Roberts and her husband Scott.

The couple had lived through the hurricane in New Orleans' Lower 9th Ward and documented the emergence, force, and aftermath of the hurricane with a $20 video camera that Kim had just bought. Combining this footage with material taken later by the documentary crew, *Trouble the Water* shows up close water flooding into neighborhoods and people climbing to their attics or roofs to avoid drowning. The failure to evacuate hospitals and prisons is depicted, and when the military arrives to control camps and public grounds, they are adversarial to the people, refusing to respond to their needs. *Trouble the Water* also deals with the aftermath of the hurricane, showing the difficulties in rebuilding a life for people who have lost their homes and neighborhoods and the inadequate response and help from the Bush-Cheney administration.[16]

Finally, Leslie Cardé's documentary *America Betrayed* (2008) dissects the monumental failure of the Army Corps of Engineers to build a viable levee and put a hurricane protection system in place. The film focuses on the Mississippi River Gulf Outlet and its canals that failed to contain the floods from the hurricane and destroyed large parts of New Orleans. Cardé's compelling documentary delves into the history of the Army Corps of Engineers and its revolving doors from military trained engineers to corporate employees and lobbyists whom the engineers have given contracts and then hired at high salaries. Narrated by Richard Dreyfuss, *America Betrayed* suggests that the entire system of flood control, canals, and levees contributed in a major way to the failure of the system and that local and federal political administrations had failed for years to respond to criticisms of the flood control system's obvious inadequacies and dangers, chickens that came home to roost during the Katrina tragedy.

Anticipating the financial meltdown of 2008, Danny Schechter's *In Debt We Trust* (2006) and *Maxed Out* (2007), directed by James Scurlock, takes on credit card debt, targeting unscrupulous credit card companies who provide easy access to credit and charge exorbitant interest rates, driving people to bankruptcy and even suicide, as is documented in the case studies in *Maxed Out* of two college students who killed themselves after incurring enormous debt. Both films note that government provides a bad model for consumers by itself amassing almost unimaginable levels of debt, one of the financial (mis)policies of the Bush-Cheney administration that helped lead to the financial collapse of late 2008 (a point also made in Patrick Creadon's *I.O.U.S.A.*, 2008, although the latter tends to posit excessive government debt alone as the source of fiscal crisis).

Schechter's *In Debt We Trust*, subtitled "America Before the Bubble Bursts," prophetically anticipates the financial meltdown of 2008 in its comprehensive examination of how lobbyists control Congress, allowing deregulation of the credit card and financial industry. The documentary also goes into the coming mortgage crisis, presciently interviewing experts who warn of a "housing bubble zone," a bubble that was to burst in Fall 2008, along with major financial institutions. *In Debt We Trust* thus provides a comprehensive look at many of the factors which helped cause the current financial crisis and roots the problems in a dysfunctional economic and political system, needing radical restructuring.[17]

Documentary filmmakers thus took on the major scandals of the Bush-Cheney years, as well as the corporations who were unleashed to pursue maximum greed in a totally deregulated environment in which unbridled laissez-faire economics (let 'em do what they want) and market fundamentalism (a religious belief that an unregulated market economy can solve all problems) led to economic catastrophe. Documentary film of the era also provided critical visions of what was going on in the country and the way that the Bush-Cheney era was impacting on social life.

Republican Rule and Crises of Democracy

Steven Greenstreet's *This Divided State* (2005) evocatively documents the political divisions in the United States during the Bush-Cheney era and presents material for a strong diagnostic critique of contemporary conservativism. The story revolves around the response to an invitation by student leaders to filmmaker Michael Moore to give a talk at Utah Valley State campus in Orem, Utah ("Family City, USA") in the run-up to the 2004 election. The largely conservative Mormon and Republican community rose up in arms at the prospect of the Antichrist himself appearing on campus when *Fahrenheit 9/11* was creating such a sensation. Conservative students protested using school funds to bring Moore to campus, and a millionaire local businessman and Sunday school teacher, Kay Anderson, helped organize and publicize a campaign to prevent Moore from speaking and contaminating the minds of students at UVSC by peddling his "hatred and filth." Anderson and other conservatives also undertook a campaign to defame and have driven from office the student leaders who invited Moore, Jim Bassi and Joe Vogel. (The DVD recounts how Anderson had earlier spearheaded a successful attempt to fire a school official who had sanctioned an outdoor concert by a hip hop group.)

As the debate unfolded, the school decided to invite conservative Fox News pundit Sean Hannity to speak before Moore for "balance." Yet the fierce debate over freedom of speech continued, with some students and professors arguing for the virtues of allowing alternative views to be heard, while conservatives continued to oppose Moore's visit and extremists in the community militated to retaliate against the students who had dared invite him, and who continued to receive hate mail and threats. Some students interviewed pointed out that Mormons should be especially cognizant of the value of freedom of speech, since they settled in Utah after being denied the freedom to practice their religion elsewhere, but no arguments seem to work for the fiercely anti-Moore conservatives.

Sean Hannity arrived to the rapturous applause of his True Believers, and the scenes of his speech to a packed auditorium put on display the vacuousness, thuggery, and demagoguery of a certain brand of contemporary ultraconservatism. When a young philosophy professor, Pierre LaMarche, attempts to question Hannity's clichéd defense of Bush's Iraq War and Bush's denouncing of opponents to the war, Hannity interrupts, insults, and berates the professor, with conservative students booing the dissenter; one woman student is shown glaring at the heretic professor with hatred for daring to expose his liberal views. When a liberal student raises his hand to speak from the audience, Hannity grills him, invites him to the stage as if a liberal were a freak show, and insults and interrupts the good-natured young man as conservative students boo and hiss. The scene puts on display the fascist tendencies of Hannity and his followers' brand of conservatism, and the documentary evokes a strong contrast between conservatives and the more liberal students and professors who try to form arguments, engage in dialogue, and defend basic American rights, even for those with whom one disagrees. This civilized and democratic behavior is contrasted throughout to the unbridled mass chanting and mean-spirited aggression of conservatives.

Michael Moore arrives to speak, salutes the students who were open-minded enough to invite him and to come listen to him, and gives an energetic speech and his usual entertaining show. *This Divided State* clearly puts on display divisions within the country and how Bush-Cheney conservatism produced aggressive intolerance for those who disagreed with their views and policies. The film shows Kay Anderson continuing to use the legal system to sue the student leaders for what he took as misuse of school funds. In the heated atmosphere, one student leader is forced to resign and becomes estranged from the other, his longtime best friend, as pressures over the legal harassment, organized personal insults and threats, and ongoing media publicity continue.

The 2004 election itself is the subject of James D. Stern and Adam Del Deo's *So Goes the Nation* (2007). While *Unprecedented* and *Counting on Democracy* highlight questionable computerized voting machines, *So Goes the Nation* offers a conventional look at campaign strategies by both sides. Interviewing political insiders in both the Bush and the Kerry campaigns, the interviews suggest that the Bush campaign successfully mobilized voters while the Kerry campaign did not, in effect blaming the Democrats for the election result. Although the documentary shows long lines of African-American and student voters on election day, it does not explore the systematic efforts to take African-American voters off voting lists in Florida, Ohio, and other states, nor the lack of adequate voting machines in predominantly Democratic Party precincts, especially ones inhabited by low-income African Americans, contrasted to the abundance of machines in Republican precincts. Nor does the lame film note statistical anomalies that suggested election fraud, and the ways that the Ohio Secretary of State Ken Blackwell, replicating Katherine Harris's partisan manipulation in Florida in 2000, systematically attacked Democratic precincts and votes with unprecedented legal harassment while doing everything possible to facilitate Republican votes, leading several authors to write books claiming that the Ohio election and thus the 2004 presidency had been stolen, since Ohio was the decisive swing state in the election (see Gumball 2005; Miller 2005; Fitrakis and Wasserman 2005).

Simon Ardizonne and Russell Michaels' *Hacking Democracy* (2006), by contrast, takes on the scandal of computerized voting machines produced by Diebold and other companies with Republican Party connections. Focusing on citizen-activist Bev Smith's BlackBox voting project, devoted to demonstrating the problem with touch screen and optical scan voting machines, the film demonstrates how easy it is to hack computers and change results, as a Finnish computer programmer hacks a Diebold machine's memory card to dramatically alter votes. The film does not, however, deal with the broader problem of election fraud, although it clearly makes the point that without ballots that can be hand-inspected in close elections, the possibility of continued fraud and stolen elections is inevitable.

In 2008, as the fateful day of the presidential election approached, Starz TV released David Earnhardt's powerful documentary *Uncounted: The New Math of American Elections*. This hard-hitting exposé focuses on the stolen 2004 election and the ways that the Republican Party was able to block votes by scrubbing voting lists, not providing enough voting machines, actually switching votes, and other nefarious activities. Interviewing Gumball, Fitrakis, and Wasserman who had written books about the election theft in Ohio, activist Bev Harris, founder of BlackBox. org, a group dedicated to exposing the dangerous flaws of computerized voting systems, and Athan Gibbs, inventor of the TruVote voting system that produced transparency and paper ballots, the film provides ample documentation of how votes were stolen in Ohio, providing testimony involving local citizens, investigative reporters, and members of Congress like John Conyers, who released a report on the scandal.

Most compelling, the film interviews Clint Curtis, a conservative computer programmer from South Florida who was asked by Florida congressman Tom Feeney to make vote-flipping software that could be used in Florida election machines to rig elections. At first thinking Feeney wanted protection against fraud, after he invented the software that allowed hacking, it was clear to Curtis that this rigged computer program was going to be used to illicitly rig the elections. He resigned, trying to expose Feeney. Putting his affidavit online, Curtis caught the attention of Bev Smith's BlackBox voting project, as well as the filmmakers, who used Curtis's story to publicize the scandal of computer voting machines, owned by Republican Party companies, that could be rigged. The film notes how California and other states cancelled their Diebold contracts, but how most states are still using dicey machines, revealing a truly rotten worm in the core of the election system. In a side story, Curtis switches party affiliations and runs against Feeney for Congress in Florida, and then challenges the results when he is beaten in his 2006 congressional run.

Also produced with the 2008 election in mind and released for free downloads on the Internet, Michael Moore's *Slacker Uprising* documents Captain Mike's 2004 campaign to rouse up slackers to vote against Bush and for Kerry. Cameras followed Moore on his 62-city tour in swing states and showed Moore and rock star friends like Eddie Vedder and Steve Earle performing and trying to mobilize young audiences to vote. Most reviews panned the film as an advertisement for Moore and, surprisingly, although the film ended with the close Ohio race, Moore did not mention the successful attempts in the state to block Democratic Party votes, or the arguments made in several books and documentaries that the election in Ohio was also stolen (for a discussion of Moore's serious films, see chapter 3).

Taken together, the documentaries of the 2000s provide a compelling and accurate view of the scandalous period of the Bush-Cheney years, providing far more detail and critical insight than the country's official presidential historians who, in both scholarly treatises and the media, tended to ignore the misdeeds and crimes of the Bush-Cheney regime and a lifetime of scandal within generations of the Bush family.[18] The documentaries of the era are supplemented, to be sure, by a small library of books exposing the malfeasances, mendacity, and fiascos of the Bush-Cheney administration (see Kellner 2005, which draws on and references this critical literature). While the mainstream media provided propaganda coverage of the Bush-Cheney administration actions from 9/11 well into the Iraq invasion and occupation, the documentaries described above revealed the unsavory and often frightening truth of the nature and consequences of the failed Republican policies. The critical documentary films that engage the crises and scandals of the era display the maturity and sophistication of US documentary filmmakers, and comprise one of the most impressive sets of documentary films in film history.

Real Disaster Films: From *An Inconvenient Truth* and Environmental Documentaries to Animated Allegories

Environmental crisis and the un-benign neglect of climate change and global warming by the Bush-Cheney administration have been the subject of many documentaries. While the Davis Guggenheim/Al Gore film *An Inconvenient Truth* (2006) has become the best known and most rewarded environmental documentary, a wide range of others, too extensive to survey, have dealt with dimensions of the ecological crisis. In addition, a series of animated features and Hollywood fictional films have allegorically portrayed the consequences of continued environmental degradation, using genres from animated children's movies to the political thriller and disaster film to portray the crises confronting life on earth today.

Climate Change and Environmental Crisis Documentaries

Davis Guggenheim and Al Gore's *An Inconvenient Truth* (2006) dramatically documents the threat to planet Earth of climate change and severe environmental crisis. The film received a large global audience, making it the third highest grossing documentary film in history, triggering widespread debate, and helping to win an Academy Award and Nobel Peace Prize for Gore.

After environmental activist Laurie David, who helped produce a documentary on global warming for HBO, *Too Hot to Handle* (2006),[19] saw a ten-minute version of Al Gore's slide-show in 2004, she helped organize presentations for Gore on climate change in New York and Los Angeles. His highly impressive performance and well-documented multimedia presentation led to meetings with Gore, David, eBay billionaire Jeff Skoll, TV director and producer Davis Guggenheim, Quentin Tarantino's producer Lawrence Bender, advertising guru Scott Burns, producer Lesley Chilcott, and others of the Hollywood left, who undertook to make a documentary based on Gore's slide-show and lectures within the following six months. One report indicated "the schedule was so grueling that Gore jokingly referred to it as 'Kill Al Vol. III'" (a riff on Tarentino's *Kill Bill* films that Bender produced).[20]

While the film's focus is Gore's lectures and audiovisual material, the titles, graphics, and compelling documentary footage created by the filmmakers help make Gore's key arguments about global warming accessible and engaging to theatrical, home, and classroom audiences. Gore proves to be an extremely competent lecturer, as well as a committed environmentalist. On the DVD commentary, director Davis Guggenheim tells how he pressed Gore to tell personal stories of how he became devoted to environmental issues, and the result is a highly sympathetic portrait of Gore, showing him in airports and lecture halls, having conversations, and relaxing and talking on his Tennessee family farm.

An Inconvenient Truth opens on Gore's farm and portrays the quiet beauty of nature under threat. It then cuts to Gore's opening lecture joke: "My name is Al Gore. I used to be the next president of the United States." The film quickly moves to explaining global warming. Charts document a growing rise in temperature, while an animated cartoon illustrates how global warming works, and Gore's lift upon a hydraulic crane dramatizes how quickly the carbon dioxide level is increasing. Gore's lecture also addresses the dangers of population explosion, and urban and industrial congestion and pollution, and how these factors help produce extreme weather events, which charts show are on the rise. One of the more dramatic features of the documentary include warnings concerning the melting of glaciers and threats to the continental ice shelves in Antarctica and Greenland. Indeed, the most apocalyptic claims concern the weakening and break-up of the ice sheets, and graphic reproductions of how resultant rising ocean currents could flood vast areas of the east and west coasts of the US, China and India, and other highly populated coastal regions.

The latter point was claimed to be alarmist in an article by William Broad in the *New York Times*, who asserted that the tide level would have to rise over 20 feet to create the damage envisaged in Gore's graphics, but scientists predicted only a 23–24 inch melting of the ice-caps by the end of the century.[21] This argument, widely touted in the corporate media and rightwing blogosphere, presupposes only "normal" melting of the ice-caps, whereas Gore's scenario envisaged increased breaking up of the ice-caps that would accelerate melting, a phenomenon already underway and which his film dramatically portrayed with documentary footage.[22]

The film was heavily promoted by activist groups and found a large and enthusiastic audience. It received generally favorable reviews, although critics of Gore either attacked the film or Gore's persona and politics. Roger Ebert, however, was so enthusiastic that he wrote:

> I want to write this review so every reader will begin it and finish it. I am a liberal, but I do not intend this as a review reflecting any kind of politics. It reflects the truth as I understand it, and it represents, I believe, agreement among the world's experts.
>
> Global warming is real.
>
> It is caused by human activity.
>
> Mankind and its governments must begin immediate action to halt and reverse it.
>
> If we do nothing, in about ten years the planet may reach a "tipping point" and begin a slide toward destruction of our civilization and most of the other species on this planet.
>
> After that point is reached, it would be too late for any action.
>
> These facts are stated by Al Gore in the documentary *An Inconvenient Truth*. Forget he ever ran for office. Consider him a concerned man speaking out on the approaching crisis. "There is no controversy about these facts," he says in the film. "Out of 925 recent articles in peer-review scientific journals about global warming, there was no disagreement. Zero."[23]

Although there is indeed overwhelming consensus in global warming studies concerning the seriousness of the issue, *An Inconvenient Truth* revealed that of 636 reports on the global warming debate in the popular press, 53 percent put in question key aspects of the arguments. This media bias is not adequately explored in Gore's film, nor is the role of corporations and lobbyists in blocking political solutions that corporations see as threatening their short-term interests and profits. The documentary also saves its suggestions concerning what is to be done about global warming for an end-credits sequence, accompanied by Melissa Etheredge's Academy Award winning song, "I need to wake up."[24]

In addition to winning the Academy Award and becoming one of the most widely seen documentaries of all time,[25] *An Inconvenient Truth* became a global phenomenon, eliciting attention and controversy throughout the world. Gore was co-awarded the Nobel Peace Prize in 2007, when it was noted that his commitment to fighting global warming "has strengthened the struggle against climate change," and he was called "probably the single individual who has done most to create greater worldwide understanding of the measures that need to be adopted."[26]

Other documentaries dealt with global warming, climate change, and other threats to the environment. Hubert Sauper's *Darwin's Nightmare* (2005) documents the devastation created by the introduction of Nile perch in Lake Victoria in Africa in the 1960s. The highly invasive and predatory fish killed off other species, some of which fed on algae and maintained the lake's ecosystem that was now slowly dying. The film focuses on the Nile perch factories that send millions of tons of fish a day to Europe, constituting Tanzania's largest export. Poignant episodes depict the incredible poverty among those who come from the countryside to work in a factory or serve as fishermen at minimum wage, the AIDS epidemic from prostitutes who service the workers, the armies of children who sniff glue and struggle for tiny amounts of food, and the possibility that the airplanes which fly the fish exports to Europe return with guns sold to various factions that bring civil war and further devastation in Africa.[27] A revealing interview by a former teacher who works in a fish factory suggests that the struggle for control of African natural resources has traditionally led to vast inequalities between the haves and have nots, with the strongest and most powerful forces seizing control. Hence, just as the Nile perch destroy other species in Lake Victoria, so too do the predatory global powers who control Africa's resources condemn the general population to a life of misery.

Gregory Greene's *The End of Suburbia* (2006) opens with stock footage of post-World War II suburbia in the United States, and the automobile and consumer culture that accompanied its rise and expansion. It quickly cuts to how the end of peak production of oil will collapse this "American Dream" based on high consumption and suburban living. Greene marshals an impressive array of experts who warn that peak oil production is rapidly approaching, or is here already, and that there will be drastic reductions in the amount of oil available in the coming years. While the warning and wake-up call is salutary, the filmmakers do not push alternative energy and debunk most candidates to replace oil. While many alternative energy sources do have their downsides, one hopes that a critical mass of multiple new energy sources could address the crisis. The film's failure to indicate alternatives reveals a lack of vision and hope in some segments of the left.

Daniel B. Gold and Judith Helfand's *Everything's Cool* (2007) focuses on corporate shills who masquerade as scientists and attack climate change science contrast with those experts who point to the dangers of global warming. The film documents how critics of global warming receive funding from energy and other corporate entities opposing regulation and restrictions on industrial activity. Begun in 2003, the film documents a number of sites throughout the Americas that are being damaged by global warming and even shows an early version of Al Gore's speech and slide-show that became the basis for *An Inconvenient Truth*. The film also follows global warming activists, who they humanize by going to their homes and doing personal interviews, as well as presenting their analyses of the dangers of climate change and criticism of those who would deny the problem.

The 11th Hour (2007) takes off from *An Inconvenient Truth*'s warnings about the dangers of climate change and global warming, and provides a harrowing overview of the earth's various eco-crises. Using the metaphor of the 11th hour, the film dramatizes the relative shortness of human life on earth and the possibility that if current crises continue, the ecosystem will collapse, threatening the survival of the human species. Co-produced and narrated by Leonardo DiCaprio and directed by Nadia Conners and Leila Conners Petersen, *The 11th Hour* uses documentary footage and interviews with over fifty environmental experts to dramatize the dangers of global warming, escalating extreme weather events, cascading pollution, the depletion of ocean resources, deforestation, desertification, the melting of polar ice-caps, the rapid depletion of fossil fuels, overpopulation, and disease epidemics, especially in overpopulated and polluted urban areas. Multiplying the global challenges to human survival, the film postulates that a "convergence of crises" could produce apocalyptic collapse, with Stephen Hawking warning in a dramatic segment that if things continue on their present course, life on earth could end, and the planet could became an arid and lifeless orb like Venus, without atmosphere to sustain life and with sulfuric acid for rain. Further, *The 11th Hour* goes much further than *An Inconvenient Truth* by pointing to specific causes and suggesting solutions. Many experts deplore the system of corporate greed that allows pollution and environmental destruction at the cost of imperiling the earth and its resources. Reliance on non-renewable fossil fuels is cited as a major problem and the need for renewable energy sources and more sustainable products is emphasized. Accompanying interviews on the DVD elaborate on solutions, such as alternative energy sources, eco-friendly houses and architecture, green products, and how a more sustainable mode of life might be produced.

The 11th Hour strongly indicts the political class in the United States, pointing out that in the early 1970s Democrats and Republicans worked together to begin dealing with problems of the environment, but since then bi-partisan congressional action on the environment has been sorely lacking. There are also philosophical analyses that claim we need an entirely new way of viewing the world and our dependence on nature, grasping our embeddedness in the natural environmentand perceiving our need to preserve the planet for future generations. All in all, the film is a sobering look at the serious environmental problems facing the human race and the need for serious solutions.

Finally, Werner Herzog's idiosyncratic documentary *Encounters at the End of the World* (2008) provides a fascinating exploration of the relation between humans, science, and nature in Antarctica that concludes with a pessimistic warning about human extinction. Herzog interviews a wide variety of interesting people working on the relatively unknown continent, including scientists who study micro-organisms, one of whom describes frightening evolutionary battles among underwater micro-organisms, while another scientist is proud he has just discovered three new species. The barren and forbidding landscape and the precarious attempts to establish camps and tunnels to explore the novel ecology lead Herzog to meditate on the fragility of the ecosystem and the human species.

This discussion takes us to engaging Hollywood allegories of environmental crisis that portray various types of threats to the existing environment and dangers of collapse, a theme that will be developed in succeeding sections.

Animated Visions

One of the most popular documentary films of the era, French filmmaker Luc Jacquet's *March of the Penguins* (2005), evades the issue of climate change and global warming. This charming film tracks the march of the Emperor penguins in Antarctica to their seasonal mating and then separation during the harsh winter, but only in a *National Geographic* documentary on the DVD is global warming and the threat to the survival of the penguins mentioned.

George Miller's animated penguin story *Happy Feet* (2006), by contrast, shows how human plundering of natural resources is adversely impacting upon the natural world. Sean Cubitt (2005) points out the long and curious connections between animation and animals, and the tendency of animated films to anthropomorphize animals while sometimes zoomorphizing humans. Disney tended to use animated films to anthropomorphize animals for the purposes of constructing conservative ideological machines, but many recent animation films have used animal figures and narratives to make pointed critiques of human follies, including Pixar/Disney's *WALL-E* (see below).

Happy Feet's warm story centers on Mumbles, a highly individualized penguin who cannot sing and win penguin love (voice of Elijah Wood). Mumbles was born to dance, leading to his ostracizing, before acceptance by other penguin groups, themselves different from the Emperor penguins. This plotline is connected to a quest drama whereby the dancing penguin wants to discover why the group's fish supply is dwindling. En route to discovery, and after threats from predatory birds and killer fish, the group encounters Lovelace the Guru (voice of Robin Williams), who has a plastic six-pack container around his neck that he claims is a magic talisman. Mumbles soon discovers that the penguins' fish are being taken away by humans and that pollution by humans is wreaking havoc in Antarctica.

The satirical animation film *Farce of the Penguins* (2007) goes further, twice bringing up climate change as a threat to the penguin's survival, a major factor left out of the idyl of *March of the Penguins*. Indeed, *March of the Penguins* idealizes and anthropomorphizes its penguins, opening with Morgan Freeman's narration that the documentary is a "love story," and he closes on the same note, telling that it was "love" that drove the penguins to return to their mate and children against great obstacles.[28] Samuel Jackson's narration on *Farce of the Penguins* mocks the idealistic narrative of *March*, and creates an unsettling story of penguins constantly faced with threats to their survival. *March of the Penguins* also presents an idealized vision of nature and triumph over adversity, while *Farce* and *Happy Feet* present darker visions of cruelty, the struggle for survival, and the destructive interventions of humans, upsetting the balance of the natural world.

An Arctic Tale (2007), directed by Adam Ravetch and Sarah Robertson, combines *National Geographic* nature footage of the Arctic with a fable about the dangers of global warming and how it is affecting the region's species. The narrative features parallel adventures in the birth and maturation of a walrus pup named Seela and a polar bear cub named Nanu, characters constructed from composites of multiple walruses and bears filmed over several years. Scripted by Linda Woolverton, who has written Disney films, Mose Richards, and Al Gore's daughter Kristin, the film uses a story narrated by Queen Latifah to dramatize the harsh lives of the walrus, polar bear, and other species. While the film is aimed at kids and family viewing, it presents a dark vision of the predatory struggle for survival, and dramatizes how global warming robs animals of their natural habitat.

In his reading of Peter Jackson's *Lord of the Rings* trilogy (2001, 2002, 2003), Sean Cubitt (2005) emphasizes ecological themes and the harmonies between nature, diverse cultures and beings, and technology. Whereas Tolkien tended to be anti-technology and romanticized preindustrial society, Cubitt stresses that in "establishing shots of Hobbiton, Rivendell and Rohan, for example, the fit between culture and nature is celebrated in the harmony of design and environment" (p. 11). Tolkien's themes of the destruction of nature through mining and manufacturing, however, are preserved in the long fly-through shots of the underground foundaries of Saruman as a "vision of hell" (p. 18). In Cubitt's reading, ecological harmony and the preservation of nature are a major positive theme in Jackson's rendition of Tolkien's novel.[29]

Yet it is perhaps Pixar's animated film *WALL-E* (2008), directed by Andrew Stanton, that provides the most poignant animated film warning about environmental collapse and the fragility of life on earth. The film opens with images of a devastated earth inundated by garbage, a dramatic warning of how the excesses of the consumer society could overwhelm the ecosystem. The charming narrative has a garbage-compactor robot WALL-E (Waste Allocation Load Lifter-Earth-class) doing his daily work of collecting and compacting garbage and industrial waste into mangeable units that he diligently stacks on top of each other, producing an artwork of sorts, as his creations begin to resemble skyscrapers. Although it appears that WALL-E's labors are a Sisyphean task – the mounds of refuse are endless and violent storms force him to seek refuge in his makeshift shelter – WALL-E makes the most of his bleak existence, collecting items for his warehouse home, one of the most valuable of which is an endlessly replayed tape of parts of *Hello Dolly*. He also seems to have cultivated a relationship with an indestructible cockroach, perhaps the only surviving living thing on earth.

WALL-E's harsh and repetitive life presents a critical vision of alienated labor under capitalism, but WALL-E struggles to have a meaningful private life in his collection of discarded objects from the consumer society. His routine is interrupted one day, however, by the arrival of a robot probe EVE (Extraterrestrial Vegetation Evaluator), just at a moment when the first fragile shoots of plant life reappear on the planet. While WALL-E is a poignant figure of industrial labor – with his box-like shape, mechanical parts and functions, and a life spent in repetitive labor – EVE represents a more high-tech post-industrial age with her sleek cylinder form (and resembles Apple computer products, the corporation that partly owns Pixar), multiple tasking, and complex functions.

The early scenes with WALL-E and EVE on earth highlight the wonder of things – their shapes, light and color, properties and functions – as the two discover beauty and meaning in their desolate surroundings and attempt a primitive form of communication. As they leave earth to return to the mother ship that sent EVE, the spectacular images evoke the wonders of space, technology, and earth. Just as earlier the Disney team anthropomorphized animals to produce morality tales for humans, in *WALL-E* machines are anthropomorphized to produce a critique of a mechanistic techno-capitalism and to embody admirable human traits like love and resistance.[30]

EVE had been sent by a corporation named Buy 'n' Large, which had evidently covered the earth with megastores whose waste and excess have inundated the planet. The corporate elite and wealthy consumers have apparently left earth hundreds of years ago on a space ship where they are served by robots, move around on reclining hoverchairs, communicate through video screens, slurp food through straws, and have grown into almost identical, fat, middle-aged infants, controlled by machines. The president of the corporation who rules the world (possibly modeled on George W. Bush and played by Fred Willard) utters pleasant banalities to "stay the course" and assure the overgrown consumers that all is well, but the ship is really run by a sinister computer named Auto, voiced by Sigourney Weaver and modeled on *2001*'s villainous computer HAL. This trope plays into fears of domination by technology, harking back to *2001* (1968), *THX-1138* (1971), and other technophobic science fiction films of the last decades (see Kellner and Ryan 1988: 245ff).

When the ship's captain learns from EVE that a fragile plant has appeared on earth, suggesting that life may be sustainable again, the orbiting spaceship prepares for a return to earth, but Auto opposes the plan, driving WALL-E and EVE, assisted by the captain, to lead resistance and take the ship back. The segment on the ship contains a powerful critique of technocapitalism whereby giant corporations provide consumers with basic needs and confine them to a life of leisure and consumption. When the captain realizes the computerized program that has ruled their existence for 700 years is enslaving the crew and passengers in a life of indolence and passivity, he has an awakening. While the computerized mechanism of the ship wants to confine him to his quarters, the captain uses the public address system to rally the passengers to a return to earth. With the help of WALL-E and EVE, the mission is accomplished.

In a Disneyesque happy ending, it appears that romance between WALL-E and EVE is now viable, that life on earth may be sustainable, and that the human race can rest assured that although it may have been exiled from its homeland for 700 years or more, a happy return is possible. The captain joyously tells the returned inhabitants of planet earth that they can do things like farm and produce their own food, and a final pan shot shows that indeed green plants are being restored to the barren planet.

Allegories of Catastrophe: Social Apocalypse in Disaster, Horror, and Fantasy Films

As we have seen in the previous sections, global warming, climate change, and the horrors of an unrestrained corporate globalization endanger the earth. Contemporary cinema has addressed a wide range of environmental issues and threats to the survival of humanity and nature. In an earlier era, films warned about nuclear war by portraying post-nuclear holocausts, ranging from the highly realistic and frightening BBC film *War Games* (1965) by Peter Watkins, to more allegorical films like *Blade Runner* (1982), which portrayed a post-holocaust Los Angeles, or *Escape from New York* (1981), which portrayed a post-holocaust New York.

In the Bush-Cheney era, allegories of disaster and visions of social catastrophe emerged, ranging from environmental disaster films to a number of dystopic visions of the future found in a fusion of science fiction and horror.[31] Whenever social anxieties proliferate, films and fantasy evoke social apocalypse, a trope evident in the Hollywood films of the 2000s that articulate worries about environmental crisis and socioeconomic and political collapse.

Environmental Meltdown

Roland Emmerich's *The Day After Tomorrow* (2004) uses the conventions of the disaster film to dramatize the dangers of climate change and global warming, ignored by the Bush-Cheney administration.[32] In an eco-disaster extravaganza featuring tornadoes devastating Los Angeles, a massive tidal surge sweeping through Manhattan, and the freezing of the northern hemisphere, Emmerich takes the disaster film to new extremes. The film opens in Antarctica where Professor Jack Hall (Dennis Quaid) and other scientists confront a polar ice-shelf cracking. At a New Delhi environmental conference, Hall warns that a change in the Gulf Stream caused by global warming could bring about a dramatic decrease in temperature. The Dick Cheney look-alike vice-president (Kenneth Walsh) is skeptical and notes the adverse effects of the Kyoto accord on the economy. Yet a Scottish scientist (Ian Holm) tells Hall that his studies of plummeting ocean temperatures in the North Atlantic support the hypothesis that sudden climate change could produce another Ice Age.

Highlighting the global nature of ecological crisis, *The Day After Tomorrow* portrays extreme weather events in India, giant hailstones in Japan, and a Tsunami tidal wave inundating New York, followed by a hard freeze of the entire northern hemisphere, with international astronauts viewing the murderous storm systems wreaking havoc. In an ironic reversal, the film shows people from the northern hemisphere desperately trying to cross the border into Mexico, with Mexican police attempting to turn them away.

The climatologist Jack Hall warns the US government that "in seven to ten days, we'll be in a new Ice Age." When the clueless president (Perry King) in

Roland Emmerich's *The Day After Tomorrow* uses the conventions of the disaster film to dramatize the dangers of climate change and global warming.

a baseball hat is confronted with the magnitude of the cataclysm, he asks his now-chastened vice-president, "What do you think we should do?" Such images transcode popular perceptions of Bush as incompetent and disengaged, and of Cheney running the presidency, and highlight the dangers of having an administration which ignores serious problems.

The Day After Tomorrow puts on display the potentially devastating effects of failing to take ecological crisis seriously and not having plans to deal with environmental problems. Resonant images of a wall of water crashing down on Fifth Avenue in New York, the Empire State Building and New York skyscrapers cracking apart, the Statue of Liberty half-buried in a frozen ice block, and tornadoes ripping the letters off the Hollywood sign, produce an imagination of disaster that provides cautionary warnings about environmental breakdown.

Indie auteur Jim Fessenden's *The Last Winter* (2006) provides a cautionary eco-horror/disaster film about the consequences of global warming. Set in the high Arctic Circle, the film opens with a PR documentary discussing how a corporation, North Industries, has just received a government contract to begin exploration in an area previously denominated a wildlife preserve, geared to discover new oil supplies to make the US more energy independent. The oil explorers and scientists already stationed in the wilderness are beginning to suffer stress, with young Maxwell (Zach Gilford) roaming the empty tundra on his own at night and mumbling about mysterious gases and images. Project manager Ed Pollack (Ron Perlman) returns to discover that Hoffman (James LeGros), an environmental activist who's been hired to monitor the project, has become convinced that the ecosystem is melting down and that with winter temperatures well above normal, the permafrost is melting, making "ice roads" needed to bring in heavy equipment impossible. Further, Hoffman is sleeping with Abby (Connie Britton), Pollack's second in command and previous lover, leading to conflicts between the corporate oil officials who want to drill, baby, drill, and the ecologists worried about effects on the environment.

As it quickly turns out, Maxwell is getting weirder, mumbling about the revenge of nature against human meddling and exploitation of the environment, and that oil, which consists of dead fossils and animals, is emanating strange phenomena after centuries of resting undisturbed. Indeed, the cracking ice and wind are emitting mysterious sounds, and a sour gas may be driving Maxwell crazy (although a Native employee mentions Wendigo, native spirits in the area). After Maxwell's death from freezing, and increasingly bizarre sights and events, the macho Pollock and the ecologist Hoffman leave for help after a plane that has flown to rescue them inexplicitly crashes into their station. The ending is not a cheerful one, but the film closes with chirpy and brightly lit newscasts reporting strange weather occurrences around the world, suggesting climate change and global warming, which the corporate media, however, are apparently failing to investigate.

Horror Shows

Crises of the 1960s and 1970s were often represented allegorically in horror, disaster, and other genre films (Kellner and Ryan 1988). The nightmares of the Bush-Cheney regime were represented in a cycle of genre films depicting social apocalypse. The first in a social apocalypse genre franchise, *Resident Evil* (2002) was based on a popular Japanese video game and inspired a cycle of films. Directed by Paul W. S. Anderson, *Resident Evil* has a strong corporate conspiracy subtext and opens with a detailed description of how a mega-corporation has taken over the US:

> At the beginning of the 21st century, the Umbrella Corporation had become the largest commercial entity in the United States. Nine out of every ten homes contain its products. Its political and financial influence is felt everywhere. In public, it is the world's leading supplier of computer technology, medical products, and healthcare. Unknown, even to its own employees, its massive profits are generated by military technology, genetic experimentation and viral weaponry.

Resident Evil opens with the release of a deadly gas that sets off a biohazard warning signal and is soon killing people who are regenerated as zombies. An elite crew is sent to contain the infestation, but as it gets out of control the Red Queen computer that controls the underground facility orders a shutdown, so the crew must struggle against zombies, infected dogs, corporate henchmen, and a malevolent computer to escape. The crew – led by two super kickass women, Alice (Milla Jovovich) and Rain (Michelle Rodriguez) – appears to shut down the Red Queen, but countless zombies escape, giving rise to sequels in the franchise. At the end of the film, the main character, who we will learn in sequels is Alice, survives, but observes that the city above the underground research facility has been overrun by zombies and she faces a desperate future.

While the first *Resident Evil* film took place largely underground in a claustrophobic environment where new evils and challenges appeared around every corner, *Resident Evil: Apocalypse* (2004) takes place amid an urban apocalypse in which Alice, endowed with genetic superpowers, fights zombies, monsters, and corporate thugs, teaming up with some other survivors, including two strong women, to escape before the quarantined city is nuked by the evil corporation. Alice and a couple of her companions make it out for the sequel, but *Apocalypse* ends with the nuclear attack covered over by the Umbrella Corporation as the malfunction of a nuclear power plant, playing on fears of government cover-ups. Further, news reports claim that earlier stories of corporate malfeasance were false and that people should be grateful to the Umbrella Corporation for preserving their way of life, a barely disguised allegory of lying by corporations and the state during the Bush-Cheney era.

In *Resident Evil: Extinction* (2007), urban life has been destroyed globally and Alice and a small band of survivors try to survive amid the zombie hordes in a mostly desert environment. Directed by Australian Russell Mulcahy, this zombie gore film shamelessly rips off *Mad Max* and *The Road Warrior* with endless battle scenes, highlighted in an attack by a flock of virally infected birds, who make Hitchcock's flock look tame and harmless by comparison. Superpower-endowed Alice fries the birds and hooks up with Claire Redford and her band of uninfected survivors, who are falling fast to the zombies taking over the world. Las Vegas is in ruins and the only hope for the group is to make it to Alaska, where reports say there are survivors (obviously they haven't seen *30 Days of Night*, which shows Alaska overrun by vampires).

The ultra-violent and nihilistic *Resident Evil: Extinction* is a right-wing survivalist fantasy. After the collapse of civilization only the most violent can survive in a dog-eat-dog and zombie-eat-the-few-humans universe. The *Resident Evil* films articulate fears of evil corporations and uncontrolled biotechnology, human beings dominated by technology, and outbreaks of deadly biochemical plagues – a fear inflamed by the anthrax attacks (never explained) following 9/11. Cumulatively, the franchise falls into a subgenre cycle of zombie films, all ripping off George Romero copiously, who returns, as we shall shortly see, to pastiche himself.

A series of other mutant zombie films focuses on the dangers of science and technology careening out of control and producing catastrophic consequences. Danny Boyle's *28 Days Later* (2003) opens in a research lab in which monkeys have been injected with a pure aggression virus to study violence and its control. Animal rights activists inadvertently "liberate" the monkeys, who begin a murderous rampage, infecting the entire population with a rage virus that turns people into zombie-like killers. Produced in 2000–2001 – when an epidemic of foot-and-mouth disease in Britain forced the slaughter of hordes of cattle, and the anthrax attacks after 9/11 were creating anxiety – the film appeared during the outbreak of the SARS epidemic in 2003. Thus the pandemic shown in the film had great resonance in the real world.

The DVD commentary and documentary dramatize the dangers of global pandemics. Fear of an out-of-control military is another subtext of the film, as a small group of survivors flees to a military camp in the north of England, responding to a broadcast message that survivors associated with the military are seeking a cure to the virus. The group finds the military encampment, but the survivors include a young black woman (Naomie Harris) and a teenage girl (Megan Burns), and it is soon evident that the military seek to make them their sex slaves in a scheme to repopulate the earth (and satisfy their sexual desires), thus positioning the audience against predatory masculinist militarism.

A sequel, *28 Weeks Later* (2007), directed by Spanish filmmaker Juan Carlos Fresnadillo, articulates specific fears of the US military out of control. A continuation of the previous story but with completely new characters, the film envisages a US-led Nato occupation of Britain to deal with the dangers of another outbreak of the virus after the initial hosts appear to have died. Predictably, the virus and monster rampage reappear and US-led troops – some of whom were complaining about the lack of "action" – begin shooting the zombies, with some of them exulting in the kills. In the context of the US occupation of Iraq, the Code Red order to exterminate survivors of the first virus wave along with the newly infected, and the protracted slaughter and eventual fire-bombing of a rehabilitation camp, produce resonances with real-world horrors.

Both films have a survivalist and Darwinian subtext, but also express fears of societal breakdown and resultant unrestrained aggression. The hand-held jittering camera and quick editing in the action sequences of *28 Weeks Later* especially, create a sense of existence careening out of control, of being thrown into an unbearable chaos, vividly evoking fears of everything going to shit. A refrain throughout both films – "It's all fucked" – expresses the ultimate anxiety, suggesting that everything is indeed so fucked there is fuck all to do to improve things or provide any hope for the future.

Perhaps Alfonso Cuarón's *Children of Men* (2006) is the most complex and thought-provoking meditation on the breakdown of the contemporary political system in its allegory of a world spinning into apocalyptic collapse and Orwellian fascism. In its science fiction premise, based on a novel by P. D. James, the story presents a world fallen into terror and hopelessness when global infertility mysteriously erupts after a flu pandemic in 2009. Set in London in 2027, the truly frightening scenario shows political tendencies of the present leading to chaos and collapse. Using long shots and long takes, Cuarón's camera forces the viewer to explore an environment that looks very much like present-day reality, only more drab, dangerous, and frightening. Opening television images present a montage of a world in collapse where "only Britain soldiers on":

> *Newsreader:*   Day 1,000 of the Siege of Seattle. The Muslim community demands an end to the Army's occupation of mosques. The Homeland Security bill is ratified. After eight years, British borders will remain closed. The deportation of illegal immigrants will continue.
> Good morning. Our lead story.

Since the economy and social order have disintegrated everywhere except in Britain, streams of refugees flood into the country where they are sent to internment camps. A revolutionary group called the Fish fights for immigrant rights and the end of the police state, and plans a violent uprising. All hope is gone after the death of the youngest human, Baby Diego, throws the world into despair. A government bureaucrat, Theo, played in his best anti-hero mode by Clive Owen, leaves a café that is bombed by terrorists and is kidnapped by them. His ex-wife Julian (Julianne Moore) is a member of the group and she helps persuade him to get exit visas for a refugee pregnant woman, Kee (Claire-Hope Ashitey), to take her to the Human Project, where attempts are being made to regenerate human life.[33] Observing the horrors of state repression, Theo becomes an active participant in the quest to smuggle Kee and her baby out of the country. This plotline provides the occasion for a stunning montage of a police state, terrorism, refugee internment camps, and accelerating social disintegration – intensifying tendencies in the present and providing a warning that if things are not dramatically changed we will slide into catastrophe.

While *Children of Men* calls attention to growing fascism and the collapse of democracy and civilization, it has a conservative subtext. The disintegration of civilization makes one yearn for the good old days and the film celebrates childbirth as the key to humanity. The revolutionaries are shown to be brutal terrorists, who gratuitously shoot Theo's lovable friend, Jasper (Michael Caine), and who plan a quixotic "uprising" that appears to be leading to more destruction and their own probable extinction. While the film valorizes political activism and charts Theo's transformation from a depressed cynic into a committed activist, hope is projected onto a nebulous Human Project and the birth of a lone child who becomes an object of religious adoration. Throughout there are media images of Islamic terrorism, and one long scene near the end,

Children of Men depicts an apocalyptic future police state with caged immi-grants.

where Theo and Kee seek to escape and deliver the child to a boat that will take it to the Human Project, features a menacing demonstration of what appears to be an Islamic radical group, thus reproducing the con-temporary tendency to fear Arabs and Islam.

Yet, on many levels, the film provides prescient critical visions of the present era, evoking the horrors of militarism and a fascist police state. The images of social decay and the faded and saturated colors of *Children of Men* provide a gloomy vision of where contemporary trends may be leading us if action is not taken and change embraced.

In a fascinating article on the proliferation of zombie themes in popular culture, "This Zombie Moment," Gendy Alimurung argues that the dazed and lumbering zombies bent only on survival stand in for figures of millions who as a result of Bush-Cheney Republican economics have lost jobs, stock market wealth, and pension funds, are unable to pay healthcare and mortgage costs, and are worn down by years of war and escalating societal violence.[34] As my analysis suggests, the proliferation of zombie films indeed provides allegories of deadened masses of people and irrational violence that has specific societal origins and references with the politics of the 2000s. While conservative catastrophe films show evil coming from sources external to the existing system or from more supernatural sources, a socially critical tradition exhibited in many of the 2000s catastrophe films discussed here, shows evil and monstrosity emerging from out-of-control aspects of the existing society. George Romero's *Land of the Dead* (2005) and *Diary of the Dead* (2007), for example, provide updated constructions of his zombies-returning-to-life series that provide critical allegories of the present moment. If the zombies in Romero's *Night of the Living Dead* (1968) could be read as the silent majorities threatening the counterculture in the 1960s, and *Dawn of the Dead* (1973) could be read as an allegory of how consumerism makes zombies out of people, *Day of the Dead* (1985) could be seen as a satire on the greed and violence of the Reagan era, while *Land of the Dead* can stand as an allegory for the deterioration of life in the Bush-Cheney era.

In *Land of the Dead*, after years of zombie attacks on one of the few urban sites of safety, society is divided between those living in high-rise luxury apartments (a fitting figure for gated communities) and the lower classes living in squalor. A small cadre of police tries to protect the upper classes from the zombies and to scavenge supplies from the countryside. The class division represents the growing discrepancy between rich and poor during the Bush-Cheney years, and the zombies initially appear as working-class types who have had the life sucked out of them and are distracted by firework displays which keep them entertained. In Romero's vision, however, the zombies are becoming more intelligent, learning to communicate, use weapons, and organize their forces to assault the city of the living and privileged.

The high-rise city is ruled by Kaufman (Dennis Hopper), an impervious dictator who is resonant of Donald Trump and Donald Rumsfeld (in a DVD video accompanying the film, Hopper said he intended to play the character like Rumsfeld). In a scene where a rogue policeman (played over-the-top by John Leguizamo) threatens to use stolen weapons against the compound, Kaufman snaps: "We don't negotiate with terrorists," an obvious jab at the Bush-Cheney administration.

Led by an African-American zombie, Big Daddy (Eugene Clark), who has learned to use weapons, the zombies attack the gated high-rise, an image of revolutionary insurrection against the ruling elites. A fireworks display fails to distract them, a symbol of growing revolutionary class consciousness, and the zombies continue systematically to assault the ruling-class refuge in the film's fantasy of class revenge.

Romero's later *Diary of the Dead* (2007) goes back to the beginnings of his *Dead* mythology to show the emergence of the Living Dead zombies. In the film's narrative conceit, a student filmmaking crew from the University of Pittsburgh is filming a horror film in the woods when media reports tell of a strange eruption of people returning from the dead to feast on the living. When the students observe the phenomenon themselves, a young filmmaker, Jason, resolves to capture the horrors on video, to produce a document of the event in which "everything changed." They obtain media coverage from Internet video and discern that the government is lying, covering up the enormity of the horror. The young crew resolves to shoot footage of what is really happening and upload it on the video, pointing to a era of new media and sources of news and information in which "viral video" can be quickly distributed across the world via the Internet.

Of course, the theme of a lying media evokes the US corporate media in the run-up to Iraq and during large stretches of the Bush-Cheney era. The film is full of topical commentary, as when a radio talk show speaker announces "the real immigration problem" is now about people crossing the line between life and death, a dig at conservative commentators who wax hysterical about immigration problems. In a larger sense, in the current environment, the very notion of the Dead returning to life points to the cycle of death and vengeance, endemic for centuries in the Middle East and other parts of the world, that the US has stirred up with the Pandora's Box of its Iraq intervention. Compared to real-life horrors, Romero's zombie films seem relatively tame and subdued.

Richard Rodriquez's *Planet Terror*, the first half of his *Grindhouse* (2007) double bill with Quentin Tarantino, also provides a critical twist to the zombie horror extravaganza, as the film off-handedly explains its zombie killer mutations as resulting from a biological-chemical weapons experiment used in Iraq and gone awry in the US. The ghoulish mutations ravage citizens – an allegory of the system producing monsters in the military who will return to wreak havoc on the populace. The film's major villains are US military thugs trying to sell the biological-chemical weapons developed in Iraq, and played with tongue-in-cheek irony by Bruce Willis and Tarantino himself.

Interestingly, there have been waves of post-apocalyptic thrillers whenever conservative Republicans serve two terms of office, increasing gaps between rich and poor, the haves and the have nots, and generating economic crisis. During the Reagan years the *Mad Max* films, *Escape from New York*, *Blade Runner*, and countless lesser vehicles showed civilization collapsing into chaotic violence, a conservative nightmare that law and order would disappear, largely caused (although the films would never let you know this) by conservative economic policies.

The number of post-apocalyptic films in the Bush-Cheney years dramatically proliferated as conditions of life worsened for many and crisis intensified. Such films offer allegories of social collapse, dystopias that provide warnings that trends in the present age can spiral out of control and produce catastrophic disaster on a grand scale. While allegories of catastrophe may reproduce the politics of fear exploited by rightwing politicians, they also suggest subliminally that the Bush-Cheney era of unregulated market fundamentalism, rampant militarism, Social Darwinism, and fear may produce the sort of societal collapse evident in *Land of the Dead*, *28 Days Later*, and *Children of Men*. These films can thus be read as allegories of the disintegration of social life and civil society, and the emergence of a Darwinian nightmare where the struggle for survival occurs in a Hobbesian world where life is nasty, brutish, and short. The zombies and monsters represent not only conservative nightmares, but also visions of where the ultra-right Bush-Cheney regime has been taking us.

Notes

1 Many conservative scholars like John Dean (2004, 2006, 2007) and Kevin Phillips (2006) wrote books excoriating the Bush-Cheney administration for rightwing extremism and authoritarianism, claiming it had betrayed true conservativism. While there is no question but that the Bush-Cheney administration was the most hard-right in recent history, it's also true that there are definite ideological and policy continuities with Reaganite conservativism, so I am using both the terms *rightwing extremism* and *ultraconservativism* to discuss the administration's ideological orientation and policies.

2 On the bankruptcy of corporate news media in the US, see Kellner (1990) and McChesney (2000, 2007).

3   Curiously, reviews and later retrospective articles describe *Unprecedented* as one of Robert Greenwald's productions (see, for example, Charles Musser, "War, documentary, and Iraq dossier film truth in the age of George W. Bush," *Framework* 48, 2 [Fall 2007]: 11f). In fact, however, although Greenwald loaned editing machines and gave advice on distribution, the film was an independent production of Sekler and Perez (interviews with Joan Sekler, Los Angeles).

4   While the vote recount story is admittedly complex, a media consortium that inspected and counted ballots indicated that if "intent of the voter" was used as a criterion, and if undervotes and overvotes were counted under this rule, and if all of the Florida election districts would have actually recounted the votes, then Al Gore would have clearly won the election; see Kellner (2001) and the sources in note 6, below.

5   There were allegations that there were also many irregularities in computer voting and other problems in the 2004 election, which many claim was also stolen by the Bush-Cheney-Rove Gang; see Miller (2005), Fitrakis and Wasserman (2005), and Gumbel (2005).

6   See the articles collected at Bushwatch at www.bushwatch.com/gorebush. htm (accessed June 3, 2008) and Robert Parry, "Gore won," November 21, 2001, at www.consortiumnews.com/2001/111201a.html (accessed June 3, 2008). Undervotes were votes on ballots that were not counted, in some cases because the machines were full of chad and the vote registered as a "dimple"; these would have been counted according to strict "intent of the voter" criteria. Overvotes were ones where either a voter voted for two presidential candidates, as on the Butterfly Ballot that had two separate pages, or handwrote the name of the candidate after punching in the vote. There were tens of thousands of these overvotes signaling that the voter intended to vote for Gore. If these had been counted he would have handily won. A spokesman for the Florida Supreme Court indicated that the court had planned to count all undervotes and overvotes in all Florida counties according to "intent of the voter" criteria when the Supreme Court stopped the counting (see Kellner 2001).

7   See Wilson's (2004) account of his clash with the Bush-Cheney-Rove Gang. Cheney's Chief of Staff I. Lewis "Scooter" Libby was indicted for lying about his attempt to destroy Wilson's wife's CIA career, but the sentence was commuted. Although there was speculation that Rove would also be charged, he has so far dodged the bullet, eventually resigning from the Bush-Cheney White House in 2007 to write a book on the scandal-ridden administration and try to profit on the lecture trail and as a commentator on Fox News.

8   The film was rereleased in October 2004 for theatrical showings in an 87-minute version with the title *Uncovered: The War on Iraq*. This version

included more material on the lead-up to the Iraq War and a revealing interview with UN weapons inspector David Kay.

9 Musser, "War, Documentary," p. 9ff situates *Uncovered* in a genre of "legal film truth" documentaries in which the filmmaker puts on trial members of a political administration or legal system, and places the results in question, as Errol Morris does with *The Thin Blue Line* (1988).

10 A short primer on Dick Cheney: after Cheney was asked by presidential candidate George W. Bush in the lead-up to the 2000 election to help him choose a vice-presidential candidate, he quickly chose himself, coming to play a major role in what many see as the Bush-Cheney presidency. Earlier, when Cheney was CEO of Halliburton in the mid-1990s, while on a hunting trip on the same ranch where he was later to shoot a 78-year-old lawyer in the face, Cheney shook hands with the CEO of construction company Brown and Root on a merger, which was subsequently quickly carried out. It soon emerged that Brown and Root had pending asbestos suits that threatened to bankrupt the new Halliburton entity, but Cheney saved the day by securing billions of no-bid contracts to Halliburton in the early years of the Bush-Cheney administration and pushed hard on the Iraq invasion to win more lucrative no-bid contracts for Halliburton, thus pushing up the stock, saving his investments, and paying off Halliburton for the $33 million-plus financial settlement they gave him to leave and go work for Bush (and the corporation). Cheney also pushed through a hard-right ideological agenda and got many other juicy contracts for his ideological allies in an epic scandal that should someday make a good Oliver Stone movie. On Cheney, see Nichols (2004) and Gellman (2008).

11 On Brave New Films, see www.robertgreenwald.org/index.php (accessed September 20, 2008).

12 On the documentary activist strategies of Greenwald and his associates, see John Haynes and Jo Littler, "Documentary as political activism: An interview with Robert Greenwald," *Cineaste* (Fall 2007): 26–8. On Greenwald's documentary work, see also Musser, "War, documentary," p. 13ff.

13 Greenwald continued to make short films exposing Fox News' corruption of journalism and affronts to documentary, distributed on his website and other sources; see www.robertgreenwald.org/ (accessed November 28, 2007).

14 Ken Lay and Jeff Skilling were found guilty in courtroom proceedings in 2006, but Lay was found dead, allegedly of a heart attack, before the sentencing hearing. Skilling was sentenced to 24 years in prison and fined $45 million. Fastow plea-bargained and received a six-year jail sentence.

15 For a revealing interview with the filmmaker, see Gary Crowdus, "Why we fight: An interview with Eugene Jarecki," *Cineaste* (Spring 2006): 32–8. For the film's informative website, go to www.sonyclassics.com/whywefight/ (accessed October 17, 2008).

16   For more information on *Trouble the Water*, see the website at www.
troublethewaterfilm.com/ (accessed June 8, 2009).

17   Danny Schechter has a new book based on *In Debt We Trust titled
Plunder: Investigating Our Economic Calamity and the Subprime Scandal*
(2008) and claims on his website to be working on a new documentary to
explain the economic crisis; see www.indebtwetrust.com/index.php
(accessed May 24, 2009).

18   The only critical biographies of the Bush family dynasty published so far
were written by Republican maverick Kevin Phillips (2004) and Kitty Kelley
(2004). Official presidential historians have so far failed to document the
misdeeds of three generations of the Bush family.

19   For Laurie David's activism, see her website at www.lauriedavid.com/bio.
html (accessed December 21, 2007).

20   See Tina Daunt, "Feeling warm all over," *Los Angeles Times*, March 13,
2007: E1, 10; other production information was culled from the DVD commentary by the director and others in the creative team.

21   See William J. Broad, "From a rapt audience, a call to cool the hype," *New York
Times*, March 13, 2007. Broad's article provided fodder for a bevy of rightwing
attacks on Gore, but for a thorough demolition of Broad's hatchet-job, see
Bob Somerby's analysis and critique on his Internet site *The Daily Howler*
from March 14–20 and beyond, saved in his archive at www.dailyhowler.
com/archives-2007.shtml (accessed December 29, 2007).

22   The scientific jury is still out on the rate of melting of the polar ice-caps, the
reasons for the disappearance of snow on Mount Kilimanjaro in East Africa,
whether polar bears are drowning in large numbers in a quest to find ice,
and a couple of other details, leading a British High Court judge to rule that
the film could only be shown in British schools if it was accompanied with a
pamphlet indicating that there was no strict scientific consensus. See BBC
News 11/10/07 at news.bbc.co.uk/go/pr/fr/-/1/hi/education/7037671.stm
(accessed December 29, 2007). Corporate and rightwing media in the US
used the British ruling unethically to make false claims that the judge had
ruled there were nine errors in the film that required supplementation if it
was to be used in British schools. See, for example, a *Washington Post* article
headlined "UK judge rules Gore's climate film has 9 errors," October 12,
2007: A12, and an October 13, 2007: A18 editorial "Gore vs. Bush," where
the *Post* describes Gore's achievement as "impressive and important, not-
withstanding factual misstatements and exaggerations such as the 'nine significant errors' in the film cited by a British judge Wednesday." As Bob
Somerby points out, neither the word "significant" nor the word "error"
appeared in the British judge's ruling and the judge threw out the lawsuit
seeking to prevent *An Inconvenient Truth* from being shown in British
schools, ruling: "Gore's presentation of the causes and likely effects of

climate change in the film was broadly accurate." See Somerby's analysis at www.dailyhowler.com/dh101707.shtml (accessed January 11, 2008).

23 Roger Ebert, "An Inconvenient Truth: Disaster movie," at www.rogerebert. suntimes.com/apps/pbcs.dll/article?AID=/20060601/REVIEWS/60517002/ 1023&template=printart (accessed December 21, 2007).

24 On the DVD commentary, director Davis Guggenheim claims he insisted that the positive agenda to fight global warming be thus restricted so as to keep the documentary focused on demonstrating the existence of the crisis and to keep the film non-partisan; he also believed motivated viewers could check the website for information on what they could do.

25 As of January 2, 2009, *An Inconvenient Truth* had grossed over $49,749,351; see www.boxofficemojo.com/movies/?id=inconvenienttruth.htm.

26 See Alan Zaremo and Johanna Neuman, "Peace prize for Gore stirs hope and speculation," *Los Angeles Times*, October 13, 2007: A1.

27 Sauper indicates that his initial impulse was to document the arms trade, but this theme became sidelined by documentation of the systematic ecological and human ravaging of the area by forces of corporate globalization. See Joshua Land, "Darwin's director Hubert Sauper on the ethics of free trade and filmmaking," *Village Voice*, August 2, 2005, at www.villagevoice.com/ film/0531,voiceover,66468,20.html (accessed February 8, 2008).

28 Conservatives warmed to *March of the Penguins*, claiming it was "pro-life," made "a strong case for intelligent design," affirmed "traditional norms like monogamy, sacrifice and childrearing," and in general championed conservative values; see Jonathan Miller, "March of the conservatives: Penguin film as political fodder," *New York Times*, September 13, 2005. Yet, as critics insisted, *March of the Penguins* embodies the basic principles of evolution and survival of the fittest; penguins have at best a seasonal monogamy and change partners frequently, and may even be gay; see Andrew Sullivan, "Not-so-picky penguins muddy the morality war," *Sunday Times*, September 18, 2005. In *Encounters at the End of the World* (discussed above) Werner Herzog asked a penguin expert if penguins were gay. The response was skeptical. While the scientist stated he had never observed gay penguins, he had seen some penguins involved in a ménage-à-trois and what could be interpreted as penguin prostitution, as female penguins, in search of stones for their nest, engage in sex with male penguins guarding stones and then run off with the stones after the deed.

29 While arguing for a multiperspective allegorical reading of Jackson's *Lord of the Rings* trilogy, I tended to stress the conservative and militarist elements of the films, but accept that they have multiple dimensions and can give rise to a wealth of conflicting readings. See Douglas Kellner, "*The Lord of the Rings* as allegory: A multiperspectivist reading," in *From Hobbits to Hollywood: Essays on Peter Jackson's Lord of the Rings* (New York:

Rodopia, 2006), pp. 17–40. A picture circulated on the Internet in 2004 of George W. Bush as Sauron, exhibiting the One Ring; see Steven Hart, "Who's Sauron – bin Laden or Bush?" Salon, February 28, 2004, at www.dir.salon. com/ent/feature/2004/02/28/lord/index.html (accessed February 6, 2009) and Luis Yerovi, "Free trade and the ring of power" at www.goecuador.com/ magazine/editorials/ringofpower.hmtl.

30 In his banal commentary on the DVD version of *WALL-E*, director Andrew Stanton denies that he had any political intentions or message to convey, but the ecological subtext and critique of consumer capitalism comes through clearly in the film, causing many rightwing bloggers and critics to attack it and liberals to extol it. For an interesting attempt by a conservative to insist that *WALL-E* embodies genuinely conservative values, see Charlotte Allen, "*Wall-E* doesn't say anything," *Los Angeles Times*, July 13, 2008: M5. In fact, *WALL-E* contains a contradictory mix of radical messages and cinematic form with a conservative love story and formulaic narrative segments. See Kenneth Turnan, "Out of this world," *Los Angeles Times*, June 27, 2008: E1.

31 Kirsten Thompson (2007) sees a rise in apocalyptic fears in end-of-the-millennium US cinema, but her analysis is too caught up in contextualizing the films in terms of religious problematics and (following Robin Wood) grounding contemporary horror films in a crisis of the family. In his intro-duction to his edited collection *Crisis Cinema: The Apocalyptic Idea in Postmodern Narrative Film*, Chris Sharrett interprets the theme of apoca-lypse in contemporary cinema largely in Baudrillardian postmodern terms as the collapse of the subject, the social, and meaning in postmodernity (1993: 2ff). Socioeconomic determinants of crisis and catastrophe are thus erased in the (idealist) postmodern vision of cultural collapse. Stroup and Shuck (2007) argue that a "column of juggernauts rolls over the identity of con-temporary citizens in leading democracies," leading to cultural pessimism and a diminished sense of self and the future. While there are clearly multiple determinants to cultural pessimism and visions of apocalypse, in retrospect, I would argue that the anticipations of social apocalypse in the cinema and popular culture of the 1980s and 1990s were prescient of a catastrophic col-lapse of the economy fueled by decades of neoliberalism and particularly the Reagan and two Bush regimes that pushed through massive deregulation and a conservative economic agenda, amassed crippling debt with corporate give aways and tax breaks for the rich, and thus widened gaps between rich and poor, while deregulating housing and fiscal markets. Hence, while I would agree that there are multiple factors that account for the rise in visions of social apocalypse in popular culture in the cinema of the 2000s, I contextualize the apocalyptic catastrophe films of the 2000s, by contrast to books cited above, in real fears of social collapse – of the environment, polity, economy, and world order – generated in part by the policies of the

Bush-Cheney administration and neoliberal globalization, which I claim have produced often-unconscious social dread – as well as real fears that have a rational grounding, as was made clear in the global economic melt-down in late 2008.

32 On the disaster film, see Kellner and Ryan (1988). *The Day After Tomorrow* grossed an astonishing $544,272,402 worldwide; see www.boxofficemojo. com/movies/?id=dayaftertomorrow.htm (accessed January 2, 2009).

33 Heather Collette-VanDeraa has suggested to me that while the name Theo evokes theology, the name Kee evokes the Chinese root Chi for the life-force and the Egyptian Ka for the immortal soul, brought together in Kee, who is also the "key" to life and a successful narrative conclusion in the film.

34 Gendy Alimurung "This Zombie Moment," *LA Weekly*, May 15–21, 2009: 21–7.

2

Hollywood's 9/11
and Spectacles of Terror

The September 11, 2001 attacks on the World Trade Center in New York and the Pentagon near Washington, DC were shocking global media events that dominated public attention and circulated a spectacle of terror that generated fear and panic throughout the United States. The attacks were intended to terrorize the US by selecting symbolic targets: the World Trade Center (WTC) was an apt symbol of global capitalism in the heart of the New York financial district, while the Pentagon stands as an icon and center of US military power. The attacks were also intended to promote Jihad against the West and undermine the global economy.[1]

Powerful media spectacles help shape social memory, constructing individuals' views of history and contemporary reality.[2] Resonant images help construct how people see and interpret the world, and the oft-repeated images of airplanes hitting the WTC, the buildings burning and then collapsing, and piles of rubble left in their wake were among the most compelling ever witnessed by global media culture. This chapter relates the cinematic mode of representation of the 9/11 attacks to an earlier wave of Hollywood disaster films, and then discusses representations of 9/11 itself in some contemporary Hollywood films including *United 93* (2006), *World Trade Center* (2006), and the TV docudrama *The Path to 9/11* (2006). This analysis is followed by discussion of some more marginal cinematic efforts that depict forms of terrorism in a contemporary realist mode and the Christian "Left Behind" allegories. At stake is how cinematic culture deals with a catastrophic event like 9/11, the politics of its modes of representation and effects, and how popular media shape social memory and perceptions of the recent past and present that are still alive in the political discourse and struggles of the day.

The attack on the twin towers in New York traumatized the US and eventually generated a cycle of films dealing with terrorist attacks.

9/11 as Disaster Film and Spectacle of Terror

In 1993 the WTC was attacked by Islamist radicals linked to Osama bin Laden, providing a preview of the more spectacular 9/11 attack. In 1994 the bombing of the Alfred P. Murrah Federal Building in Oklahoma City, killing 168 and wounding more than 500, was first attributed to Arab terrorists, but it was soon linked to a white American terrorist, Timothy McVeigh, with the help of accomplices.[3] The bin Laden group assaulted US embassies in Africa in 1998 and a US destroyer harbored in Yemen in 2000, dramatizing the dangers of global terrorism.

Palestinians and other groups from the Middle East, as well as separatist groups from the former Soviet Union, have also used spectacular terrorism to advance their goals. In a global mediascape, highly orchestrated spectacles of terror have been constructed to gain worldwide attention, to dramatize the issues of the groups involved, and to achieve specific political objectives. Spectacles of terror have also been used by states like Israel and the Bush-Cheney administration in its assaults on Afghanistan, Iraq, and other parts of the world.[4]

While the al Qaeda group had systematically used spectacles of terror to promote its agenda, 9/11 was the most deadly strike on US targets in its history, and the first foreign attack on the continental US since the war of 1812, showing the vulnerability of the US to lethal force and the kind of indiscriminate violence suffered by much of the world. Spectacles of terror use dramatic images and narrative to catch attention, and intended thereby to catalyze unanticipated events that will spread further terror through domestic populations. These made-for-media events become global spectacles that create fearful populations more likely to be manipulated by reactionary forces who give simplistic answers to contemporary anxieties and problems.

The live television presentation of 9/11 and continuous replay of the spectacle in the following days made it appear like a disaster film, leading Hollywood director Robert Altman to chide his industry for producing extravaganzas of devastation that could serve as models for spectacular terror attacks. Indeed, was *Independence Day* (1996) – in which Los Angeles and New York were assaulted by aliens and the White House destroyed – the template for 9/11? The collapse of the WTC also had resonances with *The Towering Inferno* (1975), in which a high-rise building catches fire, burns, and collapses, or even *Earthquake* (1975), which portrays the collapse of entire urban environments. In these latter disaster films, however, the calamity emerged either from within the system or from nature itself. In the 9/11 terror spectacle, by contrast, the assumed villains were foreign terrorists obviously committed to wreaking maximum destruction on the US, and it was not certain how the drama would end or if order could be restored in a "happy ending."

New York and Washington, DC are among the most media-saturated cities in the world. For days, 9/11 played out its deadly drama live on television, capturing a global audience. The images of the planes hitting the WTC and its collapse were broadcast repeatedly, as if repetition were necessary to master a highly traumatic event. The spectacle conveyed the message that the US was vulnerable to terrorists who could create great harm, and that anyone at any time could be subject to deadly terrorism, even in Fortress America. The suffering, fear, and death that many people endure on a daily basis were brought home to US citizens. Suddenly, the vulnerability and anxiety suffered by many people throughout the world was also deeply experienced by US citizens, in some cases for the first time. The terror attacks thus had *material* effects – harm to the US and global economy – and *psychic* effects – traumatizing a nation with fear.

The live "you are there" drama of 9/11 deeply involved spectators. The planes striking the twin towers and bursting into flames, people jumping out of windows in a desperate attempt to escape, the collapse of the buildings, and the subsequent chaos provided unforgettable images. The drama continued throughout the day, with survivors being pulled from the wreckage. The poignant search for individuals still alive and attempts to deal with the disaster produced iconic images that seared deeply into spectators' memories. Many people who witnessed the event suffered from nightmares and psychological trauma similar to soldiers' post-traumatic stress disorder. For many spectators, 9/11 provided a powerful set of images that would continue to resonate for years to come.

The 9/11 attacks in New York were claimed to be "the most documented event in history" in a May 2002 HBO film, *In Memoriam*. This documentary pulled together a collage of images assembled from professional news crews, documentary filmmakers, and amateur videographers and photographers, who in some cases risked their lives to document the event. As with other major media events, 9/11 took over TV programming for the next several days, without commercial breaks, as the corporate television networks focused on the attack and its aftermath.

The 9/11 terror attacks were a genuine disaster for the American people. The events would become a global catastrophe when the Bush-Cheney administration's "war on terror" mutated into a terror war that included an invasion of Afghanistan and Iraq, a clash between Israel, Hezbollah, and Hamas that resulted in widespread bombing and destruction in Lebanon and Gaza and rocket attacks on Israel, terrorist attacks all over the world, and general fear and insecurity on a global scale (Kellner 2005; Mayer 2008).[5]

Representations of 9/11 in Hollywood Film: *United 93* and *World Trade Center*

While a large number of film and television documentaries, and some TV movies, dealt with 9/11, *United 93* (2006) was the first major Hollywood film to deal with the catastrophe. The story recreated the hijacked flight during which the passengers allegedly stormed the cockpit and forced the plane to crash in Pennsylvania. The narrative was thus intrinsically tragic, but with a heroic conclusion that demonstrated American will and capability in a time of crisis.

United 93 presented no Hollywoodesque individualized heroes in its ultra-realistic, low-key, and understated portrayal of the events leading to the crash. Deploying hand-held and sometimes erratic camera movements, quick editing, and tight focus on both the interior of the plane and

United 93 shows passengers charging the terrorists who have taken over the plane in a heroic but failed effort to save themselves.

the federal agencies monitoring air traffic control, British director Paul Greengrass deftly explored internal spaces, social relations and group activities, and how individuals responded to crisis and catastrophe.[6]

The four Muslim hijackers are introduced praying before their suicide mission, and throughout are shown fervently engaged in prayer, but they are also portrayed as conflicted and afraid. The passengers on the plane are portrayed initially as ordinary citizens, involved in the petty cares and mundane rituals of everyday life, as they fidget with their cell phones, exchange banalities with each other, and eventually become aware of the disaster unfolding. Likewise, the pilots are shown as quite ordinary people, as are the members of the federal bureaucracies and US military that respond to the day's calamity. Greengrass's focus in the film is on the institutional space of the airplane and federal bureaucracies, and the ordinariness of the people involved. He explores people interacting in public and bureaucratic spaces in airports and in an airplane, in air traffic control centers, and in the Northeast Air Defense Sector (NEADS), located in Rome, New York.

As the passengers board the United 93 flight, the film cuts to the Federal Aviation Administration (FAA) air traffic control center at Hendron, Virginia, where the newly appointed head, Ben Sliny (playing himself), arrives for work. The film cuts back and forth from the airplane, whose take-off is initially delayed, to the air traffic control centers, as an alert controller overhears bits of a conversation on an American Airlines 11 flight that leads him to suspect it is hijacked. Co-workers discuss this, and

FAA employees and then the NEADS center grapple with the possibility of catastrophe, as a plane hits the WTC and others go missing on their radar screens.

The most critical aspect of the film is the incompetence with which the government agencies and military respond to the hijackings. While air traffic controllers overhear conversations that suggest a hijacking, they seem not to communicate effectively with the FAA or the military. The different agencies fail to see the big picture, appear to have no coordination, and are depicted as powerless spectators of the calamity. Especially disturbing, the military not only does not seem to have clear lines of communication with the various federal agencies or the White House, but also seems not to have enough armed planes ready to deploy, and when they finally send up a plane, it is directed the wrong way.

Equally disturbing, the FAA starts off slowly, not reacting seriously to threats of an airplane hijacking, and then keeps losing track of planes, or tracking ones as hijacked which are not. Even after the two hijacked planes are shown crashing into the WTC, the response seems chaotic and disorganized. Not only are the air traffic controllers and the military unable to communicate with each other, but they are also unable to contact the president or vice-president, who are the only ones who can ratify military action. Thus, while the film in its low-key and understated style does not blatantly assert the failures of governmental systems, it shows a thoroughly dysfunctional government and air defense system which – despite all its high-tech instruments and professionals – are not able to prevent or intelligently address the catastrophe.[7]

By contrast, the passengers on United 93 evidently grasp the magnitude of the event, as they learn from cell phone conversation with friends and loved ones of the WTC crashes, and organize to overpower the hijackers and storm the cockpit to seize control of the plane. The participants had previously been depicted as quasi-anonymous members of the crowd and no one is presented as an individual hero in the traditional Hollywood sense. Collectively, however, they organize and fight the hijackers, causing the plane to crash.

United 93 thus operates on the terrain of everyday life and institutional space, rather than in the Hollywood space of highly individualized characters and relations, using an aesthetic of naturalism rather than melodrama. The hijackers are portrayed as frightened but committed young Muslim men, and there is no comic-book caricature or demonization of Arabs and Muslims such as one finds in typical generic Hollywood thrillers (see Shaheen 2001). Likewise, in this most un-Hollywood movie, it is ordinary people who are the self-organizing protagonists who stand in for their fellow citizens and take heroic action. They attempt to crash the plane and thus prevent it being used as a weapon (it is widely speculated that United 93 was headed for Washington and perhaps the Capitol or White House).

The subtext of *United 93* appears to be that US citizens cannot trust their government for national security or to protect them from terrorists. All of the government agencies portrayed in the film repeatedly receive misinformation, make mistaken assumptions and decisions, and do not adequately communicate. Higher government officials are absent from the film, as they seemed to be absent during 9/11. The film suggests that groups of people must decide to protect themselves and organize to fight for their own survival.[8]

The Oliver Stone movie *World Trade Center* (2006) was also quite low key in its depiction of Port Authority police saving the lives of victims. In some ways, *World Trade Center* is the ultimate un-Oliver Stone film: restrained, understated, often slow and somber, and conservative. The film is shamelessly sentimental, focusing on the heroism, entrapment in the ruins, and rescue of two working-class policemen, who represent the ordinary people who bore the brunt of 9/11. It is conservative in following traditional Hollywood generic forms and storytelling, in failing to deal with the political context, and in developing several key themes discussed below.

Based on their true stories, the film opens with Port Authority Police Sergeant John McLoughlin (Nicholas Cage) waking up, lovingly observing his wife and children sleeping, and dutifully going off to work. We then see Latino Port Authority policeman Will Jimeno (Michael Peña) leaving his modest home in New Jersey for work, with his radio blasting Brooks and Dunn's country and western song "Only in America." He enthusiastically sings along, coding himself as a working-class patriot.

Opening scenes quietly depict the people of New York City beginning their day: butchers, fish sellers, and small businessmen open their shops; workers clean up the neighborhood; pedestrians head to work; subway riders banter about baseball; and homeless people face another day on the streets. Interspersed are iconic images of Wall Street, the Statue of Liberty, New York skyscrapers, and the twin towers of the WTC. The intensely populist focus of the movie encodes the message that the victims of 9/11 were innocent people, comprising a variety of races and ethnicities. *World Trade Center* suggests that terrorism, which senselessly and indiscriminately strikes at civilians, is monstrous. Its victims are ordinary people trying to get on with their lives and raise their families. The film also shows families and communities pulling together in response to the tragedy, and discovering new resources of strength and capability, conveying the message that the United States will surely pull together to fight its enemies.

Stone's drama is perhaps too understated, failing to address even minimally the political context of the attack and the existence and strategy of the perpetrators. The Port Authority policemen gather at headquarters for a typical day's work, in this case, looking for a young runaway at a bus station. Then the catastrophe strikes. A brief shadow of an airliner passing over a building denotes the attack – Stone refrains from showing the iconic pictures of the plane hitting the WTC. Curiously, no mention is made of al Qaeda or terrorism in the movie. This omission will have sinister connotations near the end of the film when one of the characters is cited as joining the military and going to Iraq, as if Iraq was involved in the attack.

The film draws on generic features of the disaster film, showing people on the street reacting to the horror and TV images of the event. Sent to Ground Zero to rescue workers, several of the Port Authority policemen are themselves trapped in the ruins and much of the film deals with how they cope with their plight, the effects on their family and friends, and their eventual rescue. The scenes of the multi-ethnic police volunteering for the mission and being chosen by the sergeant evoke the codes of World War II films in which ordinary soldiers become heroes or victims. The slow-moving entrapment scenes evoke the horror of entombment, and as one policeman kills himself after suffering a fatal injury, and all but the two main characters disappear. Here, the film takes on aspects of the horror film, with the trapped police facing gruesome deaths.

World Trade Center shifts to family melodrama as focus moves to the effects on family members, with typically emotional tear-jerking scenes. The eventual rescue takes on the triumphalist form of Hollywood happy endings, mediated by aggressively religious themes and highly (dangerously) conservative motifs that reproduce the Bush-Cheney administration discourses and ideology of the "war on terror." A subplot deals with an ex-Marine Dave Karnes (Michael Shannon), an accountant watching the televised attacks on the WTC in his Connecticut office, who goes to his evangelical church to pray, gets a standard Marine buzz haircut, and travels to Ground Zero to help in the rescue operation. Already coded as devoutly religious, he is linked to a vision of Christ seen by the trapped Latino policeman Jimeno, conveying the pleasing message to Christians and conservatives that Jesus himself is watching over America in its time of trouble. Another young man, who volunteers to help save people lost in the rubble, reveals that he used to be a medic, and quickly becomes one again, providing the possibility of redeeming himself with courageous action, as does the Marine.

There is thus an underlying Christian fundamentalist theme in the film, which was marketed aggressively to conservatives. Indeed, one leading rightwing columnist, Cal Thomas, called it "one of the greatest pro-American, pro-family, pro-faith, pro-male, flag-waving God Bless America films you will ever see."[9] To construct the Christian motifs, Stone uses chiaroscuro lighting effects throughout, with shadowy and muted lighting to depict the entrapment of the police (sunrays of hope sometimes burst through), punctuated with hellish fireballs that incinerate some of the trapped police and endanger the two main protagonists. The eventual rescue shows light dispelling darkness, as the trapped men emerge alive with triumphalist music signaling the victory of valor and goodness in a kind of religious epiphany. Stone quickly cuts to more tragic motifs such as the smoldering, dark ruins of the buildings, while voices note the many who have died, illustrated by tracking shots of rows of photos in a hospital ward of those still missing and presumably dead.

The ex-Marine Karnes expresses a need to avenge the murders. Closing titles indicate that he reenlisted and served two terms in Iraq. Such a linking of Iraq and revenge for 9/11 is doubly pernicious in that al Qaeda and Osama Bin Laden are never mentioned in the film, so it reinforces the big lie that Iraq was involved. This lie was covertly and overtly promoted by the Bush-Cheney administration, and was believed by an astonishing number of American people a long time after 9/11 and the disastrous Iraq invasion.[10]

Stone's film is thus deeply conservative. It extols the humanity and courage of ordinary Americans, but fails to explore the reasons for the attack. Moreover, Stone uses the most manipulative aspects of the family melodrama to elicit sympathy for the trapped policemen and their families, and ends with the triumphalist Hollywood ideology of heroism overcoming adversity. The only footage of George W. Bush shows him firmly and resolutely committed to fighting back and unifying the nation – precisely the image that the Bush-Cheney regime wanted projected.

World Trade Center also presents a questionable vision of American unity in which racial differences are overcome. One key focus is on the close bonding of the Anglo McLoughlin and the Latino Jimeno, whose pregnant wife in turn is Anglo (Maggie Gyllenhaal). In one poignant scene near the end, McLoughlin's wife bonds with and hugs an African-American woman in a vision of racial harmony overcoming divisions in the face of adversity. While this is a noble vision, it collapses existing racial divisions in the US and the intensification of racism – mostly projected on Muslims and Arabs since 9/11, who are constructed as enemies and threats. In addition, all the heroes of the film are men, while women are assigned the stereotypical roles of wife and mother. The police are Men's Men, strong and stoic, courageous and manly, although when threatened with death they are able to affirm their love for each other, as pain and fear permit the two trapped heroes to express their emotions.

Stone's *World Trade Center*, coming after the financial and critical disaster of *Alexander* (2004), did strong box office, got some good reviews, but deeply disappointed many critics and fans, who admired his socially critical and often unconventional works. While in principle it might have been salutary to deal with 9/11 in a non-partisan and non-political fashion, Stone's film helped promulgate the Bush-Cheney administration's version of events and aided and abetted the intense partisanship with which the Republican regime and its supporters exploited 9/11 to push through their rightwing agenda. Yet Oliver Stone remains Oliver Stone. Seeking to redeem himself in Europe while promoting his deeply flawed work, Stone stated in a widely reported Associated Press story that President George W. Bush has "set America back ten years," and that he was "ashamed for my country" over the war in Iraq and US policies after 9/11.[11]

The same week in September 2006, *Washington Post* reporter Bob Woodward attempted to redeem himself after publishing two books that were widely read as apologetics for the Bush-Cheney administration's post-9/11 policy. His highly critical *State of Denial* exposed the lies, flaws, and highly dangerous failures of the administration's foreign policy and the utter incompetence and disarray in the White House. Redemption is obviously a major theme of Hollywood film, US culture, and everyday life, but those who exploited 9/11 to push through destructive and extremist policies, while viciously smearing critics as traitors and un-American, will have their work cut out to redeem themselves.

Disney Television Republican Propaganda: *The Path to 9/11*

The exploitation of 9/11 by the right wing was most blatantly on display in *The Path to 9/11*, which is perhaps the most controversial and problematical TV movie in recent US history. As the fifth anniversary of 9/11 arrived, media culture in the US presented a plethora of commemorative events. While images of the fateful attack were clearly inscribed in social memory, the meanings and background of the attack were not. The Bush-Cheney administration had exploited the spectacle to push through a rightwing agenda, including a highly unpopular war in Iraq. Yet the origins, meaning, and effects of the initial attacks were not clear to the public at large, and were highly contested by different political factions. While resonant images like the planes hitting the WTC and the traumatic aftermath were burned into the collective memory, no coherent mainstream narrative of the events was able to contextualize, explain, and enable the public to understand them.

Social memory is constructed by historical narratives and political discourses, as well as resonant images. In this context, a two-part TV movie, *The Path to 9/11*, scheduled to begin on the eve of the fifth anniversary of 9/11 and to conclude on September 11, 2006, became a pivotal event in a rightwing partisan Republican construction of the origins, meaning, and story of the terror attacks. *The Path to 9/11* was broadcast by the Disney-owned channel ABC. The film is a blatantly rightwing piece of political propaganda, which blames 9/11 on the deficiencies of the Clinton administration, while presenting the Bush-Cheney administration as inheritors of a disaster which motivates them to heroic struggle and resolute action. We shall see that this event was orchestrated to showcase the Republican Party line on 9/11 for the upcoming 2006 congressional elections, when the Republicans were doing very poorly in the polls. *The Path to 9/11* was part of a Republican effort to counter the bad publicity for the failed Iraq invasion and failures of the Bush-Cheney administration on multiple fronts, and to present an image of the administration as the most competent force to combat terrorism. It can thus now be read as part of a campaign that presented the Bush-Cheney administration as stalwart in the war on terror and the most reliable defender of the American people in a time of trouble. An earlier TV movie, *DC 9/11: Time of Crisis* (2003), had also projected the myth that George W. Bush was a strong leader.[12] As Sheldon Rampton reminds us:

> This is not the first time that Hollywood has used 9/11 as a pretext to air pro-Bush propaganda in the guise of a docudrama. On the second anniversary of the terrorist attack, the Showtime cable network broadcast "DC 9/11: Time of Crisis," written by conservative Republican Lionel Chetwynd. Dubbed "a [2004] reelection campaign movie" by *Washington Post* TV critic Tom Shales, the film starred actor Timothy Bottoms in the role of George W. Bush, depicting him as a leader of Churchillian stature who takes personal charge in the 9/11 aftermath while brushing off worries about his own safety with declarations such as, "If some tinhorn terrorist wants me, tell him to come on over and get me. I'll be home!" In reality, as opposed to the bizarre world of docudrama, Bush's safety on 9/11 was guaranteed by hustling him off to an undisclosed location, while Cheney went into hiding for months.[13]

Rampton points out that *The Path to 9/11* is different from the Showtime potboiler by its claim "to be based on the report of the National Commission on Terrorist Attacks Upon the United States (also known as the 9/11 Commission)." *The Path to 9/11* was cowritten and co-produced by a rightwing Iranian-American, Cyrus Nowrasteh. The narrative features the struggles against al Qaeda by FBI agent John O'Neill (Harvey Keitel) and counterterrorism official Richard Clarke (Stephen Root). Both are portrayed as heroes, deeply worried about a terrorist attack by the al Qaeda group. Both run into constant bureaucratic obstacles when seeking to attack al Qaeda or bin Laden.

Over 800 DVDs of the TV movie were prereleased and circulated to conservative groups and media to hype up viewers and publicize the event. But some copies got into the hands of former members of the Clinton administration, leftwing activists, and critical members of the media. A campaign unfolded to get the Disney network to cancel the pro-Bush and anti-Clinton propaganda film, and probably never has there been such a fierce movement to block release of a TV movie.

Max Blumenthal revealed that the director of *The Path to 9/11*, David Cunningham, was a longtime extreme rightwing Christian-conservative activist. Moreover, both Cunningham and Cyrus Nowrasteh were connected to David Horowitz's far-right group that for years has been attacking the mainstream media, trying to establish a rightwing presence in Hollywood, and attempting to blame 9/11 on Bill Clinton. As Blumenthal reports:

> On this project, a secretive evangelical religious right group long associated with [David] Horowitz, founded by *The Path to 9/11*'s director, David Cunningham, that aims to "transform Hollywood" in line with its messianic vision, has taken the lead. [Cunningham] is in fact the son of Loren Cunningham, founder of the right-wing evangelical group Youth With A Mission (YWAM) ... that advocates using stealth political methods to put the United States under the control of biblical law and jettison the Constitution.
>
> Early on, Cunningham had recruited a young Iranian-American screenwriter named Cyrus Nowrasteh to write the script of his secretive *Untitled* film. Not only is Nowrasteh an outspoken conservative, he is also a fervent member of the emerging network of right-wing people burrowing into the film industry with ulterior sectarian political and religious agendas, like Cunningham.[14]

As revelations concerning the ultraconservative credentials of those producing the 9/11 propaganda film unfolded, and as rightwing groups began promoting it after receiving the prescreening DVDs, former members of the Clinton administration and progressive media activists intensified pressure on ABC to cancel the event. Responding to pressure, the Disney network made some minor edits, but basically aired the attack on Clinton and pro-Bush-Cheney positioning on terrorism intact.[15]

In response to the mounting criticism before the broadcast, ABC first claimed that the representation of 9/11 was "objective," and then claimed the TV movie was not a documentary, but a "dramatization, drawn from a variety of sources including the 9/11 Commission Report, other published material and personal interviews. As such, for dramatic and narrative purposes, the movie contains fictionalized scenes, composite and representative characters and dialogue and time compression."[16]

Former governor Thomas Kean, who was co-chair of the 9/11 Commission and an adviser to the series, claimed that the TV movie was truthful: "This is the story of how it happened," Kean asserted. He indicated that he had corrected inaccuracies during filming.[17] As Joe Conason notes, Kean's involvement with the series seriously discredited the former governor, and perhaps the 9/11 Commission he chaired, which was long under attack for not more vigorously investigating the 9/11 attacks.

Eric Alterman pointed out that it was "particularly odd" that the same corporation, Disney, which owns ABC, had

> decided to forgo hundreds of millions of dollars when it refused to distribute another movie, *Fahrenheit 9/11* ... [which] took a differing view of this same historical event because, as one of its executives explained [concerning why it did not distribute *Fahrenheit 9/11*], "it's not in the interest of any major corporation to be dragged into a highly charged partisan political battle."[18]

There were reports of clashes on the set and over editing, as some of those in the project fought with the rightwing activists involved in the production who were constructing a propagandistic version of 9/11. Indeed, the original FBI adviser quit in disgust because "they were making things up."[19] Harvey Keitel reported fierce conflicts over his own portrayal of FBI agent John O'Neill, and his concern not to misrepresent the facts of 9/11. A *New York Post* story on the production set notes:

> Meanwhile, sources on the set told *The Post* that during filming there were arguments over the veracity of the content.... When Oscar nominee Harvey Keitel signed on to play Deputy FBI Director John O'Neill, who perished in the World Trade Center attacks, he thought the film's aim was to be historically correct, he said. "It turned out not all the facts were correct," which led to "arguments," he said on CNN.[20]

Even before *The Path to 9/11* was broadcast, critics challenged its errors of detail, as well as major theses. In addition to misspelling Madeleine Albright's first name in the title graphics, in one of the opening scenes American Airlines is depicted as ignoring a security warning about hijacker Mohammed Atta, whom we see going through security in Boston. In fact, Atta departed on a US Airways flight from Portland, Maine to Boston. American Airlines threatened to sue over the depiction of its security personnel as lax.[21]

Moreover, both before and after the broadcast, people portrayed in the movie (Bill Clinton, Richard Clarke, Madeleine Albright, and Sandy Berger) raised factual objections. Richard Clarke, a major adviser on terrorism to both the Clinton and Bush-Cheney administrations, and portrayed as a hero in *The Path to 9/11*, strongly contested a scene which showed US soldiers on the ground in Afghanistan poised to attack and take bin Laden, and then canceling the assault because of bureaucratic objections raised by Clinton administration national security adviser Sandy Berger. Clarke insisted that at no time were US military or CIA personnel on the ground in Afghanistan with bin Laden in their sights. Clarke further insisted that, contrary to the movie, Afghan Northern Alliance leader and US ally Ahmed Shah Masoud was never anywhere near the bin Laden camp with CIA advisers, and never spotted or observed him as the TV movie presented. Clarke explained that the CIA cancelled a proposed attack on the bin Laden camp portrayed in the movie because there was only a single source for the report that bin Laden was present and only a small chance that a cruise missile would actually hit him.[22]

The Path to 9/11 lasts nearly four-and-a-half-hours in two parts, with an epic panorama of characters and places, from New York and Washington to Afghanistan and the Middle East. Often employing jerky handheld camera shots, tight close-ups, and fast editing, the film attempts to overwhelm viewers with visual and audio techniques and images in order to frighten them about terrorist threats. This cinematic strategy is especially effective given that these kinds of camera techniques and editing style are associated with documentary film and news broadcasting. Indeed, these techniques endowed the film with an aura of reality, as does the actual news footage interspersed throughout.

Thus, while *The Path to 9/11* is cartoonish in character and a distortion of the facts, it attempts to be realistic in style. The first half of the film explores the terrorist threat, starting with the 1993 bombing at the World Trade Center. The narrative focuses on the Clinton administration's failure to stop al Qaeda. Throughout the film there are shots of an unsavory looking Bill Clinton, shown in unflattering clips, including scenes from the Monica Lewinsky sex scandal, which the docudrama implies crippled his efforts to deal with terrorism. The film does not, however, depict the right wing's attempted impeachment of Clinton, which obviously diverted the administration from any number of issues and caused a major constitutional crisis, cost millions of dollars, deeply polarized the nation, and produced no positive results.

In one scene that recreates the terrorist attack in 1998 on the US embassy in Nairobi, Kenya, a CIA agent yells at CIA head George Tenet that they should have ordered the killing of bin Laden when they had a chance and that Clinton now "has to do something!" The drama then cuts to Clinton's new Secretary of State Madeleine Albright, who is depicted as reluctant to go after the Taliban and bin Laden in Afghanistan. At this point, failed attempts by the Clinton administration to bomb a location in Afghanistan where bin Laden was supposedly hiding are portrayed, followed by bombing of an alleged al Qaeda chemical weapons factory in Sudan. The latter turns out to be a pharmaceutical factory, and Republicans and their rightwing media apparatus at the time mocked Clinton for this failure. These events are alluded to in the TV movie when a reporter mentions that Republicans and pundits are claiming that Clinton was trying to divert attention *à la Wag the Dog* from the Lewinsky scandal through reckless military action (whereas later they attacked him for not doing enough to stop al Qaeda).[23]

Albright herself objected to a scene in which she was portrayed as insisting on warning the Pakistani government before the air strike on Afghanistan, with the movie insinuating that the Pakistanis had warned bin Laden, who escaped the attack. Albright stated she had not told the Pakistanis of the attempt on bin Laden until the missile was in the air and so "the scene as explained to me is false and defamatory."[24]

The first part of *The Path to 9/11* ends with bin Laden discussing "the plane operation" with Khalid Sheikh Mohammed. The second part begins on the day of 9/11 and top Bush-Cheney administration officials' response. The film flashes back to the 2000 election showing Bush campaigning and then gaining the presidency, after the Supreme Court decision to stop the counting of the vote, arguably the greatest crime in US history (see Kellner 2001). The ascension of George W. Bush to the presidency is portrayed in *The Path to 9/11*, however, as the coming salvation for the nation, as Bush is generally positively portrayed in documentary montage.

There is, admittedly, one shot of Bush entering the Florida classroom where "The Pet Goat" was read with students for seven minutes after the announcement of the 9/11 bombings, memorialized in Michael Moore's *Fahrenheit 9/11*. But the main focus in this episode is on President Bush's speech to the nation, where he appears resolute and ready for revenge. It also shows Condoleezza Rice reading the CIA threat assessment that "bin Laden [was] determined to strike at US" and had plane hijack plans. Yet the movie does not depict her showing the assessment to Bush, or Bush dismissing the threat while on his uninterrupted August vacation at his Crawford, Texas "ranch" just weeks before 9/11. At this meeting, Bush allegedly brushed off the warning, telling a CIA agent who briefed him on imminent al Qaeda threats that he had "covered his ass" with the report concerning the bin Laden assessment and the agent could now leave the president alone to vacation (see Woodward 2006).

As well as blaming 9/11 on the Clinton administration, *The Path to 9/11* is deeply racist and sexist. Scenes portraying the al Qaeda camps use red filters, so that the desert and buildings appear soaked in blood. The camera pans on terrorists training, intercut with shots of children shooting guns. Quick jump cuts move to show bomb-making, computers, and an assortment of weapons in the terrorist camp, with the fast editing and overload of images inducing fear in Western spectators confronted by an apparatus of terror and violence. However, the terrorists who actually carried out the plane hijacking are portrayed in a surprisingly sympathetic fashion, and are depicted as serious and dedicated, perhaps rendering them even more frightening than standard Hollywood caricatures. Yet the visual framework for the film contrasts chaotic, disorderly, and violent non-Western scenes with the ordinary, modern, and "civilized" government buildings, apartments, and restaurants of the West, producing a dialectic throughout of civilization against barbarism. The terrorists are presented in a way highly prejudicial to Islam. In one scene in an al Qaeda camp, "strange" music and sound effects punctuate the desert air with the sand filtered red. An erratic hand-held camera generates the appearance of chaos and disorder, as the scene quickly cuts from one character to another. As some of the eventual 9/11 hijackers meet al Qaeda figures, they repeatedly evoke Allah, as if Muslims typically intone the magic name as they prepare for killing, and as if all they can do is chant rather than articulate arguments and make conversation.

Indeed, throughout the film, Muslims and Arabs are depicted in the most negative stereotypes, displaying an extremely racist, Manichean, and Orientalist imaginary. The heroes are the two white men diligently fighting the al Qaeda threat: FBI agent John O'Neill and counterterrorist official Richard Clarke, who are confronted with incompetent bureaucrats and aggressive and even sinister women. Madeleine Albright is represented as a clueless bureaucrat who does not understand the al Qaeda threat, while the US ambassador to Yemen, Barbara Bodine, is depicted as an overbearing and domineering bureaucrat, aggressively preventing O'Neill and his FBI crew from going after al Qaeda suspects. Even more revealingly, and displaying profound sexism, Condoleezza Rice is portrayed as sinister, as she holds back warnings about al Qaeda attacks and does not cooperate with Richard Clarke. The actress who plays Rice (Penny Johnson) is well known to US TV audiences as the manipulative and evil wife of the (good) African-American president on the TV series *24*, so her very presence creates unease for audiences already exposed to her. It is as if it is the fault of one African-American woman that the Bush-Cheney administration was not more focused on al Qaeda threats, thus taking other members of the administration off the hook.

The only positive image of a major female character is fictional agent Patricia Carver (Amy Madigan), who shares O'Neill's and Clarke's obsessive determination to stop al Qaeda. Relentlessly Manichean, the film divides characters between Westerners and terrorists, and then divides the Westerners between those who discerned the terrorist threat and acted accordingly and those craven bureaucrats who dismissed it.

On the whole, *The Path to 9/11* shows an incompetent Clinton administration and a resolute Bush-Cheney administration committed to fighting terrorism. In fact, before 9/11 no major figures in the Bush-Cheney administration had terrorism on their agenda; the top administration security "principals" group refused to meet with counterterrorist adviser Richard Clarke in the nine months before 9/11 and demoted him just before the attack. Moreover, Clinton's national security adviser Sandy Berger claimed that when he tried to impress upon Bush's national security team the dangers posed by al Qaeda, they ignored him, as had Bush, who allegedly ignored Clinton when the former president warned him about al Qaeda the day he left the White House. Indeed, the Bush-Cheney administration ignored copious warnings from multiple sources in the days before 9/11 of imminent attacks from al Qaeda by means of airplane hijacking.[25]

The Path to 9/11 was positioned by Republican activists to aid the party in the 2006 congressional elections with the message that 9/11 was the fault of the Clinton administration, that Democrats were weak in the "war on terror," and that Republicans were the strong and trustworthy party that patriotic Americans should support and vote for. Bush himself interrupted the broadcast of the second part of *The Path to 9/11* with a speech on terrorism commemorating the fifth anniversary of 9/11, thus seamlessly segueing into the narrative that showed his administration as tough on terror, unlike the "wimpy" Democrats. The Bush-Cheney-Rove clique had long planned a sequence of events publicizing their efforts against terrorism to carry them into the November 2006 congressional elections. *The Path to 9/11* was part of this campaign and conservative groups went all out to promote the event.

However, the Republican project seems to have failed. *The Path to 9/11* was panned by critics, and the first part lost out in the ratings to a football game. The broadcast deeply discredited the ABC/Disney network and everyone associated with it. Furthermore, in an interview on Fox News with Chris Wallace shortly after the broadcasting of the film, former president Bill Clinton fiercely defended his administration and attacked Fox TV itself for their consistent attempts to blame 9/11 on his watch. Clinton defended his attempts to stop al Qaeda and bin Laden, while admitting his failure. Clinton thus disrupted the Bush-Cheney administration narrative that his administration alone was primarily responsible for not stopping bin Laden and al Qaeda. Clinton angrily claimed that he tried his best to capture bin Laden, while the Bush-Cheney administration did nothing in its first nine months in office to stop al Qaeda before 9/11, despite copious warnings of the danger and imminent threats of an attack by US intelligence agencies and others.

Just after this fierce rebuttal on Fox television, another Rupert Murdoch owned media outlet, the *New York Post*, gave secretary of state and former national security adviser Condoleezza Rice an opportunity to attack Clinton and defend the Bush-Cheney administration. In an article titled "Rice boils over at Bubba," Rice assailed Clinton's claims that Bush-Cheney failed to mount a program against terrorism when they took over in 2001, neglected plans put together by the Clinton administration, and demoted Clinton's counterterrorism chief Richard Clarke.[26] Without interruption or questioning by the reporter interviewing her, Rice claimed that the Clinton administration had not given her a counterterrorism plan, that Clarke was not demoted, and that the Bush-Cheney administration had been vigilant and concerned about an al Qaeda attack.

As critics were quick to point out, this was completely false. The 9/11 Commission Report had documented the Clinton administration's plan to fight al Qaeda, Clarke had been demoted, as he himself noted in his memoirs (2004), and Bob Woodward (2006) detailed meetings a month before 9/11 indicating that Rice herself had brushed off dangers of imminent attacks by al Qaeda in a top-level briefing with CIA and counterterrorism experts and had failed to address the issue in a serious way as Bush's national security adviser.[27] After the Woodward report, Rice first denied that the meeting had taken place and then tried to spin the episode, claiming that the CIA had not warned about a specific attack "in the US," but "on the US," which could include domestic targets as well as US interests throughout the globe. Critics quickly pointed out that this was a specious defense and Rice was compelled to keep spinning to explain why she did not take terrorist warnings more seriously just before 9/11.

In late September 2006 a National Intelligence Estimate was leaked and then partly published that indicated that Bush-Cheney's Iraq policy was helping to recruit terrorists and threatening US national security.[28] In addition, Bob Woodward (2006) presented the Iraq War as a disaster, exposed Bush-Cheney administration mendacity in selling the war, and presented Bush as a weak leader and his war cabinet as divided and dysfunctional. Following these assaults on the administration, a sex scandal erupted, revealing Republican Florida Congressman Mark Foley to be a sexual predator, when it was disclosed that he had been sending salacious emails to teenage congressional interns for years. The broadcasting of the emails, the reporting of his illicit activities with young pages, and criticism of failures by the Republican House leadership to address the issue created national revulsion and caused Foley to resign in disgrace. Shortly thereafter, another sex scandal occurred when Ted Haggard, a major evangelical liaison to the Bush-Cheney administration, admitted he had sex with a male prostitute who also sold him illegal crystal meth. These incidents seriously undermined the Republican hope to maintain control of Congress in the 2006 elections and indeed contributed to the Democrats taking over the House and Senate.[29] The Republican Party also lost major governorships and local governments throughout the country. Exit polls indicated that voters were concerned about corruption, the economy, Iraq, and terrorism, but many who cited the latter as the key issue voted for the Democrats. Hence, the Republicans lost their long-held monopoly as the party of national security.

It is obviously too soon to judge the effects of 9/11 films and documentaries on US politics, but it is safe to say that the artifacts examined so far in this chapter do not deal adequately with 9/11 and its aftermath. *United 93* is an honest attempt, but it is highly specific and does not engage with broader contextual issues or the sheer magnitude of the terror attacks and their consequences. *World Trade Center* follows conventional genre codes and presents a conservative take on 9/11. Like *United 93*, the film provides some solace in portraying ordinary Americans pulling together to maintain order and community in the face of disaster, but the restricted focus of the film does not allow understanding of the enormity of the event or provide any particular insights.

While *The Path to 9/11* is a ludicrous and despicable piece of extreme rightwing propaganda, it tries, mendaciously and unsuccessfully, to provide a narrative of the events, with heroes and villains, and a rigidly delineated Manichean universe. Its manipulative aesthetic tries to overwhelm the viewer, while its message is blatantly ideological and was sharply contested. In retrospect, it can be seen as a bold attempt by the Republican right in the US to hold onto power in the face of its systematic failures and alienation from broad sectors of the public.

Hollywood's Terror War

By 2006, terror war was a dominant subtext to the political thrillers of the epoch. Both the popular TV series *24* and the Hollywood thriller franchise *Mission: Impossible III* (2006) had plots focusing on the dangers of catastrophic terrorist attacks and featured villains within the US government, raising questions about who could be trusted.

The popular *Mission: Impossible* TV series (1966–1973) and the two previous *M:I* films frequently featured the dangers of terrorism in a global context. The 1996 film *Mission: Impossible*, directed by Brian de Palma, dealt with the effort to prevent a list of US agents falling into the hands of international arms dealers, a far from apocalyptic threat that registered the decline of Cold War tensions. John Woo's *Mission: Impossible II* (2000) presents a deadly virus and a pharmaceutical company whose evil scientist wants to unleash it in Sydney, a plot anticipating the WMD hysteria that would soon emerge in US and global politics.

TV director J. J. Abrams' *Mission: Impossible III* (2006) ups the threat level, depicting nefarious forces within the US government, as well as international arms dealers seeking to put WMDs into the hands of terrorist organizations. Owen Davian (Philip Seymour Hoffman), who has provided numerous weapons to terrorist groups around the world, seeks to steal a doomsday weapon from China and sell it to terrorists. In a fast-paced shift of its narrative from Berlin to Rome to Shanghai and sites from the west to the east coast of the US, the film points to the global nature and amorality of the illicit arms trade and dangers of terrorism from multiple sources. Like the TV series and previous *M:I* movies, *M:I III*'s spy operatives work as a team, demonstrating the importance of combining individual initiative with group efficiency, and features sudden reversals of fortune, as control shifts from the Bad Guys to the Good Guys. The brisk narrative moves back and forth in a ballet of capture, escape, pursuit, action-adventure exploits, high-tech explosives, fights, and resolutions. Tom Cruise's Ethan Hunt assumes masks and fake identities, showing the social construction of identity and how espionage involves masks and deception. Following the codes of the TV show, a dynamic white man stands at the center of the team, which consists of a loyal and dedicated multicultural cast including an African-American man, Luther (Ving Rhames), an Asian-American woman, Zhen (Maggie Q), and a pretty-boy white guy, Declan (Jonathan Rhys-Meyers).

Most significantly, *MI:III* features and legitimates torture and murder in fighting evil terrorists and their accomplices. The team uses similar torture methods to the villains, presenting torture as natural and normalizing it as part of the rules of the game. The film thus legitimated torture at a time of furious debate as to whether its use by the Bush-Cheney administration was really effective, whether it exposed US forces to violations of the Geneva conventions and international law, and whether the US should sacrifice higher moral values and political ground in the name of national security.[30]

Likewise, torture in fighting terrorism was also normalized in the TV series *24* (2001–), which featured its operatives using more and more extreme methods as terrorist threats intensified. Yet the fifth season of *24* (2006) provides one of the more radical attempts to deal with US politics and terrorism in a post-9/11 context. The first four seasons demonized a series of Muslim, Arab, Slavic, Russian, and other ethnic terrorists, duplicating the Manichean discourse of the Bush-Cheney regime and intensifying the fear that the administration exploited to push through its rightwing agenda and invade Iraq.[31] The fifth season, however, featured a paranoid and warped president in league with terrorists in a never-clearly delineated attempt to control oil supplies in the former Russian republics. The president and a cabal of operatives worked with terrorists to block a move toward an anti-terrorist détente between the US and the Russian Republic. Terrorists representing a part of the old Soviet Union promised access to their oil if the US covertly promoted the independence of anti-Russian countries that were formerly part of the Soviet Union, a policy promoted by the Bush-Cheney administration and also embraced by John McCain in the 2008 presidential election.

In season five the threat on *24* came from within as well as without. The series played on the ambiguity of not knowing whether members of various US government agencies were aligned with the president or fighting to foil his nefarious schemes. The president happened to look remarkably like Richard Nixon and took on some of his expressions and mannerisms. Moreover, *24*'s narrative of a rightwing political cabal aligned with rogue US intelligence forces in the interests of securing long-term oil interests for

US corporations and markets sounded suspiciously like what many believed were Bush-Cheney administration motivations behind the Iraq invasion and occupation, and other secret policies. Crucially, season five showed that US government officials – up to and including the president – could act in completely illegal and unscrupulous ways to promote their own political agenda (as Richard Nixon and George W. Bush actually did). The fictional president on *24* assassinated the popular ex-president David Palmer (Dennis Haysbert) to keep him from exposing his conspiratorial agenda, suggesting that presidential power could warp an individual and throw a system out of control.

While the political-allegorical dimension could be directed at the Bush-Cheney administration and mobilize suspicion and distrust toward it, there were other elements of *24* that could well promote the mindset and extreme policies of the Bush-Cheney administration. To be sure, the fifth season undermined the Manicheanism of Bush-Cheney administration discourse, which is central to conservative political thrillers, by showing levels of ambiguity in both US government officials and some of the villains, who believe they are supporting defensible aims. But the series on the whole explicitly legitimates torture and political assassination. Throughout the series the key operative, Jack Bauer (Kiefer Sutherland), exerts extreme force on terrorist suspects. By season five he and his anti-terrorist agencies were systematically and explicitly applying torture to suspects, as well as being captured and tortured themselves. After assassinating a turncoat former-US political operative and corporate executive for his involvement in the conspiracy to kill the ex-president, Bauer even goes to Washington to torture the president, to get him to admit his involvement.

Thus, while providing startling allegorical visions of the criminal activities of the current US political administration, the series also legitimated torture, political assassination, and other breaches of international law. The first episodes of season six in January 2007 portrayed a dirty nuclear bomb exploding and creating a mushroom cloud over Los Angeles, which led rightwing ideologues to exclaim in glee that the series dramatized the danger of a nuclear terrorist attack – something that the liberal media and pundits allegedly downplayed.[32]

Other allegories that helped generate fear of terrorism could be found in Hollywood films of the epoch. Steven Spielberg's *War of the Worlds* (2005) uses the 1898 H. G. Wells science fiction story of an alien invasion, but with imagery deeply reminiscent of 9/11. This highly paranoid film opens with a voice telling us we are being watched, and as soon as the aliens attack, characters evoke terrorism as a cause. Collapsing buildings, hysterical crowds, ash floating through the air, mountains of smoldering rubble, the remains of a crashed jet, and rows of photos of missing people evoke memories of 9/11 – so much so that many found it unbearable and shamelessly exploitative.[33] It could be that this blockbuster hit of summer 2005 contributed to the mood of fear and terror that the Bush-Cheney administration exploited.

Spielberg's version of the Wells novel shows total chaos erupting in the face of catastrophe and a Hobbesian state of war against all. His narrative and visual hook is to have the alien mechanical killing machines (the "Walkers" in Wells' story) emerge from underground to destroy great chunks of urban and suburban life, rather as if a terrorist sleeper cell emerges from earth to wreak havoc. The mob scenes evoke the chaos that could unfold in the face of a massive attack on the US, cruelly terrorizing audiences.

However, while Spielberg's *War of the Worlds* certainly deserves opprobrium and vilification, it can also be read by diagnostic critique as an unfolding of the dysfunctionality of the American family and a crisis of patriarchy. The narrative centers on Ray Ferrier (Tom Cruise), who returns from a job as crane-operator on the Jersey docks to receive from his ex-wife his two children, Rachel (Dakota Fanning) and Robby (Justin Chatwin), for the weekend. Cruise is obviously playing a failed father in a failed marriage, so the narrative must redeem him in good Spielbergian fashion. But the images that stick in the mind are the Cruise character's deep alienation from his children during much of the movie, his hysterical outbursts and tirades, such as throwing a peanut-butter sandwich against the wall, and his blundering confusion as the catastrophe unfolds. His daughter Rachel is a spoiled brat who is emotionally manipulative and screams hysterically throughout the film. The son Robby is presented as an alienated teen: when the aliens strike, he behaves rudely toward his father, and then takes off with the military to fulfill his irrational desire to strike back at the enemy, leaving his father behind with the screaming daughter.

War of the Worlds unwittingly puts on display the ineffectiveness of the government and military, and their inability to protect the country, as the aliens block all attempts to attack them and relentlessly destroy everything in their path. Playing on primal fears, Spielberg also makes the aliens bloodsuckers who drain the blood from their victims, shown in startling visual sequences. *War of the Worlds* was claimed by its scriptwriter to be an allegory of the failed invasion of Iraq.[34] In the film, a survivalist character tells Ray: "We are the resistance. Occupations always fail." The mutterings of a madman, however, do not a leftwing political allegory make, and on the whole the film is repellant and largely reactionary.

Of course, the father is redeemed at the end and, as in the Wells novel, the aliens are killed by microbes to which humans are immune. In a sappy conclusion to the mayhem, Ray and his daughter reach the mother's parents' house in Boston and the daughter is reunited with her mother, her brother (who somehow made it to Boston by himself), and her grandparents. Though the final images are of a reunion and celebration of the family that has survived the hard times intact, memories of dysfunctionality linger on: the parents are divorced, the father is deeply alienated from the son, and the daughter is hysterical – hardly a recipe for Spielbergian family happiness. Thus, the film reveals yet another crisis of patriarchy, with the father under attack and losing power and authority, a theme in many films of the 2000s.

Spielberg's extravaganza of special effects, high-tech spectacle, and redemptive narrative puts on brutal display the fissures and dysfunctionality that his Hollywood ending wants to patch over. The film can be contrasted with a low-budget version of *War of the Worlds* (2005) directed by David Michael Latt and released by B-pictures company The Asylum the same year as the Spielberg film. Latt's B-version is much closer to the Wells novel, featuring the main character (C. Thomas Howell) on a Pilgrim's Progress to meet up with his wife and family in Washington after the alien attack. In scenes evocative of a Dark Night of the Soul, he encounters a priest, Pastor Victor, who tries to comfort a bereaved woman and eventually loses his faith. The resulting dialogue presents an interesting interrogation of religion confronting unthinkable evil, and also plays with conservative evangelicals' fantasies of Apocalypse, with explicit references to the popular *Left Behind* series of novels, which feature similarly catastrophic "last days."

Christian Allegories of Apocalypse

The *Left Behind* novels, written by Christian evangelist Tim LaHaye and Jerry B. Jenkins, transcode the Christian right's apocalyptic vision of Armageddon. Beginning in 1995, the series of 16 bestselling novels has been accompanied by three films: *Left Behind: The Movie* (2001), *Left Behind 2: Tribulation Force* (2003), and *Left Behind 3: World at*

War (2005).³⁵ The storyline concerns the Rapture, which takes away good Christians – presumably to a life in heaven with Jesus and God the Father. However, the narrative deals with the trials and tribulations of those left behind. *Left Behind: The Movie* focuses on Global News Network reporter Buck Williams (Kirk Cameron), who learns that the explanation for the mysterious disappearance of scores of people is the Rapture, and that the salvation of those left behind depends on becoming a true Christian and joining a resistance movement against the forces of darkness creating a secular society.

The films and the novels depict Christians finding each other and forming a "tribulation force" resistant to the secular reign of the Antichrist, who uses the United Nations to form a Global Community (GC) that gets sovereign nations like the United States to give up their weapons and power in the name of world peace. *Left Behind 2: Tribulation Force* explores the horrors of the tribulation and the evil Antichrist Nicolae Carpathia gaining world power, but shows the rise of a Christian community and hopes for salvation of the believers. *Left Behind 3: World at War* has US President Fitzhugh (Lou Gossett Jr.) come to realize that Carpathia is the Antichrist and that he plans to destroy the United States. In an early scene, an oppositional militia, eventually coded as positive resistance forces, attacks the president's caravan, since he has in their view betrayed the country by ceding power to the Global Community. The film puts on display rightwing fears of global power and legitimates violent resistance against a state that it believes is ungodly and betraying US interests. Exploiting fears of terrorism after 9/11, the film shows the Antichrist Carpathia putting anthrax in Bibles to spread a deadly virus among the Christian community. Christians learn – too late for the survival of some of the main characters – that the wine drunk in the Christian sacrament is the antidote.

The *Left Behind* novels and films were given new cultural resonance post-9/11. Fears of terrorism and war in the Middle East bringing about Armageddon created a combination of hysteria and hope for deliverance on the Christian right. The films transcode rightwing Christian views of the Apocalypse and demonize liberals and liberal institutions as sources of evil. They thus fit into the Bush-Cheney Manichean vision that sees the world as divided between the forces of Good and Evil, a view intensely propagated by the right in the wake of 9/11.

A new genre of Christian films appeared in the 2000s, when various production companies targeted the audiences that flocked to see Mel Gibson's

The Passion of the Christ, and some replicated the *Left Behind* films. *2012: Doomsday* (2008) presents a countdown to the end of the world complete with Rapture, poor souls left behind, and a chosen group who survive to carry on the gospel teaching. The film's form is that of a disaster movie, with scientists detecting unusual seismic and volcanic activity so intense that the west coast of the US is evacuated (surely a rightwing fantasy). Set in the heart of Mexico in the final days of the Mayan calendar which mark the end of time, disparate individuals are drawn to the region. Signs appear that pull a group of four strangers together, who learn that their mission is to proceed to an ancient Mayan temple for the Apocalypse in order to survive and carry on the teachings of Jesus.[36]

The State of Terror

By 2005, US culture was apparently ready for the emergence of 9/11 films. Both low-budget B-movies and major Hollywood films exploited fears of terrorism. In Ben Rekhi's *Waterborne* (2005), Los Angeles' water supplies have been contaminated by a biological agent, people are dying, and the media create hysteria. As water supplies disappear, tensions and conflicts emerge. The film focuses on how the crisis effects three sets of characters who converge on a convenience store at the end, where a young man goes beserk and pulls out a gun to rob water when he is shot by a National Guardsman.

Waterborne has an interesting subtext concerning how Sikh Americans are demonized in the crisis, drawing on real-life attacks on Sikhs after 9/11 who were mistakenly believed to be Muslims. However, despite having a disturbed white guy as the villain with no apparent motive – thus undercutting the film's media (and perhaps audience) suspicion that it's a Muslim terror attack – the film ultimately is very conservative. A narrator intones that in such situations one comes to appreciate the little things in life, like the flow of water, and "people close to me." Thus, ultimately, sentimentalism trumps the film's often acute insights into how people might react during a terror crisis.

Another low-budget Los Angeles-based terrorist film, this time by first-time director Chris Gorak, *Right At Your Door* (2006), shows ordinary people going to work when dirty bombs are exploded around the city. Brad (Rory Cochrane), an unemployed musician, frantically tries to phone his wife, Lexi (Mary McCormack), who has gone off to work. Attempts to find her fail when he sees the neighborhood is blockaded by police. Returning home, and with the aid of a handyman from next door, Brad follows the advice of radio announcers and uses duct tape and plastic to seal his house, so that no toxin-contaminated air or person can get inside. At that point, of course, a coughing Lexi shows up, demanding entrance. The couple tries to negotiate when it will be safe for her to enter the house proper, as Brad keeps her cordoned off in "safe areas." The radio and government officials give wrongheaded advice and make matters worse, a resonant theme following Hurricane Katrina.

The dichotomy between bad terrorists and good Americans is undercut in Uwe Boll's savage satire, *Postal* (2008). This totally over-the-top post-9/11 film attacks American business, religion, commodity culture, cultural clichés, Islamic terrorists, and the director's home country, Germany. Interspersing 9/11 jokes about airline hijacking and suicide bombing, the film presents Osama bin Laden and George W. Bush as good ole buddies, and ends with them walking into the sunset holding hands as a nuclear blast is about to destroy the earth. Full of bad taste, it puts on display how deep cynicism and deranged irony have returned with a vengeance to contemporary cinema whereas irony was supposedly banned after 9/11.

Contemporary fears among youth were articulated in the 2008 films *Cloverfield* and *Diary of the Dead* (see chapter 1), both of which take the form of youth/horror films that deploy the "film captured on video" technique of *The Blair Witch Project* (1999). Directed by Matt Reeves and produced by J. J. Abrams, *Cloverfield* uses a rampaging monster scenario to provide the backdrop for an apocalyptic terrorization of New York City. Playing on post-9/11 fears, the film uses 9/11 imagery of falling skyscrapers, panic in the streets, dust and blood-soaked mobs running from the disaster, and general chaos portending social collapse. After an opening sequence documenting the morning after of a twenty-something couple and a trip to Coney Island, the action unfolds in a New York loft. *Cloverfield*'s hand-held digital camera documents the action by means of a narrative conceit in which a friend films the going-away party of Rob, who has accepted a job in Japan. The young, affluent crowd down excessive quantities of alcohol, with one young woman shown passed out on a couch, while another, Marlina, who becomes a major character, is shown drinking herself into oblivion. Rob apparently has not called back Beth, whom he was with in the early romance sequences, and she shows up at a party with a date, triggering drama and tensions. Pressures, conflicts, and anxieties explode into social chaos as a thundering crash signals the rampaging of the monster.

The panicked crowd hits the New York streets in terror, joining other hysterical people, and the jerky camera movements provide an analogue to the social catastrophe in which the characters and city are thrown. The monster is never really clearly shown and the footage of the crowds and collapsing buildings reveals the film to be a 9/11 exploitation flick. Yet the decapitated head of the Statue of Liberty that appears in a crowd scene in lower Manhattan suggests a broader theme of the end of innocence even for the affluent young, in the era of bin Laden and Bush-Cheney, where spectacles of terror had become part of everyday life.

There have also been epic Hollywood political thrillers dealing with global terrorism, like *Syriana* (2005), and a series of anti-Bush-Cheney films that I will engage in chapter 4. In the next chapter, we will see how Michael Moore's films address the conflicts and controversies of the era, making him the most popular and controversial documentary filmmaker of all time.

Notes

1   The contextualization of 9/11 in this analysis draws upon Kellner (2003a, 2005).

2   On media spectacle, see Kellner (2003a, 2003b, 2005, 2008). The concept of social memory refers to the socially constructed images of the past and present in a given society. In a media-dominated society, social memory is often constructed in terms of significant media spectacles, and the discourses, resonant images, and narratives that frame those spectacles. This is arguably so with the 9/11 terror attacks that continue to be a highly resonant and contested phenomenon.

3   Timothy McVeigh was allegedly outraged by an FBI assault on a religious cult's compound in Waco, Texas that killed a number of people the previous year and he set the bomb in Oklahoma City as revenge. There were allegations of a wider conspiracy of white supremacists and one associate of McVeigh, Terry Nichols, is serving life imprisonment for helping McVeigh plan and buy material for the bomb. Since McVeigh was executed by the Bush-Cheney administration, his version of the story of the Waco bombing remains untold. On the Waco incident and Oklahoma City bombings, see Jones (2001) and Kellner (2008), the latter of which puts acts of domestic terrorism and school shootings in the context of crises of masculinity and "guys and guns amok."

4   For further examples and analyses of spectacles of terror, see Kellner (2003a, 2005, 2008).

5   Since the term *war on terror* is thoroughly ideological, enabling one to do and justify anything in the name of fighting terrorism and evil, the term *Terror War* best describes the epoch from 9/11 to the present (see Kellner 2003a). The concept of terror war includes al Qaeda and Islamicist terror, the state terrorism of the Bush-Cheney administration, and other states using "terrorism" as an excuse for military aggression. For an excellent BBC documentary series on terror war, see Adam Curtis's *The Power of Nightmares* (2004), which interrogates the background to the outbreak of global terrorism in the 2000s and the respective roles of al Qaeda and militant Islam facing off against the neoconservatives who served in the Reagan and two Bush administrations. Curtis shows the similarities between the US neoconservatives who emerged during the Reagan administration and the radical Islamicist forces who became al Qaeda and the Taliban. Both are Manichean, dividing the world into Good and Evil, Us and Them, and both identify with Good and see their enemies as absolute Evil. The US neocons were inspired by German exile philosopher Leo Strauss, who argued that strong myths are needed to govern liberal, pluralist societies and that manipulation of the masses, including Big Lies, was necessary to pursue national interests. *The Power of Nightmares* argues that in general after the fall of ideology and big political ideas, governments have promoted fear, demonized enemies, and claimed to protect citizens against often exaggerated enemies, suggesting that rightwing forces in the US exaggerated the threats of the Soviet Union, Saddam Hussein and the Iraqis, and Islamic terrorism to create an atmosphere of fear and to push through a militarist rightwing agenda. Adam Curtis also directed the outstanding BBC series *The Century of Self* and *The Trap*. On his work, see Paul Arthur, "Waking life: an interview with Adam Curtis," *Cineaste*, December 2007 and online at www.accessmylibrary.com/coms2/summary_ 0286-33734218_ITM (accessed January 2, 2009).

6   Former TV and documentary director Paul Greengrass teamed up with an independent production company, Sidney Kimmel Entertainment. Much of the film was shot at Pinewood Studios in the UK, hence the film should be seen as an independent and global production. As of January 2, 2009, *United 93* had grossed over $76,286,096 worldwide at www.boxofficemojo.com/movies/?id=united93.htm.

7   Neither the film nor Greengrass on the DVD commentary addresses the conspiracy theories that suggest the government did not act to prevent 9/11 because it was planning to exploit the tragedy to push through its rightwing extremist agenda. The Wikipedia "9/11 Conspiracies" site lists salient points and sources of various conspiracy analyses and arguments against

them; see www,en.wikipedia.org/wiki/9/11_conspiracy_theories (accessed July 11, 2009).

8   Elaine Scarry argued that the lesson of the United 93 event was that citizens should assume democratic responsibility to protect themselves and not trust government; see "Citizenship in emergency: Can democracy protect us against terrorism?" *Boston Review*, November-December 2002 at www.bostonreview.net/BR27.5/scarry.html (accessed November 5, 2006). The film seems to bolster her argument.

9   Cited in Patrick Goldstein, "Oliver Stone's Ground Zero," *Los Angeles Times*, August 8, 2006: E10. As of January 2, 2009, *World Trade Center* had grossed over $162,970,240 worldwide (www.boxofficemojo.com/movies/?id=wtc.htm).

10 See Ruth Rosen, "Oliver Stone, 9/11, and the Big Lie," *Z-Net*, August 18, 2006 at www.zmag.org/content/showarticle.cfm?ItemID=10775 (accessed September 28, 2006).

11 September 30, 2006. In 2008 Stone released *W.*, which deals with the life of George W. Bush (for discussion, see the conclusion to this book).

12 I say "myth" because books on the Bush-Cheney administration, including Bob Woodward's *State of Denial* (2006), present Bush as disengaged and incompetent. In the words of Michiki Kakutani: "In Bob Woodward's highly anticipated new book, 'State of Denial,' President Bush emerges as a passive, impatient, sophomoric and intellectually incurious leader, presiding over a grossly dysfunctional war cabinet and given to an almost religious certainty that makes him disinclined to rethink or reevaluate decisions he has made about the war." See "A portrait of Bush as a victim of his own certitude," *New York Times*, September 30, 2006 at www.nytimes.com/2006/09/30/books/30book.html?_r=1&&pagewanted=print (accessed December 31, 2008).

13 Sheldon Rampton, "Hijacking 9/11" (posted September 5, 2006, accessed September 29, 2006), at www.alternet.org/story/41288/. For a thorough critique of the background and text *DC 9/11: Time of Crisis*, see Danny Schecter, "9/11 propaganda, Hollywood style" (posted September 8, 2003, accessed September 28, 2006), at www.alternet.org/story/16735/.

14 Max Blumenthal, "The right-wing roots of ABC's 9/11 Movie" (posted September 13, 2006, accessed September 29, 2006), at www.alternet.org/story/41546/. On the scriptwriter Cyrus Nowrasteh, see also the post at www.thinkprogress.org/2006/09/01/nowrasteh-conservative-activist/ (accessed September 12, 2006). In 2009, Nowrasteh released a movie *The Stoning of Soraya M* which he co-wrote and directed that exploits the topic of Islamic stoning of women to present a viciously anti-Iran and anti-Islamic movie. In a panel after its presentation at the Los Angeles Film Festival on June 20, 2009, Nowrasteh indicated that he conceived the film in 2005, just

as his fellow neo-conservatives in the Bush-Cheney administration were talking of invading Iran.

15 *Editor and Publisher* compared the originally circulated DVD with the final version and found it one minute shorter, cutting slightly the scenes with Sandy Berger allegedly refusing to sanction a CIA hit on bin Laden; see E&P Staff, "ABC airs 9/11 film – contested scenes remain" (posted September 10, 2006, accessed September 30, 2006), at www.editorandpublisher.com/eandp/news/article_display.jsp?vnu_content_id=1003119721. The original uncut version has become a cult classic on YouTube. Cyrus Nowrasteh has shown the uncut scenes in lectures and gave them to Fox TV, which broadcast the edited scenes and criticized ABC for censorship on *Hannity's America* on January 28, 2007.

16 Cited in William Triplet, "Pols pound 'Path,'" *Variety* (posted September 8, 2006, accessed September 29, 2006), at www.variety.com.

17 Cited in Joe Conason, "Jersey hustler," *Salon*, September 15, 2006 (accessed September 28, 2006), at www.salon.com/opinion/conason/2006/09/15/kean/.

18 Eric Alterman, "Lying about 9/11? Easy as ABC," *The Nation*, October 2, 2006: 10.

19 See "FBI agent who consulted on Path to 9/11 quit halfway through because 'they were making things up,'" September 7, 2006 (accessed September 30, 2006), at www.thinkprogress.org/2006/08/07/fbi.agent-quit/.

20 Philip Recchia and Jennifer Fermino, "Cast's on-set turmoil revealed," *New York Post*, September 10, 2006: 29.

21 See www.imdb.com/news/sb/2006-09-18/ (accessed November 5, 2006). A number of other mistakes and "inaccuracies" are compiled at a Wikipedia site on *The Path to 9/11*. The site has a wealth of information about the production, text, and reception of the TV movie, as well as its controversies, and continues to expand; see www.en.wikipedia.org/wiki/The_Path_to_9/11#_note-33 (first accessed November 5, 2006 and reaccessed May 28, 2009).

22 See Laura Barcella, "More 9/11 lies" (posted September 6, 2006, accessed September 29, 2006), at www.alternet.org/bloggers/41365/.

23 *Wag the Dog* (1998) was a popular film in which a president distracts attention from a Clintonesque sexual scandal by creating a fake war. The phrase "wag the dog" entered the US political lexicon as a criticism of military action allegedly taken to distract attention from domestic or personal political problems.

24 See Albright's letter at www.i.a.cnn.net/cnn/2006/images/09/07/iger.letter.pdf (accessed September 12, 2006).

25 These facts were known right from the immediate aftermath of 9/11 and are documented in detail in the 9/11 Commission Report (2004). They are discussed in Kellner (2003a, 2005).

26   See Ian Bishop, "Rice boils over at Bubba – rips 'flatly false' claim on Bush's bid to get bin Laden," *New York Post*, September 25, 2006.

27   For a critique of the Rice interview, see Gal Beckerman, "*New York Post* could learn from Fox's Chris Wallace" (posted September 26, 2006), at www.cjrdaily.org/politics/new_york_post_could_learn_from.php. For Rice's failures as national security adviser, see Clarke (2004) and Woodward (2006).

28   See Mark Mazzetti, "Spy agencies say Iraq War worsens terrorism threat," *New York Times*, September 24, 2006. For the released portions of the report, see www.npr.org/documents/2006/sep/redacted_nie.pdf (accessed January 5, 2007).

29   For an overview of the Foley scandal, see *Salon*'s "War Room" on October 4, 2006 at www.salon.com/politics/war_room/?calendar=200609#archive Calendar (accessed October 4, 2006). For the Haggard scandal, see the CNN report "Church forces out Haggard for 'sexually immoral conduct,'" November 4, 2006 at www.cnn.com/2006/US/11/03/haggard.allegations/index.html (accessed January 5, 2007).

30   For succinct analysis of the Bush-Cheney administration's use of torture and its dubious results, see Mayer (2008); for an account of the failures of torture to provide accurate and timely information and the need for other interrogation methods, see Alexander and Bruning (2008). Alexander served in the US intelligence forces during the Bush-Cheney years and saw the failures of their policies at first hand.

31   For a fierce critique of *24*, see Slavoj Žižek, "The depraved heroes of *24* are the Himmlers of Hollywood," *Guardian*, January 19, 2006, at www.guardian.co.uk/media/2006/jan/10/usnews.comment (accessed December 31, 2008).

32   Rightwing pundits praised the season six nuclear explosion episode, claiming it dramatized the real dangers in the "war on terrorism" that liberals were supposedly avoiding (see Rush Limbaugh's comments at www.rushlimbaugh.com/home/daily/site_011607/content/rush_on_24.LogIn.html) (accessed September 22, 2008). During the same period, members of the US military demanded a meeting with *24*'s creators, claiming that *24*'s nonchalant affirmation of torture was unduly influencing US military and intelligence agents in the field, by suggesting that torture was the quickest and most effective way to obtain information. US military experts argued this was not the case and pleaded with *24*'s creators to show torture did not work and how other methods might be more effective. *24*'s executive producer Joel Surnow missed the meeting and a *New Yorker* article at the time had him confessing he was "a rightwing nut job." See Jane Mayer, "Whatever it takes," *New Yorker*, February 19, 2007, at www.newyorker.com/reporting/2007/02/19/070219fa_fact_mayer?printable=true (accessed September 22, 2008).

33   For critics appalled by the film's exploitation of 9/11, see Stephanie Zacharek, "War of the Worlds," *Salon*, June 29, 2005; and Timothy Noah, "9/11 was no summer movie," *Slate*, July 19, 2005, who argued that the film's "appropriation of 9/11 imagery can only be described as pornographic."

34   David Koepp is cited in Craigh Barboza, "Imagination is infinite," *USA Today*, June 19, 2005, at www.usaweekend.com/05_issues/050619/050619spielberg. html (accessed September 12, 2006).

35   For a penetrating analysis of the religious sources, themes and theology, and effects of the *Left Behind* novels, see the study by Stroup and Shuck (2007: 51–86); the authors do not, however, engage the films.

36   *2012: Doomsday* was harshly criticized by viewers on the Blockbusters site for the film, with audiences complaining: "Ouch, I am very depressed. I could only stomach 30 minutes of this movie.... Please, please, you don't know me, but trust me in saying that you will waste a portion of your life that you will never get back if you watch this movie." And: "People who made this waste of time movie should be banned for life from the movie industry. What a piece of crap. This thing gave me such bad stomach ache." No one had anything good to say about the film. See www.blockbuster.com/ browse/catalog/movieDetails/390184 (accessed October 15, 2008).

3

Michael Moore's Provocations

I'm not trying to pretend that this is some sort of fair and balanced work of journalism.

Michael Moore[1]

Michael Moore's *Bowling For Columbine* (2002) and *Fahrenheit 9/11* (2004) are the two highest grossing documentary films in history, and he has emerged as one of the most successful and controversial filmmakers of his day. *Bowling* won an Academy Award for best documentary and in 2002 was chosen by 2,000 members of the International Documentary Association (IDA) as the best documentary of all time. *Fahrenheit 9/11* was even more successful at the box office and garnered a perhaps unparalleled legion of passionate fans and bitter detractors alike.[2]

In addition, Moore has a stack of bestselling books, and a popular website that promotes his products and receives millions of hits. He engages in lecture tours with packed houses and adoring audiences, has produced two TV series still circulating on VHS and DVD, and has been a frequent presence in the mainstream media. This success is surprising given that Moore is one of the most high-profile critics of corporate capitalism, US military policy, the Bush-Cheney administration, the US health industry, and the manifold injustices of US society.

What is the secret of Moore's success? He is a populist artist who privileges his own voice and point of view, inserting himself as film narrator and often as the subject of his films' action. Moore plays the crusading defender of the poor and oppressed, who stands up to and confronts the powers that be. He uses humor and compelling dramatic and narrative sequences to engage his audiences. Moore's films deal with issues of fundamental importance, and he attempts to convince his audience that the problems he presents are highly significant and concern the health of US democracy. Moreover, despite the severity of the crises he portrays, the films and filmmaker often imply that the problems can be subject to intervention, and that progressive social transformation is possible and necessary.

In this chapter, I interrogate Moore's aesthetics and politics by providing critical readings of his three major documentary films – *Roger and Me* (1989), *Bowling For Columbine* (2002), *Fahrenheit 9/11* (2004) – with some concluding comments on *Sicko* (2007). I attempt to specify Moore's particular documentary strategies, aesthetics, and politics, and contrast his work with that of documentary filmmaker Emile de Antonio, *cinéma vérité* directors, and other non-fiction filmmakers.[3] I argue that many of Moore's critics fail to understand his partisan radical documentary tradition and his own unique mode of filmmaking. At stake is appraising the contributions and limitations of Michael Moore's political documentaries and what strategies work best for progressive documentary filmmaking within the cinematic/political wars of the past decades.

Michael Moore, Emile de Antonio, and the Politics of Documentary Film

> *Movies are lies that tell the truth.*
>
> Bernardo Bertolucci

Among contemporary filmmakers, Michael Moore's role as outspokenly leftwing documentary provocateur is parallel in some ways to that of Emile de Antonio, although their work has major differences as well as similarities. Emile de Antonio (1919–1989) was one of the United States' greatest documentary filmmakers, although he is relatively forgotten today.[4] His works present a history of Cold War America from the McCarthy era through the Kennedy assassination, the Vietnam War, the Nixon era, and Reaganism. De Antonio's films made a significant impact on both the form of documentary cinema and the political practice of filmmaking. His politically committed and engaged cinema critiqued ruling-class figures, while sympathetically portraying oppositional political movements. De Antonio made use of archival footage, original interview material, and complex sound editing to create a montage of images and sound to present his vision and interpretation of the events of the era.

In terms of style, de Antonio eschewed voice-of-God narration and even commentary, using the juxtaposition of archival with interview material without narrative or commentary. By contrast, Moore inserts his personality and voice into the center of his films and provides point-of-view commentary on the events. Both de Antonio and Moore use documentary montage to speak truth to power, juxtaposing statements by corporate and political figures with footage that refutes or ridicules them. Both Moore and de Antonio are masters of montage and use interview material and documentary footage to assault dominant institutions and authority figures in US society, and both positively portray voices and forces of critique and rebellion.

Whereas Moore's films and politics are accessible and populist, de Antonio is a more orthodox modernist in his aesthetics and Marxist in his politics. As a modernist, de Antonio is highly innovative and experimental, meticulous in shaping a distinct formalist structure where every image and sound resonates within a whole. He combines a radical artistic and political vision with a highly original documentary style that varies significantly from film to film over the three decades of his cinematic career.[5] While de Antonio is a modernist who creates difficult works that require an active audience, Moore's more populist films attempt to make his message clear and comprehensible to mass audiences.

Moore is more rooted in popular entertainment than modernist aesthetics, and is apparently more interested in politics than art (although he too is a highly skilled creator of original and engaging documentary form, as well as purveyor of highly charged political content). Fittingly, Michael Moore's first film, *Roger and Me*, appeared the year of de Antonio's final film, *Mr. Hoover and I* (1989). Moore draws on de Antonio's aesthetic-political strategies, but has created a unique documentary style that combines partisan and interventionist cinema with his personal voice and vision, combining the personal with the political, pathos and humor, expository argumentation with strong point of view critique. There is no evidence that de Antonio had a direct influence on Moore, although the similarities are striking.[6] Both combine serious historical and political analysis with irony and humor, although de Antonio goes further in using documentary to tell the history and dissect the politics of the time, while Moore takes on specific issues that characterize his contemporary epoch and constitute its key problems.

Both de Antonio and Moore are leftwing partisans and eschew the ideal of so-called "objectivity," admitting they are making committed and interventionist political films. Both sharply criticized *cinéma vérité*'s aesthetic, which held that documentary itself would reveal the truth if the filmmaker simply used the camera to capture events without intervening a narrative voice or point of view.[7] Against this, de Antonio claimed that choice of subject matter, framing, and editing created a construct that contained a filmmaker's vision and politics and that pure objectivity is both impossible and undesirable. De Antonio spoke frequently of the "myth of objectivity," noting:

> The very idea of *cinéma vérité* is repugnant to me. It is as if the filmmaker owned truth of some kind. I have never felt that I owned truth. I tried to be as truthful as I can but I know I am a man of deep-seated prejudices and many assumptions about the nature of society which color all my thinking and feeling and the work that I do. For me, there is no concept of objectivity. Objectivity is a myth.[8]

This myth of documentary objectivity came from a variety of sources, including a tradition of photography that saw it as a mode of reproducing reality; journalism schools which reacted against the tradition of yellow and political journalism dominant in the US in the nineteenth century and held objectivity as an ideal; and documentary filmmakers who followed a realist aesthetic and objectivist notion of truth.[9] Moore appears to agree with de Antonio that objectivity is a spurious ideal, often making clear his biases, point of view, and politics,[10] although, as we shall see, critics frequently claim that Moore is not honest in his use of documentary montage and editing.

In the following discussion, I argue that Michael Moore's most popular films deploy three types of documentary strategy: personal witnessing, exploratory and confrontational quest dramas, and partisan political interventions. These categories, to be sure, are ideal types and to some extent overlap and characterize all of his work which provide sharp critique of the dominant institutions of the era in highly partisan cinematic attacks on the dominant ideology and ruling powers and institutions of contemporary US society.

Roger and Me and the Documentary of Personal Witnessing

It's not an NBC White Paper, not an episode of Nova. To the guardians of documentary, I apologize that the picture is entertaining.
                                        Michael Moore[11]

A proliferation of documentary films of personal witnessing emerged in the 1960s and 1970s when members of the civil rights, women's, gay and lesbian, and other social movements told their personal stories to bear witness to injustices and explore social problems. Emile de Antonio's *Mr. Hoover and I* (1989), his most overtly personal work, exemplifies this category in which the personal becomes a vehicle for the political, and in which he tells his life story through use of material from his FBI files.

Michael Moore's first documentary film, *Roger and Me* (1989), puts on display the hardships that the closing of the Flint, Michigan auto plants caused for working-class people. The film opens with images of Moore growing up in Michigan in a working-class family with his father employed in a Flint GM auto plant. Moore quickly cuts from home movies showing him clowning in a Popeye suit and happily playing with his family to montage of Flint in the post-World War II era of prosperity. The sequence establishes the filmmaker and his locale as the center of the film.

Roger and Me unfolds with a fast, kinetic pace, intercutting home movies, newsreel footage of the Flint plant, and TV footage of Pat Boone and Dinah Shore singing ads for GM cars. Like de Antonio, Moore chose resonant music and a soundtrack that is as rich and evocative as the visuals. Throughout the film, the soundtrack provides a strong counterpart to the visuals and Moore's own voice confirms his involvement in the events he is narrating.

Newsreel footage establishes Flint as the birthplace of General Motors, portrays the giant automobile plant, assembly lines, crowds of workers, parades, and images of the good life in Flint. After a quick look at his work as a journalist for ten years in the Flint area and a brief sojourn in San Francisco to edit *Mother Jones* (one of Moore's few failed projects),[12] the film changes tone as Moore returns home to Flint in the mid-1980s in the midst of GM's closing of automobile plants and the subsequent decline of the town's fortunes.

Moore's central focus in *Roger and Me* is class and the impact of corporate restructuring and downsizing on the working class. The film presents illuminating contrasts between the rich and poor, the working class and the corporate elite, continually cutting from images of working-class devastation and despair in Flint as GM continues its closures, to upper-class prosperity and obliviousness to the plight of the workers and the poor.

The narrative hook for the film, expressed in the title *Roger and Me*, is Moore's quest to talk to Roger Smith, president of GM, and convince him that he should come to Flint to observe the consequences of his corporate restructuring. The quest takes Moore to a variety of offices, clubs, elite restaurants, and hotels where Smith is allegedly to be found, interspersed with images of people in Flint thrown out of their houses, neighborhoods deteriorating, and dejected workers losing their jobs and homes.

Moore's personal involvement in the lives of the rich and the poor bears witness to and illustrates class differences and growing working-class oppression. As a longtime inhabitant of the area, Moore manages to obtain access to a wide range of local characters, from poor blacks and whites and a number of laid-off workers, to public officials and PR functionaries, and visiting celebrities. The film establishes Moore as a major portrayer of Americana, an astute analyst of class and capitalism, an advocate for the poor, and someone personally involved in presenting the effects of class oppression.

In retrospect, *Roger and Me* is a remarkable first film. When he began, Moore reportedly did not know anything about film production. Documentary filmmaker Kevin Rafferty served as one of his cameramen and taught Moore how to set up a shot. Rafferty himself made the successful and engaging *The Atomic Café* (1982) and an exposé of the white supremacist movement in *Blood in the Face* (1991) that Moore himself participated in, obviously giving him a taste for documentary filmmaking.[13]

Moore's satirical and biting critical representations of the upper-class elite in Flint, enjoying life while misery engulfs the underclass, brilliantly capture the decadence, shallowness, and class privileges of the rich. Moore's satire was so biting that he was sued by one of the Flint elite, showing that Moore was willing to take personal witnessing and stinging satire to levels where he opened himself to litigation. The film showed the annual Flint Great Gatsby Ball, an annual charity event in which the Flint elite dressed up in Roaring Twenties affluent styles. The sequence included unemployed blacks and workers standing as human statues. A tuxedo-attired local attorney, Larry Stecco, made light of the unemployment, stressing that others were still working. When asked about the good aspects of Flint, Stecco glibly answered, "Ballet, hockey. It's a great place to live."[14] He sued Moore for defamation under "false light invasion of privacy."

Moore proves equally effective at getting celebrities and public officials to hang themselves with their own words in front of the camera, presenting Flint native and TV's *The Newlywed Game* host Bob Eubanks in a bad light, telling a horribly anti-Semitic joke about Jewish women and AIDS. *Roger and Me* skewers as well local politicians in Flint, attacking their efforts to bring a Sheraton Hotel, a convention center, and an Auto World theme park to town when obviously the city needed programs that would provide better housing, jobs, and human services to its working and underclass. There is also a brief segment in which Ronald Reagan comes to Flint, has pizza with workers, and provides his usual upbeat patter.

On this point, critic Harlan Jacobson – in one of the first detailed interviews with Moore – took him to task for reordering the historical sequence of events, as Reagan actually campaigned in Flint in the early 1980s, while the (later bankrupt) Sheraton and failed convention center and Auto World were begun in the mid-1980s. By contrast, Moore's narrative is focused on footage from around 1986 to the late 1980s. Yet it appears from Moore's sequencing that the Reagan visit and building campaign came after the lay-offs that Moore presents.[15] Moore protested to Jacobson that he was telling a story, condensing hours of footage to present Flint's tragic recent history, and that his story about Flint was largely accurate.[16] As Moore and de Antonio claim, all films are constructs, editing is highly subjective, and there are other criteria besides objectivity and accurate historical sequencing to judge documentaries. Since Jacobson's critique, however, there has been a cottage industry of Moore critics who have attacked his editing and alleged distortions. In fact, Moore's films are of a unique genre, often departing from standard documentary conventions. Moore readily admits that he is doing polemics and satire, and, as the epigraph to this section indicates, he presented his first film as entertainment. By the time of *Fahrenheit 9/11*, however, Moore had published entire books documenting statements and claims made in his films, and used his website to attack his critics and defend his work on a factual and documentary basis.

From a critical perspective, *Roger and Me* brilliantly puts on display the class privilege, racism, and sexism of the upper classes and their lack of social conscience and humanity. Privileged corporate and political figures deserve satire and critique and the public deserves to see their unguarded and revealing moments. Yet, *Roger and Me* provoked questions as to whether Moore does or does not exploit the working-class characters and lower-echelon functionaries in his film. One example of this accusation focuses on his portrayal of the "pets or meat" rabbit lady, Rhonda Britton, a young woman struggling to pay her bills by raising rabbits that could be sold either as pets or meat.[17] Moore returns to her in a short follow-up documentary showing her raising snakes and rats as well as rabbits, providing a poignant picture of how the struggle for survival in predatory capitalism drives people to engage in bizarre occupations – a theme that would later frequently reappear in his TV series.

In the absence of Roger Smith, Deputy Fred Ross becomes one of the major figures in the film, appearing early on as the casual and lighthearted evictor of poor people who cannot pay their rent. He claims he is just doing his job, knows many of the people he is evicting, and serves as an engaging middle man between the town elite and the poor. In one striking scene near the end of the film, Roger Smith spouts banalities about Christmas and reads from Dickens as Deputy Ross evicts a family during the holidays, carrying out a Christmas tree as a distraught woman shouts obscenities, using audiences' associations with Christmas to highlight the inhumanity of the town's socioeconomic and political structure.

Moore's mode of personal witnessing and intervention in *Roger and Me* goes beyond standard compilation film documentaries in a highly condensed, fast-moving, and entertaining montage of sequences which express a clear point of view in a well-constructed narrative about capitalism and class in the United States. This topic is seldom addressed in mainstream media and rarely has a documentary on this topic provoked so much interest and discussion. Moore managed to take political documentary film out of the ghetto of a marginalized cinematic form and into mainstream film. His innovative and successful film, however, propelled Moore into a life of public controversy.

Roger and Me began the construction of a unique genre: the Michael Moore film. Moore emerges from his first film as a storyteller, fabulist, satirist, and witness to the corporate downsizing and devastation of his beloved Flint. Yet in retrospect, Moore does not appear as a rigorous documentary filmmaker concerned about historical sequence, strict documentation of facts, or objectivity. Moore positions himself instead as an entertainer and provocateur who raises questions, attacks wrongs and wrongdoers, and speaks up for the oppressed and against the oppressors. Despite critiques of inaccuracies of historical sequences or "facts" in his films, much of what Moore says is true in the wider sense. Certainly his documentary practice strained certain conventions and traditions of progressive documentary filmmaking that uphold "objectivity" and historical accuracy as the norms, and elicited ferocious debate. As we shall see, by the time he made *Fahrenheit 9/11*, Moore would be more concerned about standard documentary conventions. Yet he would continue to develop his own unique, controversial, and hard-to-classify filmmaking in *Bowling For Columbine* and subsequent films.

Bowling For Columbine and Exploratory Documentary Montage

> *I have long admired the old filmmakers who used comedy and satire as a means to discuss or illuminate social conditions, whether it was Charlie Chaplin, Will Rogers, or even the Marx Brothers. I hope people will laugh at this movie harder than they've laughed at a movie in years – but that they will also find themselves choking back the tears.*
>
> Michael Moore[18]

An exploratory documentary tradition on the political left uses film as a medium to probe social problems, as with the work of Emile de Antonio, discussed above. In *Bowling For Columbine* Michael Moore explores connections between guns, militarism, and violence in American history and contemporary society, and investigates the question of why there has been so much violence in the United States.

Roger and Me was made for around $160,000 and turned over a $7 million profit,[19] making Michael Moore a hot item in the film and entertainment world. Moore turned next to television, using his populist "little guy against the system" persona on *TV Nation* to expose corporate and sociopolitical problems in a show broadcast by NBC and then the Fox network in 1994–1995. Moore used his mode of personal witnessing, exploring of social problems, and good-natured humor to provide highly entertaining vignettes of corporate and political misconduct.

After the unsuccessful release of Moore's one non-fiction film, *Canadian Bacon* (1995), and a mixed response to a documentary, *The Big One* (1997), focusing on a book tour publicizing his successful publication *Downsize This!* (1996), once again television beckoned to Moore, with the UK's Channel Four television taking on another Michael Moore TV series, *The Awful Truth*. The series was shown in the US on the Bravo channel in 1999, and also took on corporations, rightwing politicians, and various reactionary forces. Moore served as host in a theater packed with adoring fans, introducing filmed episodes from the stage and interacting with his audiences.

Moore's next major film was *Bowling For Columbine* (2002), which took his documentary aesthetic to new levels of complexity and controversy, eliciting both widespread praise and condemnation. By now, Moore was a genuine American celebrity, and he uses his strong persona once again to engage his audience in a quest narrative, this time to try to find out why there is so much violence with guns in the USA today. Moore's voice is again the narrative center of the film and it is more confident, self-assured, and insistent than in his earlier work.

Moore's hook was the April 1999 Columbine shooting, when two white, middle-class, small-town teenage boys took an arsenal of guns and home-made bombs to school and slaughtered their classmates.[20] The film opens with a clip from a National Rifle Association (NRA) promotional film then cuts to Moore narrating "April 20, 1999," another "morning in America," with footage of farmers, workers, milk deliveries, "the president bombing another country we couldn't pronounce," and the shootings at Columbine high school, with "The Battle Hymn of the Republic" playing in the background. Once again, Michael Moore uses a highly resonant soundtrack to highlight his themes, using ironical juxtaposition of music as a technique of social critique.

A second opening vignette shows a bank in Michigan which offers a free gun to new CD depositors. Moore joyfully enters to open an account and emerges triumphantly with gun in hand. Michael Wilson in his *Michael Moore Hates America* (2004) documentary, drawing on previous critics of Moore's editing sequences, interviews the bank employees who appeared in Moore's film, claiming he misrepresented the sequence of how one got a gun from the bank. While the film suggested guns were in a vault in the bank, the Wilson documentary claimed they were really stored in another location. Carefully observing the sequence in *Bowling*, however, shows that the employees are only too happy to be in a film, and it is a bizarre piece of Americana that the bank did give out guns to new CD depositors, including Moore, thus illustrating the US's gun fetishism, and connections between guns, capitalism, and the American experience.

As this opening sequence suggests, Moore's targets in *Bowling For Columbine* are much broader and more complex than in his previous work. Indeed, the real quest of the film is to understand America itself, in particular why the country has such an obsession with guns and so much violence. Again, Moore opens the film by situating himself in relation to his topic with footage of him receiving his first gun as a youth, accompanied by "I was born in Michigan" on the soundtrack. We learn that at 15 Moore won an NRA marksman award and has been a lifelong hunter and rifle owner.

Another montage sequence introduces a fellow citizen who grew up in Michigan, Charlton Heston, who in movie scenes holds and shoots guns, and then emerges as NRA president. Moore has again developed a dialectical structure where he poses himself against a villain. The Bad Guy in *Bowling* is Charlton Heston, Moses himself. In *Roger and Me* Roger Smith incarnated corporate greed, insensitivity, and a privileged upper-class lifestyle immune to concern for the human suffering of GM employees and others in Flint devastated by the plant closings. Now, in *Bowling*, Heston represents the NRA, which attacks all restrictions on gun ownership and use, and appears at an NRA annual meeting just after the Columbine shootings, despite requests from parents of the teenagers and the mayor of the city of Denver to stay home. Heston also represents a privileged white, upper-class lifestyle, who champions guns and conservative views while living in a gated mansion above Beverly Hills.

However, *Bowling For Columbine* has a much larger tapestry to weave, making connections between US history, culture, guns, the military, violence, and racism. A section on the Michigan militia cuts to James Nichols, brother of Terry Nichols who, along with Timothy McVeigh, was responsible for the 1995 Oklahoma City bombings. While the opening on the Michigan militia was lighthearted and followed by a comedy routine of Chris Rock protesting "bullet buyers" (suggesting that bullets should be much more expensive), the Nichols section goes into a darker side of US conspiracy mavens and gun fanatics. In one section, Nichols goes off-screen into his bedroom and proves that he has a gun under his pillow by returning on-screen with gun in hand, startling Moore and the audience with the ferocity and weirdness of his behavior.

The film continues to make "six degrees of separation" connections by moving to Oscoda, Michigan, home of the Strategic Air Command, where one of the Columbine shooters grew up, while his father worked for the military. Another scene focuses on Littleton, Colorado and the Columbine shootings, and notes that Lockheed Martin, one of the US's major military contractors, is located in the city and employed the father of one of the Columbine shooters. Further, by chance, one of the heaviest bombing raids on Kosovo took place on the day of the Columbine shootings: the film cuts from President Bill Clinton announcing the Kosovo events, and then shortly thereafter addressing the Columbine shootings.

In addition to interviews and news footage that illustrate the connections, Moore uses a montage of images (accompanied by the Beatles song "Happiness is a warm gun") to depict US violence. Another sequence uses "What a wonderful world" in an ironical, Brechtian fashion[21] against a panorama of US military interventions ranging from complicity in the overthrow of democratically elected governments in Iran and Guatemala in the 1950s, to support for Osama bin Laden's group that was fighting the Soviets in Afghanistan in the 1980s and support for the Taliban in the 1990s – followed by the horrendous spectacle of 9/11.

An animated cartoon, "History of the United States," made by *South Park* creators Trey Parker and Matt Stone, also provides a historical montage of violence in the US against Native Americans, the horrors of slavery, bloodshed in the American Revolution and Civil War, and growing class division between the haves and have nots. Interviews with Stone reveal that both he and Parker were from Littleton, went to Columbine, and modeled their highly acclaimed TV show on their oppressive experiences growing up in the Colorado suburb.

These sequences and the film as a whole suggest that US history and social organization are responsible for violence. The film questions one-sided or reductive explanations of the Columbine shooting and violence in general. Moore goes through a litany of politicians and pundits who blame the Columbine shootings on heavy metal, the Internet, Hollywood and violent films, the break-up of the family, and Satan, including a rant by Senator Joseph Lieberman, who blames the shootings on youth culture and attacks rock singer Marilyn Manson. In a long interview, Manson intelligently defends himself, and makes the moralistic Lieberman come off a fool in comparison.

In one particularly strong sequence, Moore shows how the reporting of violence on local and network news makes it seem like apocalypse on a national scale. Moore interviews sociologist Barry Glassner, author of *The Culture of Fear*, in Los Angeles's fabled black neighborhood of South Central. The two discuss how the media greatly exaggerate the violence in the US, especially by scapegoating African Americans. *Bowling* features such compelling sequences that explore connections between the media and racism, while depicting in interview and montage how African Americans are victims of poverty and inner-city violence. Moore devotes a long sequence to the story of the murder of a young black girl, Kayla Owens, by a six-year-old student at Buell High School. It turns out that her mother was forced by welfare law to bus 60 miles from her Flint, Michigan home to take two minimum wage jobs in a mall; moreover, the young boy was left with a relative from whom the boy took the gun and shot the young girl. In a tense sequence, Moore confronts *American Bandstand* and TV impresario Dick Clark on how he feels about the mother of the boy working at one of his restaurants and whether he supports the law that requires welfare mothers to work at minimum wage jobs and leave their children unsupervised. Clark coldly turns away, and another American Icon is deflated with the cameras of the iconoclastic Moore.

Other sections show how youth are scapegoated in the media and subjected to humiliating surveillance and school discipline and suspension in an attempt to blame them for the maladies of US society. Interview sequences with teenagers from Columbine and other high schools show how Moore is highly sympathetic to youth. He has gained a large audience of adoring young fans, bringing documentary film and radical politics to a group not usually exposed to such fare. Indeed, there is a youthful and rebellious aura to Michael Moore's work that makes him a spokesman for alienated youth, as well as oppressed racial and class members.

Bowling For Columbine suggests that one of the major effects of the media is to generate fear that ruling politicians can exploit. While Moore makes connections between US history and military actions, guns, the media, and violence, he does not attribute causal relationships between these forces. Instead, he suggests that they interact in a complex social environment. It's not just one thing, but many things, that cause Columbine shootings and violence in the US. *Bowling For Columbine* thus provides a multidimensional and multi-causal view of violence in the United States, gun culture, and teen shootings. It is open and non-reductive and does not provide simplistic answers.[22]

This openness is apparent in one revealing sequence in which Moore interviews Tom Mauser, father of one of the Columbine victims, about why the US has more violence and gun victims than other industrialized countries. Mauser passionately asks: "What is it?!" The scene then cuts rapidly back and forth, with Moore and Mauser repeating the query, ending with Mauser saying: "I don't know." Neither is obviously able to answer the unanswerable question, and Moore's exploration of the issue does not offer simplistic or easy answers. However, his queries are able to ferret out responses like Charlton Heston's, who in the film's penultimate sequence blames violence on American history and then the country's "mixed ethnicity," suggesting a racist response.

Moore's film closes with his infamous confrontation with Heston and a montage demonstrating fear in the United States. Moore concludes: "Yes, it was a glorious time to be an American," cutting to the titles and an upbeat version of "What a wonderful world." Moore has not really found the answer to the question why there is so much gun violence in the United States. Nonetheless, *Bowling For Columbine* suggests connections between US gun culture, history, the media, political organizations and policies, US military interventions and the weapons industry, deteriorating families and living conditions, and violence. Frighteningly, as divisions increase between the rich and the poor and alienated youth cannot find meaningful jobs, this matrix of factors is likely to produce more violence, and will require systematic social change and transformation.

Moore fails to address the issue of gender and violence, however, in a country where over 90 percent of violent crime is committed by males (Katz 2006). This oversight is symptomatic of the failure of progressive males to question gender more radically, and it may express Moore's own emotional attachment to guns, which he connects, perhaps unconsciously, with his masculinity. Moore also does not make it clear that 25 times more black inner-city teens than other groups are murdered by gunfire. At the time of making the movie, "of 10,801 gun homicides in the US, 2,900 (a little more than one-fourth) involved whites; 7 in 10 involved blacks and Latinos."[23] Further, Moore's critics insist that he exaggerates per capita gun violence and murder in the US compared to other countries.

The standard conservative critique of Moore and his films, however, is that "Michael Moore hates America" and presents a wholly negative view of the US.[24] This conservative critique misses the point of who Michael Moore is and what he is doing. Moore presents a new type of personal interventionist documentary that combines personal witness to wrongdoing and an exploratory quest for answers to social problems with satire and humor and the development of his own crusading character. Moreover, he shows the United States as it is rarely seen on film and television, which tend to idealize the US as a beacon of affluence and prosperity, or as a highly functional system where (TV) cops get the bad guys and (TV) lawyers prosecute wrongdoers. Moore shows typical Americans who are overweight, undereducated, and not beautiful or glamorous. He puts on display the more freakish and bizarre aspects of Americana and the significant differences between a corrupt upper class, its political apparatus, mid-level functionaries and operatives, and the culture of class, race, gender, and age oppression. Rarely before have so many common people, so many forgotten people, but also so many varied and interesting characters, appeared on the screen in a documentary film.

Michael Moore's films thus run counter to the dominant ideology that idealizes the "American dream," and his work undercuts the fantasy representations of life in the US as shown in countless TV series, films, and the whole apparatus of advertising. In Michael Moore's probing explorations, the US appears as a very strange country with a lot of bizarre aspects to its economy, politics, culture, and everyday life. In putting on display the underside of American life, Moore is similar to his fellow documentary filmmakers Errol Morris and Ross McElwee.[25] Moore is also akin to Soviet filmmakers like Sergi Eisenstein and Dziga Vertov, who sometimes fudged on facts or historical accuracy in order to communicate larger truths and to advocate specific political positions (mentioning Moore in the same breath as Eisenstein and Vertov speaks of his brilliance as a filmmaker, as well as his leftist partisanship). And like Emile de Antonio, Moore would take on a sitting president and highly controversial war in his most widely discussed film to date, *Fahrenheit 9/11*.

Fahrenheit 9/11 and Partisan Interventionist Cinema

I've invited my fellow documentary nominees on the stage with us ... because we like non-fiction. We like non-fiction and we live in fictitious times. We live in the time where we have fictitious election results that elect a fictitious president. We live in a time where we have a man sending us to war for fictitious reasons, whether it's the fictions of duct tape or the fictions of Orange Alerts.

Michael Moore, 2002 Academy Awards ceremony[26]

Bowling For Columbine grossed almost $60 million, making it the most successful documentary in history through 2002. While it received top honors at the Cannes Film Festival and Academy Awards, and was voted the top documentary of all time by the IDA, it also received fierce criticism. Moore was now identifying himself as a documentary filmmaker making non-fiction films in an era with a fictive president in a specious war undertaken for false reasons. In an era marked by one of the most mendacious presidents and administrations in US history, Moore felt it was important to provide an all-out assault on the Bush-Cheney administration, including evoking the stolen election of 2000,[27] and George W. Bush's limitations and failures as president.

Fahrenheit 9/11 stands as Moore's most interventionist film, taking on the sitting president George W. Bush and his Iraq War during the 2004 election season. While *Roger and Me* bore witness to the assault on working-class jobs and lives in the Flint, Michigan area and implicated General Motors in socioeconomic deterioration, there was not really an effort to change these conditions. Likewise, *Bowling For Columbine* came up with no answers or agenda; in fact, Moore seemed genuinely surprised and delighted when Wal-mart executives announced they would no longer sell 17 cent bullets, following Moore's visit to their Michigan headquarters with two surviving victims of the Columbine shootings.

It is clear, however, that Moore intended *Fahrenheit 9/11* to be an important and perhaps decisive influence on the highly contested 2004 presidential election. These exalted aims are made clear in the foreword by John Berger and introduction by Moore to *The Official Fahrenheit 9/11 Reader* (2004), which contains the film script, reviews, and documentation of some of the controversial claims and segments in the film. Berger asserts *Fahrenheit 9/11* "may be making a very small contribution toward the changing of world history.... What makes it an event is the fact that it is an effective and independent intervention into immediate world politics." Moore described the tumultuous response to the film, the thousands of emails that poured into his website, and claimed: "In an election year where the presidency could be decided by a few thousand votes, these comments were profound – and frightening to the Bush White House."

While the film was immensely popular, it also evoked fierce criticism, perhaps unparalleled in documentary film history, unleashing the entire right wing against Moore, and many mainstream critics as well.[28] In *Fahrenheit 9/11*, Moore continued to develop his own unique form of documentary film, serving as narrator and intervening occasionally in the action. While *Bowling For Columbine* examined a complex of issues centered around guns and violence, *Fahrenheit 9/11* focused more intensely on the personality and politics of the Bush-Cheney administration and in particular its exploitation of 9/11. As in his earlier films, there was a centerpiece villain who was the target of Moore's scorn and critical animus: this time, it was the president of the United States. In taking on George W. Bush and the American presidency, Moore was going after his biggest target so far. The controversy over the film, as well as the fact that it became the largest grossing and arguably most influential documentary in history, provided an index of Moore's success in provoking his audience and promoting debate over issues of key importance.[29]

Playing on the title of Ray Bradbury's novel about book-burning, *Fahrenheit 451*, *Fahrenheit 9/11* refers to "the temperature at which truth burns." The first section of the film takes on George W. Bush, beginning with his stolen presidency after the Florida election fiasco of 2000, and then going back through his checkered career and failures in the oil industry, investigation by the securities exchange for insider stock trading, failure to fulfill his National Guard service, and his family connections with the Saudis, followed by Bush-Cheney administration neglect of warnings about terrorism prior to 9/11, and Bush's slacking at his ranch and family vacation sites before 9/11. Other segments document Bush-Cheney administration responses to the 9/11 attacks, how they and the media generated fear, and how the administration manipulated that fear.

The film opens with fireworks exploding and Moore musing "Was it just a dream?" A sudden camera movement cuts to Al Gore campaigning in Florida. After a quick review of the Supreme Court intervention for Bush, a contested inauguration, and the appalling failure of the US Senate to support black congressional calls for investigation of election irregularities, an astonishing title sequence unfolds, showing members of the Bush-Cheney administration – Bush, Cheney, Rumsfeld, Rice, Ashcroft, and Wolfowitz – being made-up for a televised statement or photo-op.

The sequence suggests that the administration is a product of artifice and scripted theater (and in the case of Wolfowitz, unseemly hair management). Although the images are comic and deflating, sinister music and off-center close-ups help convey the threat and danger of the highly secretive and rarely exposed mechanics of Bush-Cheney administration image production.

After documenting the first nine months of the administration, when it appeared to be losing its agenda and support and seemed to be collapsing, Moore queries what should a guy do whose presidency is in so much trouble so soon, and answers: "He went on vacation." While a montage of images shows Bush golfing, yachting, and playing cowboy at his Texas "ranch," accompanied by a jaunty country music soundtrack, we learn that Bush spent 42 percent of his time prior to 9/11 on vacation, away from the White House.

Moore chose to represent the 9/11 attack on the World Trade Center with a black screen and horrified voices responding to the tragedy, before cutting to show how it affected a wide range of ordinary people. He then intervenes as narrator, describing 9/11 and revealing that he had a friend killed that day. Moore presents highly revealing images of Bush, such as those of him sitting aimlessly for seven minutes after being told that the nation was under terrorist attack, while "My Pet Goat" was read to a grade school class. Bush is later shown making a statement to reporters on fighting terrorism and then seamlessly shifting to take a golf shot, telling the group to "watch my drive." Moore shows him clowning and smirking before announcing to the nation that he'd just attacked Iraq. These images of Bush were shocking because most audiences had not seen such negative or revealing images of him before, portraying Bush as superficial, smug and smirkish, arrogant and incompetent. After 9/11, criticism of the presidency was taboo and the media served as a propaganda machine for the Bush-Cheney administration's "war on terror," a point Moore makes with a montage of media clips.[30]

The right wing went on ferocious attack, screaming that Moore was making false claims about connections between the Bush and bin Laden families and other Saudis, and about connections between oil companies, Bush-Cheney administration officials and US foreign policy. For them, the film was a pack of lies.[31] However, Moore did not make specific causal claims, but instead pointed to connections and raised questions for the viewer to unravel and interpret. While his critics generally had a reductive and positivist mindset that claimed Moore was making specific dogmatic claims and arguments, in fact his vision is more dialectical, focusing on connections between factors that interact in overdetermined and complicated ways. Moreover, Moore was raising issues that had not been discussed: US support for bin Laden and Saddam Hussein in the 1980s, relations between the Bush family and the Saudis, the failures of the Bush-Cheney administration to address terrorism before 9/11, and its problematic policies in the aftermath. While the film does not follow a chronological sequence (the second half especially jumps back and forth between different time periods), Moore does not noticeably juggle time sequences to make narrative and political points, as he sometimes did in his earlier films. While admitting that the film was highly partisan, Moore also published *The Official Fahrenheit 9/11 Reader* (2004) to document claims made in the film.

Moore brilliantly demonstrates the contradictory directives of the Bush-Cheney administration's manipulation of 9/11, with Bush telling people to be happy, to travel, and to go to Disneyland for a vacation, while dark warnings from Cheney and Rumsfeld evoke fears of terrorism and a long brutal war. Congressman Jim McDermott (D-Wash) characterizes these mixed messages as "crazy making," for the American people are told to do two contradictory things at once.[32] Other contradictions Moore points out are the administration promoting fear of terrorism on the one hand and cutting back counterterrorist budgets on the other, allowing lighters and matches to be carried on planes but not bottles of milk for babies, and extolling the heroism of young US soldiers in Iraq while cutting back on veterans' benefits and healthcare.

Michael Moore on the Iraq Invasion

The second half of *Fahrenheit 9/11* focuses intently on the Bush-Cheney administration's intervention into Iraq. After portraying Bush clowning in front of the camera before announcing the military assault on Iraq, a brief sequence shows a peaceful country suddenly under heavy bombardment. Other images are of US soldiers on patrol assaulting ordinary Iraqis in Samarra, hyped up on adrenaline and heavy metal before attack, and brutalizing Iraqi prisoners. Much of the film's audience had never seen such shocking images of Iraq and were horrified.

Moore was criticized for showing an idyllic Iraq on the eve of the devastating assault on the country, but the sequence allowed a contrast between life before and after the invasion and provoked empathy for audiences to consider how they would respond to an attack on their country. Moreover, the Iraq segment anticipated revelations that Iraqi weapons of mass destruction did not exist. It also presciently anticipated how the Iraq intervention would be a fiasco for the Iraqis and Americans, as it previewed the Abu Ghraib scandal of US soldiers sexually humiliating Iraqi prisoners.[33] In addition, the film exposed the lies used to sell and justify the intervention, and the ways US troops would be brutalized and made to pay the costs of the war with life and limb.

Although Moore was attacked for these negative images of US troops, the last half of the Iraq segment contains very sympathetic presentations of the US military victims of the war. It makes clear that, in addition to Iraqis, it was poor and working-class young Americans who were traumatized, mutilated, and killed. Cutting to Flint, Michigan to illustrate military recruitment of working-class and African-American youth for the Iraq War, a long sequence introduces Lila Lipscomb, a middle-aged woman who had risen from welfare mother to executive assistant at a jobs center. Lila tells how her daughter and son had joined the military, and her patriotism is demonstrated by showing the daily flag-raising at her house. Then it is revealed that her son was killed in Iraq, and the footage captures the aftermath for the mother and her extended family. In one scene Lila shows Moore a multi-colored and multicultural cross – subsequent shots reveal that her own family is multiracial and rainbow colored. Again, Moore shows great sympathy for class and race victims of US policies and takes their side against the powers that be.

After demonstrating how the Bush-Cheney administration manipulated 9/11 and the horrific Iraq catastrophe, Moore concludes with the villains of the piece: George W. Bush and the congressmen who urged the war. In one of his trademark confrontational episodes, Moore goes after congressmen who supported the war, asking them if they'd like to send their children to Iraq, highlighting again that it is the sons and daughters of the working class who are the fodder and victims of the elite.

Closing sections of *Fahrenheit 9/11* show a Halliburton ad touting its role in Iraq, revealing that the company, of which Dick Cheney was a former CEO, was garnering billions in no-bid contracts. Businessmen are seen at a conference on how to make money in Iraq, getting "a piece of the action." In a memorable sequence, the audience is shown George W. Bush addressing a group of "the haves and the have mores," telling them: "Some people call you the elite, while I call you my base!" Although this self-mocking humor is characteristic of the traditional Alfred E. Smith memorial dinner held to raise money for Catholic charities, it reveals the anti-populist thrust of the Bush-Cheney administration. The film ends with a flustered Bush trying to finish the old "fool me once" saying, finally blustering, "Fool me, can't get fooled again." Michael Moore concludes: "For once, I agree with him." The film then cuts to the credits, accompanied by Neil Young's "Rocking in the free world."

Moore's film is thus a fierce assault on the Bush-Cheney administration, using satire and parody to mock the president and his administration, raise questions about its connections to corporate elites, the military-industrial complex, and Middle East oil interests, and demonstrate the horrific effects of the Iraq War. Moore's intervention was highly ambitious: while it failed to attain its political dream of removing an incumbent president, it was recognized as one of the most popular, daring, and controversial documentary films of all time. Conservatives objected to Moore's critique of the Bush-Cheney administration and its "disrespectful" presentation of Bush. Moore used his celebrity status to campaign against Bush in the 2004 election, then temporarily retired from public view, while working on a documentary on the health system, *Sicko*, released in 2007, and *Slacker Uprising*, released in 2008, available for free Internet downloads before the 2008 election. By 2008, Michael Moore was once again intervening in public life, frequently appearing on television and in other media.

Conservative Critique

The rightwing response to *Fahrenheit 9/11* included documentaries attacking Moore and his work. Two of them were rushed into production to compete for attention and influence with Moore's film before the 2004 presidential election, in recognition that Moore's polemic might influence US electoral politics.

Celsius 41.11, produced by Lionel Chetwynd and Ted Steinberg, and directed by Kevin Knoblock, puts on display the utter intellectual and political bankruptcy of the pro-Bush-Cheney Republican right. While the movie purports to be a critique of *Fahrenheit 9/11*, it merely has a few grainy video images of Moore and some uncontextualized quotes that make him out to be an ultra-extremist. The film is a highly didactic anti-Kerry and pro-Bush diatribe, valuable mainly as a compendium of the Big Lies of the Bush-Cheney era, including fervent declarations by various rightwing ideologues about the connections between al Qaeda and

Iraq and the existence of Iraqi weapons of mass destruction. Michael Ledeen even goes so far as to state that Iraq tried to obtain nuclear-grade yellow cake uranium from Niger, despite the failure of earlier official global intelligence reports to find any evidence for this (papers appearing to document the transaction were forgeries; see Wilson 2004).

Fahrenhype 9/11 is another rush job put out before the 2004 election. Director Alan Peterson and writer Dick Morris set out to savage Moore and *Fahrenheit 9/11*, and make the case for Bush and against Kerry. The first part of the film uses repeated footage of the 9/11 attacks and talking heads like former New York Mayor Ed Koch, actor Ron Silver, and Senator Zell Miller (all one-time Democrats) to evoke the horror of 9/11 and to argue that Michael Moore underplays the threat of terrorism – a misfired critique since Moore does not underplay terrorist threats in the film. The middle part scores some small points against details in *Fahrenheit 9/11*, while the last laborious and tortured segment features Iraq War veterans and their families criticizing Moore for being unfair to US troops.

In *Michael Moore Hates America* (2004), novice filmmaker Mike Wilson undertakes to present Moore as un-American and to expose the fallacious elements of his documentary style and editing. Curiously, Wilson slavishly imitates Moore, using the same strategy as *Roger and Me* to stalk Moore and trap him into an interview. Like Moore, Wilson uses ingratiating personal narration to tell the viewer what he is doing and put himself in the center of the film. Like Moore, Wilson stresses his working-class background. While he wants to demonstrate that Moore has a one-sided and overly negative view of American life, Wilson's story of his working-class father continually being laid off by greedy corporations illustrates one of Moore's major arguments. Wilson's film also deconstructs itself: it criticizes Moore for deception in his interviews and not explaining what he is really doing, yet Wilson shows himself reluctant to tell his subjects that he is making a film called *Michael Moore Hates America*. This title alone undercuts Wilson's purported call for a more civil public sphere in which individuals can discuss differences without hostility or nastiness. To Wilson's credit, he shows himself embarrassed by his manipulative techniques. After interviewing the shrill rightwing ideologue and former communist David Horowitz, Wilson admits to feeling uncomfortable with such rigidity and aggressiveness.

Wilson scores his most effective points when interviewing subjects of Moore's films who complain that his editing misrepresented events. For example, Wilson interviews bank employees shown in *Bowling For Columbine*. While Moore appears to walk into the bank, open an account, and triumphantly walk out with a new gun, the employees claim that Moore manipulated the sequence of events and presented the scenes out of chronological order – criticisms already made of Moore's films by Harlan Jacobson, which Moore attempted to answer.[34]

While Wilson imitates Moore's own films and raises questions about Moore's documentary techniques and editing, Larry Elder's *Michael and Me* (2004) presents a mean-spirited assault against Moore's "message" that America "has too many guns." In a highly polemical rant, Elder interviews subject after subject on the importance of personal gun ownership and the NRA, while attacking Moore's position on the problem. Elder's film is completely dishonest, however, for it does not really present Elder's relation to Moore, outside of an opening shot where he ambushes Moore at an airport, camera in hand, to rant in favor of gun ownership. Moreover, Elder does not really present Moore's complex position on guns and violence, or his aesthetic strategies in *Bowling For Columbine* or other films, but simply engages in a highly repetitive tirade. While Moore's films are fast-moving, entertaining, and rich in content, Elder employs boring talking head interviews that go on and on, making the same rightwing pro-gun arguments with little other footage or relief from the hectoring. Elder dishonestly reduces Moore's argument in *Bowling For Columbine* to claiming there are "too many guns in America," while Moore presents a whole range of issues and provocations. In the one sequence where the dour Elder attempts humor, he presents a short animation that nastily caricatures Moore and reduces him to a cartoonish clown. In a film that purports to be about Michael Moore, barely two minutes are devoted to him. Instead, for 90 minutes, we are treated to a dishonest, aggressive, mean-spirited, and vile conservative rant typical of the vicious attacks gun fanatics launch when anyone questions gun laws in the US.[35]

As 2008 drew to a close and any conservative should have been ashamed to support the infamy of the Bush-Cheney regime, David Zucker released a satirical assault on Michael Moore called *An American Carol*. Zucker completely misrepresents Moore's views, indulges in the worst imaginable racist stereotypes, and uses the trope of American ghosts of General Patton, John F. Kennedy, and George Washington, who, with the help of Bill O'Reilly, persuade Moore of the errors of his ways in a contrived fictive scenario. The film bombed at the box office, its poor excuse for a satire demonstrating how laughable and irrelevant sections of the Hollywood right have become.

Sicko and the Michael Moore Genre

My films are a work of journalism, but they're journalism of the op-ed page.... [My job] is not to present all sides. My job is to present my side.

Michael Moore[36]

Moore's work is highly partisan and interventionist, asserting specific political positions, as well as attempting to inform and entertain. Broadly speaking, one can classify documentary/non-fiction films as either openly *partisan*, seeking to address a specific issue and offer a position, or claiming to be *non-partisan*, seeking to gain the truth about a situation by minimizing biases, presuppositions, or a set agenda.[37] Thus, within the documentary tradition, there are filmmakers who aspire to a norm of maximum objectivity, contrasted to those who insert themselves in a non-objective partisan camp. The films of Michael Moore obviously fall into the latter category and have given rise to assaults on his work largely by supporters of the concept of documentary he opposes, or those opposed to his politics.

I have argued that a Michael Moore film is different from the tradition of documentaries governed by ideals of objectivity and non-partisanship. In Moore's films there is also more of an interaction between documentary and entertainment, fact and narrative, and archival/shot footage and creative editing than in non-partisan documentaries. His films' entertainment value obviously accounts for their success, while many people identify with and applaud the Michael Moore character and love to see him confront the bad guys and uncover corporate or political wrongdoing. Moore is one of the few US filmmakers who is consistently critical of corporate capitalism and who explore class differences and oppression in the United States. His personal witness to problems and his presentation of them from his own point of view produces a much more subjective and interventionist text than is found in a non-partisan and "objectivist" documentary tradition.

Moreover, while one can quibble with some facts and editing sequences in Moore's films, his cinema portrays larger truths neglected by other filmmakers and the media industry, such as the fact that corporate restructuring and downsizing has been creating great misery for the working class and devastating communities. Moore was also one of the first to raise questions about George W. Bush's competency, an issue that entered the mainstream after his inadequate response to Hurricane Katrina and the economic collapse of 2009.[38]

Moore's *Sicko* (2007) combines the defining features of specific Michael Moore films that I have delineated and thus builds on his previous filmmaking. The film opens with Moore bearing witness to working-class and middle-class people who do not have adequate health insurance and the problems this creates. Moore sees inadequate healthcare as a major social problem in the US and shows how the corporate health-medical complex, the insurance industry, and conservative politicians conspire to keep an inadequate system in place. Moore then goes on a quest to discover if there are better health systems in other Western countries, visiting Canada, the UK, and France, and demonstrating that their national health services are highly popular and effective, without the bureaucratic red tape and inequities that plague the US system. In perhaps the film's most humorous extended episode, Moore goes to Guantanamo Bay, Cuba, suggesting prisoners there get better healthcare than average Americans. In a personal intervention, he takes into Cuba some non-governmental emergency workers who voluntarily served at the New York 9/11 Ground Zero site and who were not able to obtain adequate healthcare in the US, and Moore helps get them treatment from Cuban doctors.

Sicko is one of Moore's most radical films, attacking the presuppositions of a capitalist dog-eat-dog society where individuals are forced to secure healthcare on their own, and where only the rich and fortunate are able to do so. Moore takes on the laissez-faire logic that the market should dictate the terms and availability of such crucial services, and shows how other countries operate their health systems on a completely different basis. In extended sequences, Moore challenges the rationales for America's health systems by showing that many of our neighbors have a completely different view of the world, one that believes that in a truly just and healthy society everyone should have adequate healthcare.

As with Moore's other films, *Sicko* is rich with detail, information, and insights into relations between often-overlooked economic, political, and cultural forces, and in an accessible and entertaining format. Moore's critics often harp on small points of fact that are usually a matter of interpretation, or simply engage in broadside ideological critique from an

Michael Moore is an American original with his persona of Everyman and his ubiquitous baseball hat, speaking truth to power.

opposing partisan position. Many of these critics fail to see there is a longstanding and honorable partisan filmmaking tradition and that films can legitimately intervene in specific political contexts and hit specific targets without having to be "fair and balanced" – itself an ideological construct, as with the Fox News Channel.

Michael Moore is an American original, combining the crusading idealism of JFK liberalism with leftwing anti-corporate populism; the comic antics of the Yippies with the more performance oriented left, still visible in the anti-corporate globalization movement. Moore is as American as apple pie with his baseball caps, oversized body and ego, often disheveled appearance, and ability to continually redefine himself and come out on top. While Moore exposes some of the seamier and more freakish aspects of American life, and takes on major institutions and the corporate and political elite, he also embodies and presents in his films good, decent, common people, confused individuals overwhelmed by circumstances – a whole panorama of American characters portrayed in the tradition of Diane Arbus, Errol Morris, and R. Crumb.

Michael Moore himself is a complex character. Biographies, articles, and news stories written about him portray both admirable and less admirable features of his personality and work. Moore is a large character, embodying many opposites and many contradictions. He is highly controversial, intensely polarizing, and extremely partisan. Yet his works raise important questions, make connections overlooked in conventional media, provoke discussion and inquiry, and rarely fail to entertain those willing to enter his cinematic universe.

Notes

1 Michael Moore in an article by Ron Hutcheson, *Knight-Ridder/Tribune Service*, June 23, 2004, cited in Toplin (2006: 80).
2 As of January 2, 2009, *Bowling For Columbine* had grossed over $58,008,423 worldwide, while *Fahrenheit 9/11* had grossed over $222,446,882 (www.boxofficemojo.com).
3 I use a broad conception of documentary as non-fiction films concerned with depicting actual events, but the concept of documentary contains many different types of film, competing definitions, and a wealth of categories. As I will argue, Moore undercuts many traditional notions of documentary cinema, while drawing on strategies in a partisan radical film tradition, ultimately producing his own genre of Michael Moore film. For helpful comments on earlier drafts of this chapter, I want to thank Rhonda Hammer, Jeff Share, Richard Kahn, Charles Reitz, and, especially, Matthew Bernstein, who provided many useful sources and editorial suggestions.
4 De Antonio's films include *Point of Order* (1963), a brilliantly edited montage of the Army/McCarthy hearings; *Rush to Judgment* (1964), a provocative documentary on the Kennedy assassination; *In the Year of the Pig* (1969), a major documentary on the Vietnam War; *America is Hard to See* (1970), an excellent depiction of Eugene McCarthy's campaign for the presidency in 1968 which catches the political turmoil of the era; *Millhouse* (1971), a scathing indictment of Richard Nixon which won de Antonio a place of honor as the only filmmaker on Nixon's infamous "enemies list"; *Painter's Painting* (1972), a set of interviews with the luminaries of the New York art scene; *Underground* (1976), a documentary about the Weather Underground Organization which reflects on the radical movements of the 1960s; *In the King of Prussia* (1982), which deals with the 1980 attempt by the Berrigan brothers and a group of Catholic activists, the Plowshare Eight, to call attention to nuclear madness by splashing blood on the cones of nuclear weapons in an assembly factory in King of Prussia, Pennsylvania; and *Mr. Hoover and I* (1989), which tells de Antonio's life story, utilizing his FBI files, which amounted to tens of thousands of pages of material culled by means of the Freedom of Information Act. For more on de Antonio, see the introduction to Kellner and Streible (2000).

5   On modernism as a tradition in the arts that advocates a perpetual innovation of form while engaging with the modern world, see Berman (1981).

6   I am drawing on several books that provide overviews of Michael Moore's life and work, including the accessible introductory studies by Schulz (2005) and Larner (2005), which provide both critique and good political contextualization of Moore's biography and work. Larner's subsequent book on Moore, however, *Forgive Us Our Spins: Michael Moore and the Future of the Left* (2006), presents a highly problematical critique of Moore. Larner recycles old criticisms of Moore and assembles some new ones, but as I will argue in this chapter, he completely fails to understand Moore's aesthetic strategy and has a highly flawed view of contemporary politics, as Moore's views of the Bush-Cheney administration, Afghanistan and Iraq wars, and the Republican administration's subservience to corporate capitalism appear vindicated by subsequent history. In addition to these sources, I draw on a vast amount of film scholarship and Internet material on Moore, as well as his own books. In fact, Moore appears to be the best-documented and most controversial documentary filmmaker in history.

7   On *cinéma vérité* in the United States, see Mamber (1974).

8   See Emile Antonio, "Conversation with Bruce Jackson," at www.sensesofcinema.com/contents/04/31/emile_de_antonio.html (accessed August 18, 2006).

9   On mechanical reproduction in film and photography, see Benjamin (1969: 217–52). On the myth of objectivity in journalism, see Michael Schudson, *The Power of News* (Cambridge, MA: Harvard University Press, 1996).

10 Moore has said: "There's a myth of objectivity out there, whether it's a documentary or the *Philadelphia Inquirer*. We're subjective beings by nature. Even the decision of what to put in the paper, where to place it – it's all subjective." Cited in Lawrence (2004: 98).

11 Michael Moore, *Australian Financial Review*, May 4, 1990. Cited in Lawrence (2004: 110).

12 On the *Rashamon*-esque story of Michael Moore's short sojourn at *Mother Jones*, the major radical monthly publication, when Moore was hired and then fired in 1986, see the different accounts assembled in Schulz (2005: 39–60) and Larner (2005: 46–66).

13 Moore has reportedly said that Terrence Rafferty's *The Atomic Café* is the only film that influenced him (see Schulz 2005: 64), and has never, so far as I know, discussed de Antonio's work. Rafferty himself was influenced by de Antonio and thanked him in credits on *The Atomic Café*.

14 On the Stecco story, see Schulz (2005: 81ff) and Larner (2006: 74–8).

15 See Harlan Jacobson, "Michael and me," *Film Comment*, 25, 6 (1989). This text is the mother-lode of the anti-Michael Moore industry, with the pathetic Larry Elder even taking its title for his "documentary" assault on Moore.

For later critique of the sequencing of Moore's Flint narrative, see Schultz (2005: 61ff), Larner (2006: 66ff), and Hardy and Clarke (2004: 17ff). For a sharp critique of Jacobson's failure to grasp Moore's documentary aesthetic and Jacobson's rather old-fashioned perspective on documentary, see Toplin (2006: 26ff).

16 See Michael Moore in Jacobson, "Michael and Me."

17 For critique of Moore's depiction of some working-class people in the film, see Pauline Kael, "Melodrama/cartoon/mess," *The New Yorker*, January 8, 1990: 90–3.

18 Michael Moore, *USA Today*, October 11, 2002, quoted in Lawrence (2004: 58).

19 As of May 30, 2009, *Roger and Me* had grossed $6,706,368; see www.boxofficemojo.com/movies/?id=rogerandme.htm.

20 For my own take on the Columbine school shootings, see Kellner (2008).

21 On "Brecht's Marxist aesthetic," see Kellner (1997). Moore effectively uses Brechtian "separation of elements," ironically playing off soundtrack and music against image and narrative. Like Brecht, he also makes strongly political works. However, I have found no evidence in interviews with Moore or anywhere else that he was directly influenced by Brecht.

22 Moore's rightwing critics and Larner (2006) constantly claim that Moore is making reductive causal claims, whereas in fact his dialectical cinema makes connections between different phenomena and in good modernist fashion forces viewers to raise questions and make connections themselves.

23 See Mike Males, " 'Bowling For Columbine' misframes gun quandry," November 6, 2002, at www.home.earthlink.net/~mmales/bowling.htm (accessed September 28, 2008).

24 See the anti-Moore films by Mike Wilson, *Michael Moore Hates America* (2004), and Larry Elder, *Michael and Me* (2004), discussed below, or the attacks on Moore in Hardy and Clarke (2004).

25 Morris has made nine highly acclaimed documentaries, including *The Thin Blue Line* (1988), *Mr. Death* (1999), and *The Fog of War* (2003): see www.imdb.com/name/nm0001554/. McElwee's 12 documentaries include *Sherman's March* (1986), *Time Indefinite* (1994), and *Bright Leaves* (2003). See www.imdb.com/name/nm0568478/ (accessed September 28, 2008).

26 Quoted in Lawrence (2004: 51).

27 For my take on the 2000 election and first nine months of the Bush presidency, see Kellner (2001). Toplin (2006: 91ff) provides a judicious and balanced appraisal of Moore's claims about the Bush presidency, conservative critiques, and counterarguments.

28 See Brock (2004). After his 2002 Oscar acceptance speech Moore stated: "For the next couple of months I could not walk down the street without

some form of serious abuse. Threats of physical violence, people wanting to fight me, right in my face, 'F– YOU! You're a traitor!' People pulling over in their cars screaming. People spitting on the sidewalk. I finally stopped going out." *Entertainment Weekly*, July 9, 2004, cited in Lawrence (2004: 52).

29 Toplin (2006) even-handedly presents the conservative critique of the film and deals with criticisms in terms of the failure of many conservative critics to understand Moore's unique brand of filmmaking and the partisan reaction against his leftwing politics. Moore (2004) presents his own defense of the film and answers to his critics; see also his website: www.fahrenheit911. com/library/book/index.php.

30 For my take on the 9/11 terror attacks and how the media promoted Bush-Cheney administration policy without raising serious questions or debate, see Kellner (2003a, 2005).

31 See the attacks in Hardy and Clarke (2004), which includes Christopher Hitchens' demagogic and vicious assault on Moore and *Fahrenheit 9/11*. Toplin (2006: ch. 3) critically dissects the rightwing critique of Moore.

32 Thanks to Rhonda Hammer for pointing out to me the use of paradoxical injunctions in Michael Moore's films. For discussion of how paradoxical injunctions, double-binds, and the manipulation of fear can make people crazy, see Paul Watzlawick, Janet Beavin, and Don Jackson, *Pragmatics of Human Communication* (New York: Norton, 1967).

33 These photos were the subject of Errol Morris's documentary *Standard Operating Procedure* (2008); for my interpretation of the photos and their effects, see Kellner (2005); for discussion of Morris's film, see chapter 5.

34 For critique of this argument begun by Jacobson, see note 15, above. Larner (2006: 175f) fails to see the close connections with Moore's aesthetic and persona in Wilson's feeble attempt to imitate Moore. He bizarrely valorizes Wilson over Moore, claiming that the young novice filmmaker has "completely mastered" the art of making positive statements about American life and connecting with the people (p. 207). In the spirit of Wilson and Larner, Canadian documentary filmmakers Rick Caine and Debbie Melnyk made an anti-Moore doc *Manufacturing Dissent* (2007), which repeats the standard criticism of Moore's life and films, and adds some pungent Moore-bashing by disgruntled former employees and hypercritical critics. Yet the film does not really add anything substantial to the Moore controversy and has little that is new about Moore.

35 For my own take on guns and violence in the contemporary US, see Kellner (2008).

36 Michael Moore in Rene Rodriguez, "Controversial Moore documentary stirring up passions for both sides," *Miami Herald*, June 24, 2004, quoted in Toplin (2006: 80).

37   Toplin (2006) makes a similar distinction and has a chapter on the partisan and engaged documentary tradition in which Moore's work should be situated and interpreted (pp. 71ff).

38   On Hurricane Katrina and the Bush presidency, see Douglas Kellner, "Hurricane spectacles and the crisis of the Bush presidency," *Flow*, 3, 3 (October 2005) at www.jot.communication.utexas.edu/flow/?jot=view&id=1049; and Henry Giroux, *Stormy Weather: Katrina and the Politics of Disposability* (Boulder: Paradigm Press, 2006).

4

Hollywood Political Critiques of the Bush-Cheney Regime
From Thrillers to Fantasy and Satire

An exceptional number of films of the 2000s directly or indirectly launched cinematic weapons at the Bush-Cheney administration. It was almost as if a film had to take a dig at the Republican administration and its policies if it was to be taken seriously, even as popular entertainment. *Pirates of the Caribbean 3: At World's End* (2007), for instance, opens ominously with authorities intoning that *habeas corpus* has been suspended, martial law imposed, and the outcasts are to be summarily executed – a chilling reminder of Bush-Cheney administration "justice." Scores of scruffy people are being hanged, presumably without trial, because they have been accused of consorting with pirates. This is an obvious coding of pirates as terrorists and of the established regime as repressive and murderous. The *Pirates of the Caribbean* films thus have a slightly subversive bent, as they sympathize with outsiders and attack established authorities.

Another popular entertainment, *Transformers* (2007), a story of alien robotic forces invading the US, mocks George W. Bush himself. A twangy Texan voice blurts out that he knows what the invading forces are and "we know what to do with 'em," when in fact he has no idea about the robots or what to do about their threats to the country. The Bush figure's buffoonish character is emphasized when he asks one of his female assistants "could you wrangle me up some ding dongs, darlin'?" which alludes to Bush's philistine food habits. The woman complains to an associate that she didn't take a government job to carry out such dumb requests. Throughout, an official announces the president is taking decisive measures to deal with the invasion, which is obviously hot air and empty spin.

The X-Files: I Want to Believe (2008) presents prominently displayed pictures on the wall of George W. Bush and J. Edgar Hoover when Mulder and Scully return to Washington FBI headquarters after many years of retirement. The camera zooms in for a close-up of Bush, as the eerie *X-Files* theme plays. A sharp discordant note coincides with a cut to a wide shot that catches the portraits of Bush and Hoover, linking the two as frightening figures in US history.[1]

Harold and Kumar Escape from Guantanamo (2008) has two post-ethnic stoners arrested on a fake terrorism charge and sent to the infamous prison in Guantanamo, Cuba, from which they escape and engage in a cross-country tour to exonerate themselves. They are pursued by fanatical and utterly incompetent Homeland Security officials. En route, they encounter no less than George W. Bush himself, with whom they smoke some weed and discover that underneath we are all humans with the same desires and needs (and Daddy problems).

Satirical and critical cinematic slams at Bush were made until the end of his presidency. Peter Segal's satire of the spy genre and popular TV series *Get Smart* (2008) has the super-secret spy agency Control in fear of getting shut down by the ultra-controlling vice-president (read Dick Cheney). When we see the president, he is reading to school children (as Bush famously did on the morning of the 9/11 attacks). He asks what the vice-president has said about issues on which decisions are needed, not having a clue himself about what is going on. He is seen laughing inanely during the disruption of a classical music concert at the Los Angeles Disney Music Center, where Maxwell Smart (Steve Carell) and company prevent a nuclear bomb explosion. And, as I indicate below, even the satirical *The Simpsons: The Movie* (2007), based on the popular TV series, cannot resist taking shots at the current Republican regime, as well as Arnold Schwarzenegger.

In chapter 2, I discussed how some Hollywood political thrillers initially responded to the 9/11 attacks in largely apolitical or conservative fashion. In this chapter, by contrast, I argue that certain Hollywood political thrillers offer barely disguised allegorical critiques of the Bush-Cheney regime, ranging from Jonathan Demme's 2004 remake of *The Manchurian Candidate* and the *Bourne* trilogy films (2002, 2004, 2007) to Stephen Gaghan's *Syriana* (2005), which critically engages the complexity of global politics, and the ways that US oil corporations, and intelligence and government agencies, intervene in the politics of the region, often in a destructive and utterly immoral fashion. To be sure, the anti-Bush-Cheney political thrillers are countered by other films that replicate and celebrate the administration's interventionist policies, and so in this chapter I will also contrast conservative thrillers with more politically critical ones.

The Hollywood Political Thriller Against the Bush-Cheney Regime

The political thriller is often a conservative genre that idealizes government officials or intelligence agents pitted against Evil Enemies in a Manichean duality of Good vs. Evil, in which the country of the film's origin embodies goodness. There are exceptions to this, such as political conspiracy films of the 1970s like *The Parallax View, Three Days of the Condor,* and *All the President's Men,* which pitted good individuals against an evil state, reflecting public beliefs during the Vietnam and Nixon era that the state was a locus of corruption and wrongdoing (see Kellner and Ryan 1988). During the Bush-Cheney era, not surprisingly, the political thriller often took a left turn, pitting moral and righteous individuals against corrupt and depraved government officials.

Political thrillers often catch the fears, paranoia, and fantasies of their era. Richard Condon's 1950s novel *The Manchurian Candidate* and the 1962 film version could be read as a conservative-paranoid anti-communist Cold War thriller. The 1962 film showed evil Chinese commies brainwashing young Americans to turn them into diabolical tools of communist world domination. In the film's chilling finale, a young American brainwashed during the Korean War in Manchuria is poised to assassinate the presidential candidate so that the vice-president, whose wife is a communist agent, can ascend to the presidency.

Jonathan Demme's 2004 version of *The Manchurian Candidate*, by contrast, features Gulf War soldiers subjected to genetically engineered mind control experiments by a malevolent US corporate conglomerate named Manchurian Global, modeled after the Carlyle Group or Dick Cheney's Halliburton. The film opens in Kuwait in 1991 with a troop of ambushed GIs, then cuts to the present. A somewhat robotic Lt. Ben Marco (Denzel Washington) is lecturing to various groups on his war experiences and intoning that Sgt. Raymond Shaw (Liv Schreiber), with whom he served and who received a Medal of Honor, was "one of the finest and bravest men" he'd ever met. A deeply disturbed member of Marco's unit (Jeffrey Wright) appears at one of his lectures and tells him afterwards of his dreams about their Kuwait experience. These tell a very

Jonathan Demme's *Manchurian Candidate* has a malevolent US corporate conglomerate as villain.

different story about Shaw, whose fable of heroism has helped propel him on a sky-rocketing political career.

The film then cuts to a political convention, where Shaw's ambitious mother Eleanor (Meryl Streep) – a powerful senator and daughter of a major industrialist – is pushing the party toward accepting her son as vice-presidential candidate. Her opponent, Senator Tom Jordan (John Voight), is an internationalist liberal who opposes militarism and the cutting back of civil liberties in the US. He is an obvious Good Liberal standing up to policies readily identified with the Bush-Cheney administration. In the intricate plot, Eleanor Shaw gets the party to name her son as the vice-presidential candidate. In cahoots with Manchurian Global, she helps manipulate her son's brain implant to impel him to kill Jordan and his daughter (who was Shaw's only love interest, a relationship quashed by his mother).

Demme's *Manchurian Candidate* articulates fears about giant corporations getting out of control, as well as biotechnology and genetic engineering refashioning human beings and producing monsters. It also deals with Gulf War syndrome and how the military experiments on soldiers, suggesting shadowy and sinister connections between key players in the military-industrial complex and their allies in the government. Released in the election year of 2004, the film resonated as an anti-Bush political thriller at a time when an unholy alliance between the military, corporate giants, and the Bush-Cheney administration was wreaking havoc throughout the world.[2] As J. Hoberman put it:

> From the opening theme, Wyclef Jean's cover of the anti-Bush anthem "Fortunate son," through the references to "no-bid contracts," computerized voting and constant terror alerts, to the elaboration of a corporate conspiracy to install a "sleeper" as president, the remake is an unambiguous attack on the current American [Bush-Cheney] administration. Despite the Internet-fueled rumor that Meryl Streep was evoking Hillary Clinton for her character, her portrayal of the candidate's mother is far more evocative of Bush aide Karen Hughes – or perhaps even Bush's own mother who, according to Kevin Phillips's *American Dynasty*, had spoken of becoming First Lady as early as the late 1940s.[3]

The Manchurian Candidate received mixed reviews and did only middling box office, and hence probably had limited, if any, political effect. Like Condon's novel and the 1962 film, Demme's version had a strong sexist subtext in the over-the-top performance of Meryl Streep (Angela Lansbury won acclaim in the 1962 version playing the same dominating and incestuous mother). The mother is an overbearing, power-mad monster, wicked in the extreme. In both film versions the son is completely under her control and kills the good liberal senator and his daughter. In the 1962 version Janet Leigh plays an irrationally devoted and nurturing woman who nurses Marco back to health. In the 2004 version the woman who cares for Marcos is a government agent, intensifying the paranoia even further.

The 2004 *Manchurian Candidate* has a fantasy happy ending in which Marcos assassinates Shaw and his mother rather than the president, illustrating the film's conviction that there is a good and free person behind every socially constructed (in this case, genetically engineered) individual. The film articulates the fantasy that the malevolent political forces that have plotted to seize power can be painlessly removed – the Good US Republic can be restored. In 2004 this remained wishful thinking, as the Bad Guys continued their rule of infamy when the Bush-Cheney-Rove Gang stole yet another election (see Miller 2005; Fitrakis and Wasserman 2005; Gumball 2005).

The *Bourne* trilogy is emblematic of anti-Bush-Cheney political thrillers. Paul Greengrass's *The Bourne Ultimatum* (2007) fills in much of the back-story of the eponymous CIA-trained assassin (Matt Damon) who in *The Bourne Identity* (2002) and *The Bourne Supremacy* (2004) finds himself in a state of amnesia. Pursued by sinister US government forces, he searches for knowledge of his past and discovers his abilities to elude and eliminate his pursuers. Based on the fast-paced spy thrillers of Robert Ludham but shorn of their Cold War background and infused with post-9/11 paranoia, the films became increasingly relevant as "extraordinary renditions," spying on American citizens, torture, and other forms of thuggery were brought to light (Hersh 2004; Suskind 2006; Mayer 2008).

The Bourne Ultimatum begins in Moscow, where Jason Bourne seeks the daughter of one of his victims to apologize. He eludes the assassins sent to kill him, and then tracks down the masterminds behind the CIA black-ops that turned him into a cold-blooded assassin, all the while seeking to discover his true identity. The sinister head of the CIA, Ezra Kramer (Scott Glenn), is conspiring with his subordinate, Noah Vosen (David Strathairn), to refigure the assassin program titled Treadstone into Blackbriar. When a British *Guardian* reporter is leaked information about Bourne and the assassin program, Vosen assembles an assassin team to kill the reporter and to take out Bourne. Bourne meanwhile hooks up with a CIA operative, Nicky Parsons (Julia Styles), who knows of his programming and had earlier worked with him (with a hint of romantic involvement). She questions the CIA covert program and decides to help Bourne trace his programmers (opening the way for a romantic sequel).

The US intelligence agencies in the trilogy evoke fears of an out-of-control Bush-Cheney administration. In *The Bourne Ultimatum*, the CIA's deep-cover New York City office has an image of Donald Rumsfeld visible on a computer monitor. In a deleted scene featured on the DVD, there is a picture of Bush on the wall behind the evil Noah Vosen, thus evoking the real people who were doing vile and immoral deeds in real life.

The Bourne Ultimatum poses an increasingly moral and humane agent against menacing intelligence operatives who train assassins to kill. As Paul Greengrass notes in his commentary on the DVD, Jason Bourne is a new kind of action hero, without the gun-toting hypermasculinity of many other action adventure films and spy thrillers. The Bourne character is more humane, humble, remorseful, and reflective. He is both truth-seeking and intelligent, speaking a number of foreign languages and possessing incredible survival skills. Bourne's morality and humaneness are pitted against the amoral villainy of adversaries who represent the operatives and policies of the Bush-Cheney era.

Syriana (2005) uses political allegory to provide a complex vision of the complicity of US corporations and government with political regimes and oil barons in the Middle East, and how that involvement has produced terrorism. *Syriana* transcodes mistrust of oil corporations and Arab sheiks, the CIA and government agencies, and their imbrication in criminal activities and terrorism. In intertwining stories about the Middle East, oil corporations contending for markets, Gulf emirs pushing competing national and US/corporate interests, Islamic terrorists and the CIA, and politicians acting with the various interests, the film comments allegorically on the nexus of powers wreaking havoc.

Written and directed by Stephen Gaghan, who penned the screenplay for Steven Soderbergh's highly acclaimed *Traffic* (2000) about the global drug trade, *Syriana* was inspired by Robert Baer's CIA memoir *See No Evil* and takes its title from a think-tank term for a reconfigured Middle East.[4] A highly complex film, it sets out to map contemporary global capital and struggle in the Middle East between a myriad of competing forces. Action centers on Bob Barnes (George Clooney), an over-the-hill CIA agent loosely based on Robert Baer. After assassinating some Iranian arms dealers, Barnes returns to Washington and finds himself in a web of intrigue.

Major plotlines in the film's multiple overlapping stories include lawyers and executives trying to broker oil mergers, and the successor to the emir of a fictional Middle East country. The eldest of two sons, Prince Nasir (Alexander Siddig), appears interested in economic and political reform for his country and sells some oil rights to China, while the younger brother, Prince Meshal (Akbar Kurtha), appears ready to sell out to Western oil interests. The giant oil company Connex has just lost oil interests in a Middle East country and is seeking to buy out a smaller Texas oil company, run by wildcat Texan firm Killen, which has locked up the drilling rights to Kazakhstan, which allegedly has tremendous untapped oil reserves. This leads various US corporations, politicians, and lawyers to involve themselves in the merger and emir succession issues, bungling both – just as the Bush-Cheney administration bungled almost everything.

Syriana also features a Committee for the Liberation of Iran, evoking the Iraqi National Congress sponsored by the Bush-Cheney neoconservatives to push for war in Iraq. In the end, Barnes finds himself the dupe of a plot to kill the reform-minded prince, while the oil companies continue to merge and expand. In a subplot, a young Pakistani worker has lost his job in the oil-drilling fields. Bitter and frustrated at his inability to make a living, he comes under the sway of an Islamic fundamentalist, showing how terrorists are recruited out of the mess that the US has contributed to creating in the Middle East.

Released the same year, Andrew Niccol's *Lord of War* (2005) explores the complexities of arms dealing in its story of a Ukrainian immigrant, Yuri Orlov (Nicholas Cage), who gets involved in the trade. The film opens with a bullet's-eye view of arms factories and the manufacture of tons of munitions which are often sold to the highest bidder. The camera continues to follow the bullet as it is loaded into boxes and shipped to Africa, where it is put into a gun. The camera follows the bullet's trajectory and point of view into the head of a young child.

Lord of War is a geopolitical satire told as a rags-to-riches immigrant saga. Yuri provides an ironic voice-over to his own rise and fall, in a story-form much like that of a tragic gangster film. After the collapse of the Soviet Union, Yuri returns from the US to the Ukraine, where a connection with his uncle, General Orlov, gives him access to hordes of weapons that make him superrich. But Yuri is tracked by a government arms agent, Valentine (Ethan Hawke), who gets to Yuri's wife. She provides him with access to Yuri's dirty business records and he is set up for a bust. Just before his last big deal with a Liberian dictator trading "blood diamonds" for an arms cache to fight his opponents, the dictator holds up a newspaper with the 5–4 Supreme Court ruling that gave the presidency to Bush: now "the US must shut up forever" and quit lecturing others on democracy, mocks the dictator. Yuri's brother sees that the weapons will be used to kill innocent people and manages to destroy half the arms shipment before he is shot, but Yuri completes the deal.

Shortly afterwards, Yuri is arrested by Valentine, who has the full bill of goods against him. It appears that Yuri is finished, having lost wife, brother, and family, and facing years in jail. However, he tells Valentine that he is doing covert dirty work that serves the interests of the US government and will have all charges against him dropped immediately. A shadowy government figure, Col. Oliver Southern (obviously modeled on Iran-contra criminal Oliver North), orders Valentine to release Yuri, whose final voice-over points out that the world's biggest weapons dealers are not private individuals like himself, but countries like the US, Russia, Britain, and China.

Another Middle Eastern political thriller, Peter Berg's *The Kingdom* (2007), transcodes more conservative discourses in a conventional Hollywood format. The film tackles one of the most sensitive issues in US foreign policy: relations with Saudi Arabia and the latter's connection to terrorism. An opening montage encapsulates US-Saudi relations, from the 1930s when oil was discovered, to 9/11, shortly after which it was revealed that 15 of the 19 alleged World Trade Center murderers were Saudis. The film cuts to Americans in a softball game at a picnic in Riyadh, Saudi Arabia, where US oil workers live with their families in an American-style community. Mayhem ensues when Saudi guards are shot and terrorists posing as policemen invade the compound and begin killing Americans. Suicide bombers blow themselves up and take out more than a hundred people with them, including two FBI agents.

In Washington the FBI calls for the immediate insertion of an investigative team, while State Department bureaucrats and the attorney general (Danny Huston) caution against rash action. The FBI director intimidates the weak attorney general and agent Ronald Fleury (Jamie Foxx) blackmails the Saudis into letting him fly in immediately with an investigative team. The team comprises the obligatory woman forensic expert, Janet Mayes (Jennifer Garner), to help demonstrate retrograde Saudi attitudes toward women; a Jew, Adam Leavitt (Jason Bateman), to demonstrate retrogressive Saudi attitudes toward Jews and to make bad jokes; and a white southern good ol' boy, Grant Sykes (Chris Cooper), an explosives expert, to give white guys someone to identify with. The team is greeted by a local police colonel, Al-Ghazi (Ashraf Barhom), who is their babysitter and who bonds with Fleury, to demonstrate good Saudi/Arab attitudes and behavior.

The Kingdom combines aspects of a forensic crime drama with an action-adventure film and a political thriller. Saudi Islamicist terrorists are uncovered as perpetrators of the crime, putting on display familiar images of terrorists killing innocents, using the Internet to propagandize their deeds, recruiting children as murderers, and preparing to behead one of the captured team members. The film privileges Bush-Cheney administration hard-right extremism in a pointed contrast to the liberalism of the attorney general and other politicos in the film. Diplomacy and negotiation with the Saudis are shown to be futile; resolute militant action is shown as necessary. The Saudi police are represented as inefficient, obstructive, and devious, but in a few days the Americans have discovered the terrorist cell responsible for the killings (based on the 1996 bombings of a US apartment complex in Saudi Arabia). In a rousing 30-minute climax, the cell is hunted down and destroyed. The Saudis themselves are pictured as either good allies of the Americans or evil terrorists devoted to murder and mayhem, just as the Americans are divided in Manichean fashion into good, aggressive, all-American men of action contrasted to liberal, weany, do-nothing bureaucrats. The FBI agents invade a Saudi compound to blow away the terrorists, providing narrative closure with an American victory over evil terrorists.

The Kingdom is a comic-book fantasy of US revenge against al Qaeda terrorism, while more serious films like *Syriana* attempt to capture the challenges of a dangerous Middle East in complex and open-ended narratives. *Lord of War* makes clear that the US is involved in compromised relations with shady characters and complicit in an arms trade that fuels global wars and massacres. Michael Winterbottom's *A Mighty Heart* (2007) provides a nuanced presentation of the impact of terrorist actions on victims while exploring the complexity of Middle Eastern politics. Recounting the kidnapping and execution of American journalist Daniel Pearl, it focuses on the efforts of his wife, Mariane (Angelina Jolie), their friends and colleagues, and American and Pakistani officials to track down the perpetrators. Eschewing black and white stereotypes, it shows a variety of individuals from different cultures and backgrounds working together to solve the mystery of who kidnapped Pearl and how to save him. The story, as many viewers know, ends in tragedy, as the Jihadists beheaded Pearl and showed the killing on a video distributed on the Internet. However, unfolding the story captures the complexity of Pakistani politics, with a great diversity of people with differing views. The film depicts Mariane and her friends getting on with their lives and eschewing futile calls for violent revenge.

Other political conspiracy thrillers take direct aim at the Bush-Cheney administration. Paul Schrader's *The Walker* (2008) combines social drama, a murder mystery, and political intrigue in a story of how a gay man who accompanies wives of politically powerful men on shopping and cultural events uncovers political corruption. Catching the contemporary moment, there are off-hand comments throughout the film about Iraq, threats to civil liberties, and a vice-president deeply immersed in intrigue and dirty business deals. The film subtly puts on display the corrupt corporate lobbying and scandals that reached a zenith in the Bush-Cheney years, although its specific critique is more understated and indirect than many of the films analyzed here.

Star Wars Prequels as Anti-Bush-Cheney Allegory

By 2006 it was clear that the Bush-Cheney administration was a world-historical catastrophe of the highest order. While a series of Hollywood thrillers can be read as critical commentary on Bush-Cheney administration foreign policy, some popular fantasy adventure films can be directly read as allegorical assaults on the regime. I will read the three prequel episodes to George Lucas's *Star Wars* trilogy from *Star Wars I: The Phantom Menace* (1999) through *Star Wars III: Revenge of the Sith* (2005) in this way.

After a 15-year hiatus in his astonishingly popular *Star Wars* franchise, George Lucas envisaged and executed a trilogy of prequels that told the background story of Luke Skywalker, Darth Vader, and the battles between the Jedi Knights and their Rebel Alliance against the Evil Empire. This second *Star Wars* trilogy (1999–2005) can be read in retrospect as an allegorical premonition of the rise of the Bush-Cheney administration and its dangerous consolidation of presidential power, undermining of democratic rights and freedoms, and attempts at Empire.

Released 16 years after *Return of the Jedi* (1983) concluded the first *Star Wars* trilogy, *Star Wars I: The Phantom Menace* (1999) features a dark, evil, hooded villain plotting to overthrow established regimes and deploy violence and duplicity to take control of the Senate and turn the republic into an authoritarian and militarist empire. The villainous and twisted figure can be seen in retrospect as a remarkable anticipation of Dick Cheney, a power-mad individual who manipulates ruthlessly behind the scenes. In addition, Senator Palpatine who rises from Senator to Supreme Commander of the Empire, and who we later learn is the mysterious Darth Sidious, can be read as a figure representing the different faces of the Bush-Cheney-Rove Gang, ruthlessly accruing power, undermining democracy, and carrying out secretive political conspiracies and military adventures.

Of course, the *Star Wars* films are exemplars of the fantasy genre that operate on a high level of myth-symbol narratology. They can be read as articulations of a self-contained fantasy-mythic universe, as morality tales, and as examples of a spiritualist (albeit crusading militant) religious tradition.[5] Yet, on the level of sociopolitical allegory, they reveal the social and political impulses of their era, and the narratives can be articulated with dominant political discourses, struggles, and events of the time.

Kellner and Ryan (1988) read the first three *Star Wars* films (1977–1983) as an anticipation of Reaganism, including a proto-Reaganite conservatism with its crusading militarism, hierarchical patriarchal values, articulations of religion and politics, entrepreneurial individualism (Hans Solo), and celebration of the family and traditional values. To be sure, there were echoes of 1960s countercultural motifs: themes of rebellion against coercive authority, communal bonding, and motifs of freedom and individualism. But just as Reaganism itself incorporated many of these discourses and motifs, so too could the countercultural motifs of the first three *Star Wars* films be accommodated to the ruling conservative hegemony of the 1980s. Similarly, California countercultural discourses and motifs were assimilated into the high-tech "California ideology" of the Silcon Valley technoculture that became a dominant ideological and material force of the 1980s and 1990s, in which Lucas participated vis his Skywalker Sound and Industrial Light & Magic companies that revolutionized film technology.[6] An older and more politically astute George Lucas, however, conceived and began a *Star Wars* prequel trilogy at the end of the Clinton era of globalization and relative peace and prosperity in the US. While the prequel trilogy contained many of the mythic and conservative motifs of its predecessors, it projects a much darker moral and political vision and intersects with the rise of the authoritarian Bush-Cheney regime and its fantasy of Empire which provided threats to democracy and the concept of a republic based on a separation and division of powers.

Star Wars 1: The Phantom Menace (1999) opens with Jedi Master Qui-Gon Jinn (Liam Neeson) and his apprentice Obi-Wan Kenobi (Ewan McGregor) on a diplomatic mission to the planet Naboo, where they are sent to negotiate a tax dispute and blockade of the planet by the Trade Federation. The thematics of taxation and trade war reflect the dynamics of economic-political competition in the neoliberal Clinton era of globalization. The Jedi Knights soon learn that something more sinister is going on behind the scenes, as the mysterious Darth Sidious (Ian McDiarmid) is plotting to take control of the Galactic Republic. Surviving an attack ordered by Darth Sidious, the two Jedi, after noisily dismembering an army of droids, move to save Naboo's teenage ruler, Queen Padme Amidala (Natalie Portman), from possible danger. After their spaceship is attacked and needs repairs, Gon Jinn and Obi-Wan Kenobi take Queen Padme and her retinue (including her favorite droid, R2-D2) to the desert planet of Tatooine, familiar from the very first 1977 film when Luke

Skywalker entered into popular culture immortality. There the group meets young Anakin Skywalker (Jake Lloyd), a slave child with amazing potential in the Force. After a pod race where Anakin proves his mettle, the group travels to the capital world of the Republic, Coruscant, which appears as a giant planetary city, as if Los Angeles were to spread out and become a single planet.

The gnomic Yoda (voice of Frank Oz again) sees the positive potential in Anakin, but warns him and the audience that fear is the most malignant passion of all, leading to anger, hatred, and destruction. Thus, the film anticipates the Bush-Cheney regime's manipulation of fear after 9/11. The rise to power of the corrupt Senator Palpatine can also be read as an allegory of the transition from the more human rights and globalist-oriented regimes of Carter and Clinton to the militaristic and anti-democratic regime of Bush and Cheney. In *The Phantom Menace* the immature Queen Padme is manipulated by smarmy politicians into replacing Supreme Chancellor Valorum (Terence Stamp) with Senator Palpatine, who will reveal himself to be thoroughly sinister, transforming the republic into empire and setting it on the path to aggressive militarism.

Star Wars II: Attack of the Clones (2002) continues the Jedi education of Anakin Skywalker, but sketches out the beginnings of the end of the democratic republic and the rise of a militarist empire under Supreme Commander Palpatine. The film articulates disquieting worries in US culture about the fate of democracy and the country's imminent plunge into militarism and empire. It became a blockbuster hit in the troubled period after 9/11 and the US-led military intervention in Afghanistan, when the war in Iraq was already conceived in the inner circles of the Bush-Cheney administration and was beginning to be publicly debated and openly promoted.[7]

The story begins approximately ten years after the events of *The Phantom Menace*, and shows the maturing into rebellious youth and Jedi proficiency of Anakin Skywalker (Hayden Christensen). Anakin falls deeply in love with Padme, now a senator of the republic, and reveals to her his inner anger and yearnings. He is angry at his mentor Obi-Wan, who is too harsh a disciplinarian and does not recognize that he is ready for greater things. In political discussions with Padme, Anakin is impatient with democracy and believes dictatorship can be more effective, with the right man in charge – a belief shared by Bush and Cheney. Plans to assassinate Padme put her under the protection of Obi-Wan and Anakin. After another attempted murder, Obi-Wan is sent to discover the assassin, while Anakin protects Padme by taking her to her home planet of Naboo, where their love will mature.

On the planet of Kamino, Obi-Wan discovers that a secret army of clones is being developed on the orders of a Jedi Master, long disappeared, who used the bounty hunter Jango Fett as a template for the clones. Obi-Wan believes Jango is the assassin and trails him to the planet of Geonosis, where he discovers that Count Dooku (Christopher Lee) and Nute Gunray have produced a droid army. This sets up the scenario of wars between the droid army and the Jedi and their emergent clone army, anticipating postmodern war in which robotic forces play a significant role.

Attack of the Clones plays on widespread fears of the time over cloning and genetic engineering. The formation of a clone army also reflects fears in military circles that humans would be replaced by technology, rendering humans obsolescent.[8] Read retrospectively, the republic's secret building of a clone army could be conceived as paralleling the US's attempt to build a high-tech military machine that would be used to maintain hegemony and empire throughout the world. One of the unstated elements of the so-called Bush doctrine was a belief that since the US had the most powerful military force in history, it should use it to pursue US interests, including preemptive strikes and regime change in countries deemed hostile (see Kellner 2005).

For Lucas's universe of the Force, rule by empire and a mechanistic army of droids could not be allowed. *Attack of the Clones* pits the Jedi and their allies against the military forces of the empire and the Sith who control them. It takes Yoda himself to ward off destruction by the Dark Side of the Force. The film ends on a disquieting note as the (ambiguously) evil Count Dooku/Darth Tyranus meets with the hooded Darth Sidious (who we will discover is Chancellor Palpatine). The doubling and doubled figures of the villains noted here will allow us to suggest that the Evil Ones in the prequel trilogy stand in allegorically for dyads such as Bush-Cheney or Bush-Rove.

For example, Dooku/Tyranus says that the clone war has begun and Palpatine/Sidious notes his satisfaction that all is going according to plan. In 2002, when *Clones* was released, Cheney and Bush's plan to invade Iraq was proceeding inexorably to its conclusion. In addition, Yoda tells the Jedi that "lies, deceit, and mistrust" are being spread by the Dark Side. The Bush-Cheney Gang spread lies about alleged Iraqi WMDs, creating the fear and mistrust that prepared the way for their catastrophic

Iraq War. And as the US faced a new era of militarism, authoritarianism, and perhaps even fascism in 2002, so was the republic quickly mutating into the empire in the *Star Wars* saga. *Attack of the Clones* thus warns against the coming evil of the empire replacing the republic as the Dark Side of the Force gained its power.

While my reading of *Phantom* and *Clones* is obviously a retrospective one, *Star Wars III: Revenge of the Sith* (2005) can be read explicitly as an anti-Bush-Cheney allegory. As the Iraq War spun into manifest disaster, Lucas stated at the 2005 Cannes film festival:

> Because [the prequel trilogy] is the back-story [of the *Star Wars* saga] one of the main features of the back-story was to tell how the Republic became the Empire.... The issue was: how does a democracy turn itself over to a dictator? Not how does a dictator take over but how does a democracy and Senate give it away?... The parallels between what we did in Vietnam and what we're doing in Iraq now are unbelievable.[9]

While nervous executives did not want to have the film seen as a commentary on the Bush-Cheney administration and Iraq War, the film itself and Lucas's comments made such readings inevitable.[10]

Revenge of the Sith begins with the graphic title "War!" popping onto the screen accompanied by the familiar *Star Wars* theme music. The titles tell audiences that the republic is crumbling under attacks by the ruthless Sith, whose Lord Dookus has kidnapped Supreme Chancellor Palpatine. The kidnapping of Chancellor Palpatine is revealed as a ruse to persuade Obi-Wan and Anakin to rescue him. They do so, giving the chancellor the opportunity to tempt Anakin to increase his power by going over to the Dark Side of the Force (one thinks of Karl Rove and Dick Cheney tempting George W. Bush). Anakin and Padme have been secretly married and Padme is pregnant with twins, as Bush's wife Laura once was. A brooding Anakin has a dream of his wife's death. He fears he will not be able to take care of her and the twins, and needs the power that Darth Sidious has promised him. The dilemma of selling out to support and protect one's family is, of course, archetypical in many societies, but the narrative suggests that Anakin is really obsessed with power for power's sake and is increasingly meglomaniacal and violent (another uncanny parallel to the trajectory of George W. Bush).

Yoda and the top Jedi fear that Chancellor Palpatine is illicitly amassing power and planning to destroy the republic and make himself emperor. They are also rightly worried that Anakin may betray them. The Jedi Council's refusal to bestow upon Anakin the coveted Master Jedi status further alienates and inflames the young buck and makes him more easily manipulated by Sith forces. George W. Bush's failures in the oil industry made him an easy mark for unscrupulous political forces who manipulated his will to succeed and overcome his earlier failures.

Chancellor Palpatine usurps power, declaring "I am the Senate." He then turns the Senate against the Jedi, whom he claims are trying to overthrow him. The chancellor's forces set out to exterminate the Jedi, who are condemned and labeled as "separatists." The right wing in the US targeted democratic and progressive forces who questioned the expansion of militarism and the dramatic increase of presidential power during the Bush-Cheney administration. In 2005 at the time of *Sith*'s release, there was a huge debate about whether the US would remain a democratic republic or fall prey to the temptations and dangers of empire (see Johnson 2000, 2004; Vidal 2002, 2003; Mann 2003). The *Star Wars* prequel trilogy focuses on the dangers of a republic slipping into the temptations of empire and thus becomes a historically relevant warning about major dangers of the time.

The Chancellor successfully rallies the Senate against the Jedi and in the name of security and stability declares the end of the republic and the institution of empire, while the Senate wildly applauds. Palme watches the proceedings and sardonically exclaims, "This is how liberty dies, with tremendous applause." The scene becomes poignant in the light of the wild applause for George W. Bush when he made his annual State of the Union addresses from 2001 to 2006 (the applause died down in the final years).

Anakin had tried to persuade Palme that the Jedi were out to destroy him and that their future lay with the chancellor and empire, but she would have none of this. Deeply alienated from Anakin, she eventually dies while giving birth with a broken heart to her twins Luke and Leia, an event that would drive the narrative of *Star Wars IV–VI* (which of course had already appeared and would accrue new meanings and effects in the context of the prequels). In a frightening sequence, Anakin tries to convince Palme that his immersion in the Dark Side has made him immensely powerful, that he can overthrow the chancellor and that he and Palme together can rule the universe. It appears that Anakin has become completely mad, a victim of a lust for power whose humanity is hopelessly destroyed (although he will be able to redeem himself partially in a subsequent episode).

In another powerful sequence, a delusional Chancellor Palpatine tells the assembly that he has brought peace, freedom, justice, and security to "my new empire," just as Bush would brag he was bringing freedom, justice, and democracy to the Middle East (when he was really bringing chaos and disorder). In obvious echoes of Bush, Anakin intones: "If you're not with me, you're my enemy." Obi-Wan comments: "Only a Sith deals in absolutes." The Sith are allegorical stand-ins for rightwing extremist Republicans like Bush, Cheney, and the neocons.

The narrative ends with two megafights between Obi-Wan and Anakin, and between Yoda and Darth Sidious. While the good Jedi are victorious, the evil one escapes – albeit horribly maimed – to return in the next trilogy that will feature the rebel alliance against the empire. Anakin loses his hand in his saber fight and his body is grievously injured, forcing his Darth Vader incarnation to wear metallic body parts. This is suggestive of the US troops and Iraqis mutilated in the Iraq War. The slaughter of the Jedi and the survivors' predicament mirror the difficulties the US experienced in maintaining control after the occupation of Iraq, putting in question Donald Rumsfeld's doctrine that a lean and efficient military and special forces can prevail without significant numbers of boots on the ground.

In historical context, the Jedi now appear as representatives of the progressive forces of the 1960s that combined spirituality and militancy in battling the evils of global capitalism and imperialism. From 1977 to 1983 it was reasonable to see them as crusading Cold Warriors and dangerous Samurai–like militarists, although even then one could read them as low-tech warriors fighting empire and a military machine (see McVeigh 2006). But the Jedi are much less overtly militarist in the prequel trilogy and in fact battle more dangerous militarist and anti-democratic forces. Thus, in this context, they become more progressive and positive figures – "freedom fighters," if you wish.

The vision of democracy in all of the *Star Wars* films is problematic. The Senate is generally shown from a neoliberal and anti-UN position as a squabbling forum of base interests with manipulation and deception the rule. The Jedi are a genetically elite warrior caste, somewhere between Plato's guardian-philosopher kings and the warriors in his Greek republic. All groups in the *Star Wars* cosmology and polity are hierarchically ordered, ruled by the superior and most powerful, and there is evidence in Lucas's biographies that he too tends to be an authoritarian leader, completely in control of his empire and not a friend of participatory democracy. As John Lawrence (2006: 7) warns us:

> It would be a mistake to see Lucas as a pacifically inclined, articulate phi-
> losopher of democracy. In his most complex public utterances on govern-
> ing, he revealed himself as a closet monarchist – indicating a spiritual
> affinity to the Old Republic's aristocracy. Responding to Orville Schell in a
> 1999 interview with the *New York Times*, he spoke the language of "rul-
> ers" as opposed to speaking of democracy as an opportunity for participa-
> tion and shared responsibility. He offhandedly remarked that "a good
> despot" or "a benevolent despot who can really get things done" would be
> desirable, explaining himself this way: "There's no respect for the office of
> the presidency. Not that we need a king, but there's a reason why kings
> built large palaces, sat on thrones and wore rubies all over. There's a whole
> social need for that, not to oppress the masses, but to impress the masses
> and make them proud and allow them to feel good about their culture,
> their government and their ruler so that they are left feeling that a ruler has
> the right to rule over them, so that they feel good rather than disgusted
> about being ruled.... But there's probably no better form of government
> than a good despot."

Although one can interpret the Jedi as righteous warriors against the militarist empire and fascism, one should also note that they are deeply flawed. Throughout the prequels, various Jedi, including Yoda, fail to recognize their hubris and overestimate their abilities to control the situation. The Jedi Council makes mistakes and does not always have a good grip on reality, as when it alienates Anakin Skywalker and allows him to come under the control of Palpatine. As Tyson Lewis comments, the Jedi also fail pedagogically, helping to drive Anakin to the Dark Side. Their overemphasis on discipline, authority, hierarchy, and subser-vience, and their failure to address Anakin's emotions and concrete exis-tential situation, help Darth Sidious take control of him. As Lewis suggests, the Dark Side ultimately has a more effective notion of peda-gogy, as Darth Sidious gets Anakin to express his emotions, vulnerabili-ties, needs, and frustrations with the Jedi that help him bring Anakin over to the Dark Side.[11] Yet one could argue that the Sith pedagogy and Palpatine are deceptively and unethically manipulative, and that a genu-inely emancipatory pedagogy should not guide student behavior in what could be destructive ways.

The *Star Wars* prequels are thus ambiguous as a social and political allegory and are lacking in democratic and egalitarian social relations, with no just, self-governing philosophy. Yet the entire series is an impressive moral allegory of self-development and mastering base emotions, while the prequels have progressive political effects in their compelling story of a fall from democracy to empire at a time when the US and other parts of the world were confronting just such a threat.

In retrospect, one can really only grasp the ideological problematics of the *Star Wars* series as a whole at the end of the cycle when the pieces fit together, the symbols and narratives can resonate in their historical moment, and interpretation of the entire cycle in the context of contemporary US and global culture becomes possible. In the 2002 and 2005 episodes, Lucas's vision of the US losing its democracy and falling prey to the evils of empire was one that could not be easily embraced by conservative sectors of his audience. However, when the horrors of the Bush-Cheney regime became apparent in the Iraq disaster, and in its relentless undermining of democracy and democratic values, and in the face of threatened US interventions in Iran and elsewhere, Lucas's cautionary tales became prescient, with the prequel trilogy taking on even more relevancy and power for the contemporary era.

Of course, the *Star Wars* saga can also be read as mythic-poetic spiritualism that articulates George Lucas's re-visioning of Joseph Campbell's "hero with a thousand faces," enjoining individual and spiritual development, aiming at the triumph of good over evil in one's personality and in society.[12] One can also equate this mythical vision with traditional conservatism. For instance, there are militarist aspects to the cycle, when military action is deemed the most efficacious tool in a life-or-death struggle against evil. The blowing up of enemy machines, planets, and the deadly Death Star in the early post-1977 episodes can be read in the context of the video games culture at the time as programming young kids to perform nuclear war or push buttons to blow up stuff and people in Iraq. The light saber artistry of the entire series can also be equated with a militarist masculinism whereby the warrior, in touch with his inner feelings and the Force, is valorized as the highest form of human being, the flashing sabers signifying male phallic power. The light sabers' connection with the spiritual ideology of the Force arguably signifies a more organic link between individuals and technology than the mechanistic clone armies whose goal is to dominate and destroy, or the blasters, which are a pure tool of male aggression. However, the light sabers – among the most popular merchandising toys spun off the franchise – are clearly connected with aggressive male power and feudal militarism, hardly a positive role model for boys.

The prequel trilogy is nevertheless highly ambiguous toward military action, questioning its limits and its dangers, especially when a lethal military machine is in the wrong hands. Conversely, the cumulative universe in Lucas's saga is like the state of permanent war in Orwell's *1984* that justifies and helps reproduce a militarist, totalitarian, police state. Post-9/11 and post-Iraq invasion, the prequel trilogy circulated on video and DVD, often receiving cult-like attention, as well as ridicule.[13] It can be articulated with discourses critical of unrestrained militarism, the loss of democratic rights and freedoms in the construction of empire, and fears about military appropriation of genetic engineering and biotechnology.

The *Star Wars* films are thus polysemic, inviting multiple readings. My reading presents a sociopolitical hermeneutic in which popular-cultural artifacts are articulated with political discourses and struggles and interpreted as commentary on contemporary events. Popular movies tap into people's social and political unconscious, bringing to expression their deep fears and hopes. George Lucas is an especially talented storyteller and mythmaker, able to synthesize disparate pop-cultural material and provide epic stories that connect with audiences. With the first series coming after traumatic defeat in Vietnam and when the Cold War seemed perpetual, the US and its global allies needed a comforting set of redemptive myths. Lucas's 1977–1983 saga fit the bill.

George Lucas is a storyteller and mythmaker who is able to tap into the culture's worries, fears, and conflicts and provide narratives that address contemporary issues in a way to attract mass audiences. The technological exploitation of high-tech special effects by Lucas's Skywalker Sound Industrial Light & Magic companies, which made him a billionaire many times over, are an important part of Lucas's storytelling. His computer generated imagery, sound effects, and animation units have spun off into separate companies and Lucas is acknowledged king of high-tech cinema, although his critics claim too much emphasis on computer generated imagery undermines his films' characters, dialogue, and stories.[14] Indeed, one could see Lucas on the whole as part of a progressive high-tech liberal capitalist wing of the Silcon Valley California ideology, which combines pro-market and individualist values with liberal social ones.

Hence, one of the major blockbuster series of all time provides prescient warnings against the assault on democracy in the US during the Bush-Cheney era and the dangers of militarism. A vast number of films presented more realist, satirical, and allegorical assaults on the Bush-Cheney regime, as I attempt to document in the next section.

From Satire to Dystopia

Blending allegory, satire, and low-key political realism, John Sayles' *Silver City* (2004) has a dimwitted and opportunistic candidate for governor in Colorado in cahoots with rightwing forces. Groomed for office by his father, former Senator Judson Pilager (Michael Murphy), a powerhouse in Colorado and national politics, the relation between father and son, and portrait of a callow and superficial Dickie Pilager (Chris Cooper), provide a barely disguised double of the relationship between George W. Bush and his father. The name Pilager nicely pinpoints the aims of the Bush dynasty.[15]

Silver City deftly explores how conservative politicians are connected with powerful economic interests to push a rightwing agenda. It opens with a photo-op of candidate Dickie Pilager fishing, highlighting how cynical advisers present tools of conservative economic interests as environmentalist. As the camera sets up a shot for a campaign commercial, the hapless Dickie pulls from the lake the dead body of a man. Fearing a political smear by opponents, the Karl Rove-like campaign manager Chuck Raven (Richard Dreyfus) hires a private investigator, Danny O'Brien (Danny Houston), to check on political enemies who might have played a dirty trick on Pilager. These include a rightwing talk radio host (Miguel Ferrer), a former mine engineer who has become a mining industry safety critic and whistleblower (Ralph Waite), and the candidate's ditzy and promiscuous sister (Daryl Hannah), who deeply despises her brother, offering Sayles and company a panorama of issues and personalities to dissect contemporary US politics and society.

Danny visits the editor of an alternative webzine (Tim Roth), with whom he had earlier worked on a community newspaper, and discovers how the candidate is involved in a complex web of Colorado politics and economic interests. Using film noir codes of an investigative mystery unpeeling layers of corruption, the film shows Danny regaining his investigative zeal and encountering a group of characters and stories that illustrate contemporary political corruption and provide trenchant critical commentary on the Bush-Cheney administration. In a cameo role, Kris Kristofferson plays rightwing businessman Wes Benteen who, on horseback, and with a gorgeous Colorado scenic background, makes a speech about how the country's land and natural resources need to be "liberated for the people" – which means, of course, corporate forces like himself who support rightwing politicians who "liberate" the public domain for private interests.

Pilager's father is a powerful senator and scion of a Colorado political dynasty that evokes the Bush family. Like George W. Bush, there are intimations that Dickie Pilager has a drunk-driving charge in his background; like him, he has trouble putting together an unscripted sentence. Pilager is scripted by his Karl Rove-like manager, presenting the image of a politician programmed by his handlers, as George W. Bush was handled by Rove and Cheney (see Suskind 2006; Gellman 2008).

Danny learns that the deceased man was an exploited Mexican laborer who drowned in a mine being closed down to develop Silver City. This proposed land development deal crystallizes the economic, political, and environmental forces exposed in the film's plot. A subplot has Danny meet his ex-girlfriend reporter (Maria Bello), now engaged to a sharkish corporate lobbyist (Billy Zane), which provides an opportunity to expose the role of lobbyists in politicking for corporate interests, as well as the opportunity for the girl to dump the knavish fellow.

John Sayles and his crew use the form of an epic political drama with satirical overtones to criticize the Bush-Cheney administration, but the film got mixed reviews and did not find a large audience. Spike Lee's *Inside Man* (2005) uses the format of a gritty police thriller to explore the ethnicities and personalities of a variety of New Yorkers, and the relationships between the police, politicians, banks, and the power structure in post-9/11 New York. Shot in a fast-moving and quick-cutting style, the taking of a bank and hostages by a gang of crooks is punctuated by the opening confession of the main crook (Clive Owen), plus interviews, shot in a faded sepia, of customers and employees, some of whom are suspected to be part of an "inside job."

The film subverts the typical heist drama, as it appears that the four crooks have not stolen anything, the "death" they perform is faked, and they seem to have ulterior motives and a hidden agenda. *Inside Man* explores institutions, relations, and personalities rather than a standard genre storyline. It puts on display deep racial tensions after 9/11 and makes clear that Arabs and Muslims are the targets of racism, as the multicultural city struggles to come to terms with its differences and problems.

Appearing at first to be a standard bank heist with hostages drama à la *Dog Day Afternoon* (1975), *Inside Man* becomes an exploration of personalities, relationships, and past secrets, especially concerning the bank owner. In a plot twist, it turns out that the bank president (Christopher Plummer) organized the heist to steal Nazi-era treasures which he had stolen from Jews in concentration camps. Roger Ebert's website features a commentary by Jamie Cohen, "Bush: The real 'Inside Man'?," that suggests a political subtext and critique of the Bush family:

> As soon as the Nazi finance angle came in, I thought of Prescott Bush. Then, in Christopher Plummer's office, there was a picture of the Bush family on the credenza behind Plummer's desk. There was also one of Plummer with Maggie Thatcher....
>
> After the movie, I got to thinking about how Prescott's son was elected vice-president and president, and his grandson was elected president twice, despite the fact that the family got rich from helping finance the Nazi war machine. Would Christopher Plummer really have to worry about consequences in the real world, when it seems that war crimes committed by the rich and powerful don't?[16]

In the DVD commentary, Spike Lee tells how he has been asked if he intended to model the Christopher Plummer character on Prescott Bush. His answer is no, making it likely that this was the idea of screenwriter Russell Gewirtz. This episode illustrates how political messages can be inserted into genre films, including police thrillers.[17]

Taking up a different strategy, *American Dreamz* (2006) presents a direct satire of George W. Bush and the popular TV show *American Idol*. Paul Weitz's mordant satire features a president much like George W. Bush, programmed to appear on a popular TV show so as to boost his flagging popularity. Making fun of Bush's anti-intellectualism, the film opens with a reelected president (Dennis Quaid) bored and having trouble getting out of bed in the morning. Picking up a newspaper for the first time in years, he suddenly immerses himself in newspapers and books, but becomes reclusive, and his approval ratings go down. To help get him back on track, his chief of staff (Willem Dafoe), who appears as a morph of Cheney and Rove, books him as a guest judge on the hit talent show *American Dreamz*. The show's host, Martin Tweed (Hugh Grant), in a dig at *American Idol*'s Simon Cowell, is presented as a completely narcissistic womanizer and all-around rotten guy. Tweed and his staff pick as contestants an all-American Midwestern blonde (Mandy Moore), a Hasidic Jew rapper (Adam Busch), and a would-be Iraqi dancer shown training in a terrorist camp in Afghanistan (Sam Golzari), sent to the US as a sleeper agent.

Tweed beds the ambitious young blonde, breaking her naive boyfriend's heart, and the Iraqi and his terrorist friends concoct a plan to blow up the president. The joke here is that, like George W. Bush, the president is wired,[18] with handlers telling the dimwit what to say through an ear-piece. The wire connection breaks and the president is forced to ad-lib, a loose canon that could go any which way, just like George W. Bush. The comic fantasy format, of course, avoids disaster and, unlike the real world, this scenario ends with characters redeemed and the audience reassured that their president is not a complete dolt, that terrorists just want to dance and sing, and that the country's top-rated TV show is not corrupt and damaging to the well-being of the republic.

Going as far as possible into the terrain of broad political satire, Trey Parker and Matt Stone's *Team America* (2004) makes fun of the "war on terrorism" and the fetishism of high-tech special forces in sectors of the US military and Bush-Cheney administration. Making fun as well of Jerry Bruckheimer action films like *Top Gun* (1985), the film opens in Paris with the clay-puppet Team America after terrorists with WMDs. The team takes out the bad guys, but also wipes away the Eiffel Tower, the Louvre, and Arc de Triomphe – unfortunate "collateral damage" in the War on Terror. The all-American team leader decides to recruit a new member who must be an actor in order to infiltrate terrorist groups. Shown in a Broadway production spoofing *Rent*, a male singer performs in the number "Everyone has AIDS" and is whisked away to join the team in its secret hideaway behind the presidential faces on Mount Rushmore. After they destroy the pyramids and Sphinx in a mission to Egypt, they get down to the really important business of taking out Hollywood liberals like Michael Moore, Alec Baldwin, Sean Penn, Tim Robbins, Susan Sarandon, and Martin Sheen, who are shown as soft on Iraq and North Korea.

Not to be outdone by *South Park*'s animators, *The Simpsons: The Movie* (2007) develops an anti-Republican environmental satire. Based on the long-running and wildly popular TV series created by Matt Groening and produced by James L. Brooks, the film opens with the Simpsons and other

Springfield residents in a cinema watching a big-screen version of *Itchy and Scratchy*, the family's favorite TV cartoon show. Itchy becomes president and hits the fail-safe nuclear button to unload destruction on his arch-rival Scratchy, a truly scary image evoking a deranged Bush or Cheney pushing the button in the White House. The political subtext is quickly erased, however, as Homer bellows: "I can't believe we're paying for something we could get for free on TV. If you ask me, everyone in this theater is a big fat sucker," and turns to point to the spectator, "especially you."

The Simpsons: The Movie veers between insider jokes, the TV series' typical comedic antics, visual and puerile humor, and pointed political satire. The plot centers on environmental crisis and environmental politics, about which the populace of Springfield appears supremely apathetic. In an early scene, the band Green Day (played by themselves) are performing on a barge floating on Springfield Lake before a large audience on the shore. The crowd is enjoying the show until a band member tries to say a couple of words about the environment and pollution, at which point the barge is bombarded with so much debris that it sinks into the toxic lake.

The town's apathy is demonstrated when Lisa Simpson (Yeardley Smith) launches a campaign to clean up the ultra-polluted lake, and has every door slammed in her face when she tries to alert her neighbors. Persisting in the face of apathy, she makes a presentation to the town assembly titled "An Irritating Truth." Continuing the satirical references to Al Gore's lecture and film, she uses an elevated ladder to demonstrate how high the level of pollution is rising. Seeing a potential bandwagon, local politicians take measures to prevent dumping, including constructing a concrete barricade around the lake's perimeter. But Homer crashes through the barriers and deals a deathblow to the lake's ecosystem by dumping a large container of his pet pig's waste products, making Springfield the most polluted city in the country.

An administrator from the Environmental Protection Agency, Russ Cargill, brings the Springfield situation to President Arnold Schwarzenegger who, presented with five options, declares: "I was elected to lead, not to read." He blindly picks one of the choices: a giant dome around the city and quarantine for its toxic wastes and people. Satirizing the Bush-Cheney tendency to place representatives of industry and extreme rightwing ideologues in government, the EPA administrator is a thorough-going fascist who decides to use the nuclear option and destroy Springfield when it is revealed that people are escaping.

Meanwhile, the offending container of pig poo-poo is pulled out of the lake with Homer Simpson's name on it and an angry mob drives the Simpson family out of town, who then emigrate to Alaska. The government employs Tom Hanks to prepare the country for the end of Springfield, with Hanks noting that since the government has run out of credibility, it is forced to use him to sell their policies. Learning of the impending destruction of their city, the Simpsons leave Alaska and return by train to Springfield. Homer remains in Alaska and has an epiphany in a sweat lodge where he finally learns the truth: human beings are put on earth to be with and take care of other people. He rushes to Springfield to try to save it from nuclear devastation. En route, Marge cautions Bart to pipe down until they arrive: "We have to keep a low profile 'til we get to Seattle to tell the world there's a plot to destroy Springfield." Lisa whispers in response, "I don't know if you guys should be talking so loud!" but Marge replies, "No Lisa. It's not like the government is listening to everybody's conversations." The scene then cuts to the vast offices of the National Security Agency (NSA), where scores of agents are listening in on random telephone conversations. When he hears Lisa, an agent screams out with joy: "Hey everybody, I found one! The government actually found someone we're looking for! Yeah, baby! Yeah!" Fortunately for Springfield and the continuation of the TV series and film franchise, Homer makes it to Springfield and deflects the nuclear device, which instead just cracks the dome and liberates everyone.

Such tongue-in-cheek jabs at Republican administrations score points, but neither realist drama nor satire is really able to take account of the full horror of the Bush-Cheney era. For this task, a series of films use the codes of science fiction and futuristic allegory. While utopian science fiction celebrates a high-tech future, a dystopic tradition shows dangerous tendencies of the contemporary era intensified in a nightmare future, such as in *Blade Runner* (1982).

An allegorical futuristic drama in the dystopic mode which nevertheless ends with a utopia of revolution,[19] *V for Vendetta* (2005) attempts to unfold the consequences of an extreme rightwing, quasi-fascist government. Based on the graphic novel by Alan Moore and with a script by the Wachowski brothers, who produced the *Matrix* films, the story features V (Hugo Weaving), a masked and caped crusader who exposes, attacks, and avenges the wrongs of a totalitarian police state. Drawing his inspiration from Guy Fawkes and the foiled Gunpowder Plot to destroy the English parliament on November 5, 1605 – a day celebrated annually in

Britain with fireworks and parties – *V for Vendetta* uses a futuristic Britain to present allegorically fascist tendencies in the contemporary United States. The US has been largely destroyed by plague and civil war, while Britain suffers under a totalitarian police state with a Big Brother-like dictator, High Chancellor Adam Sutler (John Hurt). The regime is propped up by demagogic media, secret police, an enforced curfew, reduced civil rights, and torture for dissidents. A stand-in for Dick Cheney, Creedy (Tim Pigott-Smith), a pinched bureaucrat who is connected to the corporation that produces biological weapons like the plague and its cure, manipulates the deranged and vile Sutler. A hypocritical and lecherous bishop lends the church's support to the authoritarian government, just as hypocritical "Christian" evangelicals were point-men for the Bush-Cheney administration.

The film opens with a young woman, Evey (Natalie Portman), violating the curfew. She is confronted by secret police intent on gang raping her, but V appears to readily dispatch them. V invites Evey to observe a spectacular fireworks explosion at the Old Bailey, London's highest court. Chancellor Sutler appears on television and claims the destruction of the building was a planned demolition – John Hurt's face takes up the entire screen, as it did in his performance as Big Brother in *1984* (1984). Since many people had actually observed the destruction, individuals begin questioning the government in a process that continues throughout the film.

Parallels to contemporary American politics are obvious. Prothero, a Bill O'Reilly-like "Voice of London," speaks on what appears to be the country's only television channel. "The former United States is the world's biggest leper colony," he intones. "And it wasn't because of the immigrants, the Muslims or the homosexuals, or the war that they started. No," he says. "It's because they're godless!" Like supporters of the Bush-Cheney administration, Prothero combines religious nationalism with aggressive ultraconservatism, ending his broadcasts with the jingoistic "England prevails." Posters seen throughout the movie advocate "Strength through Unity," offering V and resistant graffitists an excellent target for the V sign, proliferating messages of resistance that inspire the opposition.

Like the Bush-Cheney administration, Sutler's administration is based on fear. He exclaims in rage "We will show him what terror really looks like" when V takes over the broadcasting network and promises more fireworks on the next Guy Fawkes night and threatens the regime with retaliation. Set around twenty years in the future, after, as one character puts its, "America's war grew worse and worse, when unfamiliar words like 'collateral' and 'rendition' became frightening," the film includes obvious references to Bush-Cheney America. In the world of *V for Vendetta*, the Koran is forbidden, homosexuals are violently persecuted, and torture is the treatment of choice for dissidents in facilities that evoke imagery of Guantanamo and Abu Ghraib.

Evey becomes V's protégé and accomplice. She learns that V was horribly misshapen in a government biological weapons experiment, but was endowed with supernatural powers that make him an effective killing machine. To give Evey a sense of real oppression, he fakes her kidnapping, imprisonment, and torture, letting her find a memoir from a supposed earlier prisoner that tells a story of how the regime tortured and murdered gays and lesbians. Later, her television-show boss (Stephen Fry) tells her he's gay. After he broadcasts a Benny Hill-type campy comedy skit, he too is arrested and murdered.

V reveals to a police detective pursuing him, Chief Inspector Finch (Stephen Rea), that the current political regime gained power after using biological weapons to create plague. It then exploited fear and panic to win the election, and produced a cure for the plague from a corporation that enriched top government officials. Finch investigates V's allegations and comes to work with him to help expose and overthrow the corrupt regime.

Meanwhile, V murders the demagogic television host and top political officials like Sutler and Creedy one by one, in a barely disguised fantasy of vengeance against monstrous political leaders. In the concluding sequence, Evey pulls the lever that will set off the subway train to blow up the British Houses of Parliament. Scores of people with Guy Fawkes masks descend on parliament. The police, whose rulers have been murdered, give way to the crowd.

V for Vendetta was attacked for promoting terrorism, although the scenario makes it clear that V's role is to act out a revenge fantasy. The emphasis is not on terrorist violence, but awakening people to the oppression of the system in order to bring about change through direct action. Yet despite lip service to anarchism, the people do not really self-organize and militate, but mainly follow the lead of the mysterious V. On the other hand, V allows himself to be murdered at the end so the masses can shed their Guy Fawkes masks and assert their own collective democratic power, as well as their individuality.[20]

While *V for Vendetta* puts on display the horrors of creeping fascism and projects a revolutionary fantasy of the overthrow of an oppressive

V for Vendetta: crowds of people with Guy Fawkes masks descend on parliament.

system, Steven Spielberg's *Minority Report* (2002) (based on a story by Philip K. Dick) provides a prescient anticipation of Bush-Cheney's domestic wire-tapping program and detention camps and government infamy to protect the system.[21] In a futuristic society, murder is eliminated by "pre-cogs" who foresee the crimes, stream their visions to police functionaries who quickly arrest the suspect, and then incarcerate them in suspended animation tubes, thus reducing the murder rate in 2040 Washington, DC to near zero.[22]

Appearing the year after 9/11, *Minority Report* presents a government that preemptively arrests crime suspects and holds them without trial, much as the Bush-Cheney administration did with terrorist suspects like José Padilla, completely denying them their basic rights. In the world of *Minority Report* no one protests against police surveillance, the violation of civil liberties, and the end of privacy, seemingly because an all-seeing surveillance apparatus makes resistance futile and an all-engrossing consumer society offers a dazzling array of commodities. In a clever visual conceit, products like cars and beer are offered personally to individuals who walk through shopping areas, as the ads scan the person's retina and send out a personal solicitation to buy the product advertised. Other frightening portents of a panopticonic future include giant artificial spiders that enter a room, scan everyone's retina, and send the data back to a central computer for identification.[23]

Tom Cruise plays John Anderton, who in opening scenes appears a perfectly programmed functionary without messy humanity, fitting in entirely with the police apparatus and doing his job. We eventually learn that the seemingly robotic Anderton is deeply disturbed by the loss six years previously of his son, is estranged from his wife, and takes drugs for maintenance. When he is himself accused of murder the next day and faces preemptive arrest, Anderton rebels, replaces his eyes to avoid retinal detection, and kidnaps one of the pre-cogs, after learning that occasionally a "minority report" from one of them raises doubts about the certainty of the forthcoming murder.

At this point, Spielberg departs from Dick's highly paranoid and politically critical story by bringing in Anderton's wife, who helps battle a conspiracy against him by the pre-crime agency, allowing Anderton to redeem himself. The saccharine Spielbergian ending of the restored bourgeois couple and redeemed father takes the bite out of Dick's relentlessly pessimistic vision and provides a sappy happy ending for adolescent viewers unable to face up to the dangers of a frighteningly repressive government. In his films of the past two decades, Spielberg just cannot help inserting his obsessive problematic of a family in crisis, solved by the restoration of order and redemption of the father.

On the other hand, *Minority Report* portrays a government willing to engage in lies and murder to maintain its totalitarian order, just as the Bush-Cheney administration did. While Spielberg typically takes socially critical and even explosive material and wraps it up in the fantasy of a redemptive couple or family, Richard Linklater's *A Scanner Darkly* (2006) provides the full force of a critical vision of a fascist future. Based on a 1977 Philip K. Dick novel, the film projects an image of the future in which a corporation linked to the government produces and sells drugs to keep the population under control and to legitimate a police state and war on drugs. Its view of future government strategies of domination is similar to *V for Vendetta* – perhaps both films were influenced by the vision of Philip K. Dick, who deeply mistrusted government and its police agencies, as well as big corporations. Such horrors, of course, mirror real-world situations: US political administrations from the Nixon era to the present have used a war on drugs to legitimate a prison-industrial complex in which over 2 million people are incarcerated (more than any other country). More than half of those imprisoned on drug offenses are African American, and prisons linked to corporations provide super-exploited labor (see Kellner 2008).

A dim ray of hope emerges at the end of *A Scanner Darkly* when an apparently burned-out character, Bob Arctor (Keanu Reeves), a government agent and drug taker whose identity became blurred, picks up one of the Substance D plants cultivated at the secret drug factory in a government prison. He mutters to himself that he will give it to one of his friends soon, suggesting the faint hope that evidence condemning the nefarious corporation will eventually see the light of day.

Gabriel Range's *Death of a President* (2006) envisages another end to George W. Bush in a futuristic docudrama with a fictional imagining of Bush's assassination after giving a talk to the Economic Club in Chicago. A unique blend of documentary footage and fictional re-creation, the film takes the form of a conventional documentary on a (fictional) event with (fictional) interviews with (fictional) members of Bush's staff, mixed in with a montage of documentary footage, itself an amalgam of actual archival material and fictional restaging. While the film set off a firestorm of criticism before it was shown at the Toronto film festival in 2006, where it won the director's prize, *Death of a President* is remarkably sympathetic to Bush and provides "balanced" presentations of his activities and entourage, while depicting protestors strongly opposing his policies. Set in the form of a quasi-mystery (whodunnit?), the film looks at the treatment of Arabs post-9/11, anarchist movements in opposition, and an African-American family involved in the Iraq War. As the filmmakers state on the DVD, it provides a snapshot of the US at a moment in time, trying to catch the post-9/11 situation and the divided country. It articulates growing anger with the Bush-Cheney administration's Iraq policy and Bush himself.

Death of a President takes real Bush-Cheney policies and extrapolates them into a fictive future. For example, when discussing suspects in the murder an official is told to "look again" to document a weak assassination case, as intelligence officials were told to look again to find (nonexistent) evidence of Iraqi WMDs. As happened with Bush-Cheney renditions, the film depicts people disappearing after the (fictive) assassination and the passing of Patriot Act III, exploiting fear once again after the (fictive) Bush assassination, which was exploited by the (fictive) Cheney administration, as was 9/11 exploited by the actual Bush-Cheney Gang. And, just as the Bush-Cheney administration constructed fallacious discourses to justify its polices which the media uncritically reproduced, so too we see false administration spins on assassination suspects that are taken up and reproduced in the uncritical media. *Death of a President* also depicts the new President Cheney wanting to go to war with Syria, but blocked by establishment opposition and public opinion. This is a hopeful fantasy that the US might be stopped from going into further wars in the Middle East.

Richard Kelly's *Southland Tales* (2006) presents a mind-boggling extension of the madness of Bush-Cheney policies in an apocalyptic future. Five years earlier, Kelly's cult film *Donnie Darko* (2001) had combined science fiction, horror, and youth film motifs to explore the life of a young teenager (Jake Gyllenhaal) growing up absurd in Southern California. At an opening dinner conversation, his sister (Maggie Gyllenhaal) tells the Republican parents she will vote for Dukakis in the 1988 election that frames the story. Throughout, images of George H. W. Bush provide part of the collage of the real/imaginary horrors faced by young Donnie Darko.

Southland Tales goes much further in exploring societal and political madness. Its futuristic science fiction opening deploys home video footage of a nuclear attack on Abilene, Texas, which triggered World War III, in which the US is at war with Iraq, Afghanistan, Syria, and North Korea. Oil shortages have wreaked havoc with the economy and a mad German corporate scientist/CEO, Baron Westphalen (Wallace Shawn), seeks a new energy source from oceanic waves, Liquid Karma, which has the

Southland Tales presents a chaotic future in an imagined World War III in which the US is at war with Iraq, Afghanistan, Syria, and North Korea.

downside of generating potential rifts in the space-time continuum that could lead to planetary collapse.

Otherwise, it's business as usual in 2008, with a presidential campaign between Hillary Clinton-Joe Lieberman on the Democratic side against an Eliot-Frost Republican ticket, while a neo-Marxist revolutionary group plans an insurrection to mark the third anniversary of the Abilene explosion. Oh, and a more repressive Patriot Act has created a government agency to control cyberspace, leading to opposition by a coalition of neo-Marxists, porn producers, and slam poets. Republican candidate Eliot inspires voice-over recitation of an inversion of T. S. Eliot's famous assertion that "the world will end with a bang and not a whimper," and indeed it may in this film, at least. Republican Vice-President Bobbie Frost is allied with the German energy consortium, which seems to be funding the neo-Marxist revolutionaries. His son-in-law had disappeared in the desert and returned with an altered identity, taking up with porn star Krysta Now (played by *Buffy, the Vampire Slayer* lead Sarah Michelle Gellar).

Images of Bush and Cheney in the film caused the AFI Fest 2007 audience I saw it with to hiss. In an apocalyptic conclusion, the corporate and political elite party in a giant zeppelin, the *New Trier*, and is attacked by a flying ice-cream truck piloted by the neo-Marxist revolutionaries.[24] As the zeppelin explodes, there is a rift in the time-space continuum bringing it all to an end, which makes a sequel to this film unlikely, but not impossible. The hallucinatory craziness of the film is an apt analogue for the lunacy of the Bush-Cheney years, which found truly mad expression in the invasion and occupation of Iraq, the cinematic representations of which are explored in the next chapter.

Notes

1   While viewing the opening sequence of *The X-Files: I Want to Believe*, I thought that Chris Carter and his team might be producing a critique of the FBI, as opening images show FBI agents marching in lock-step and beating ice with sticks to find a dead body – an eerie spectacle of the FBI as a totalitarian police force. The images of FBI headquarters also suggest a possible critique emerging, but the plot features homosexual Russians killing people for organ selling and a pedophilic priest providing "visions" of the crimes. Further, the FBI is presented, as in the TV series, as heroic, hence the film ends up being muddled, conservative, and disappointing. For my take on *The X-Files* TV series, see Kellner (2003b: ch. 5).

2   Both Frank Rich and Paul Krugman published articles that interpreted the film in terms of growing criticism of the Bush administration and the coming 2004 election. Frank Rich saw it as a highly partisan anti-Bush film in his article "3 hours, 4 nights, 1 fear," *New York Times*, July 25, 2004 at www.select.nytimes. com/gst/abstract.html?res=F3081EFC3A5E0C768EDDAE0894DC404482. Paul Krugman referred to the original *Manchurian Candidate* and did a thought-experiment satire in which a "Manuchurian" president aided terrorists to recruit followers and discredit the country, making a barely veiled assault on Bush. Although the film had grossed $96,105,964 globally as of December 31, 2008 (www.boxofficemojo.com/movies/?id=manchuriancandidate.htm), it probably had little if any effect on the election.

3   J. Hoberman, "Sleeper in the White House," *Guardian*, October 30, 2004.

4   Gaghan, Soderbergh, and George Clooney have worked on a number of films together or separately that constitute a critical cinematic mapping of the political complexities of the contemporary era. For discussion of Gaghan's *Michael Clayton* (2007), see the conclusion.

5   See Baxter (1999) and Kapell and Lawrence (2006).

6   See Barbrook and Cameron, "The California ideology" at www.alamut. com/subj/ideologies/pessimism/califIdeo_I.html. It may not be such a stretch to suggest that the droids R2-D2 and CP-30 helped circulate images that acclimated the geeks and intellectual workers of the world to the emergent computer culture of the 1980s at a time when many of us were forced (or chose) to sit in front of computers all day. Like the *Star Wars* figures, they eventually talked to us or communicated in metallic sounds.

7   As of January 4, 2009, *Attack of the Clones* had grossed $649,398,328 globally (see www.boxofficemojo.com/movies/?id=starwars2.htm).

8   On the "revolution in military affairs" and postmodern war, see Best and Kellner (2001); on how the *Star Wars* films relate to official US military doctrine and debates since Vietnam, see McVeigh in Lawrence (2006).

9   See Bruce Kirkland, "George W. Vader," *Toronto Sun*, May 16, 2005 at www.torontosun.com/Entertainment/Movies/2005/05/16/1041776.html.

10   See David M. Halbfinger, "Latest 'Star Wars' movie is quickly politicized," *New York Times*, May 19, 2005. As of January 4, 2009, *Revenge of the Sith* had grossed $848,998,877 worldwide.

11   Email from Tyson Lewis, February 7, 2007.

12   For critical views of the mythologies and spiritual dimensions of *Star Wars*, see Jewett and Lawrence (2002) and Lawrence in Kapell and Lawrence (2006). Lawrence (2006) argues that while the first three *Star Wars* films were deeply informed by Joseph Campbell, who Lucas saw as a quasi-guru, the prequel trilogy marks a break with Campbell toward a more direct political allegorical vision of the sort I describe here.

13 Contradictory responses to the *Star Wars* prequels are evident on the Internet Movie Database at www.imdb.com/find?s=all&q=star+wars &x=7&y=7 (accessed December 10, 2008). See, especially, the critical user comments, which are quite harsh and certainly varied in comparison to the adulation of the earlier films; see the user comments on *The Phantom Menace* at www.imdb.com/title/tt0120915/usercomments (accessed December 10, 2008).

14 The 2008 animated feature *Star Wars: The Clone Wars* regresses to computer-animated militarism and adds little to the series' mythology, showing how computer-animated special effects can kill creative filmmaking. The film was almost universally panned and received an embarrassing 19 percent approval rating at the Rotten Tomatoes website that reviews films; see www.rottentomatoes.com/ (accessed December 10, 2008).

15 On the Bush dynasty, see Kelley (2004) and Phillips (2004).

16 Jamie Cohen, "Bush: The real 'Inside Man'?" at www.rogerebert.suntimes.com/apps/pbcs.dll/article?AID=/20060330/LETTERS/60330004 (accessed October 29, 2008). On the connection between the Bush family fortune and its financing of Nazi businesses before World War II, see Phillips (2004) and Kelly (2004).

17 Spike Lee's political critique of the Bush-Cheney administration is apparent in a highly engaging HBO documentary on Hurricane Katrina, *When the Levees Broke: A Requiem in Four Acts* (2006) (see discussion in chapter 1).

18 See Douglas Kellner, "Media spectacle and the wired Bush controversy," *Flow*, 1, 3 (November 5, 2004) at www.idg.communication.utexas.edu/flow/?searchbyline=Douglas%20Kellner&jot=view&id=473 and Kellner (2005).

19 On *V for Vendetta* as an anarchistic utopia of revolution, see Sebastian Nestler and Rainer Winter, "Utopie im Film. *V for Vendetta*," in Markus Schroer (ed.) *Gesellschaft im Film* (Konstanz: UVK Verlagsgesellschaft, 2008), pp. 309–32.

20 For an excellent account of how *V for Vendetta* differs from classical anarchism, see Richard Porton's review in *Cinéaste* (Summer 2006): 52–4. On the film's anarchism as a utopia that combines collectivity and individuality, as in Hardt and Negri's category of multitude, see Nestler and Winter, "Utopie im Film."

21 After lawsuits by those detained for years without charge in military prisons, and various other court decisions, the US Supreme Court ruled in June 2008 that the Bush-Cheney administration was unlawfully detaining prisoners. See David G. Savage, "Constitution applies to detainees, justices say," *Los Angeles Times*, June 13, 2008: A1.

22 The story "Minority Report" is collected in Dick (1987). On Philip K. Dick, see Steven Best and Douglas Kellner, "The apocalyptic vision of

Philip K. Dick," *Cultural Studies/Critical Methodologies*, 3, 2 (May 2003): 186–202.

23   Many other films of the time depicted a surveillance society, including *Look* (2007), which unfolds a narrative from ubiquitous surveillance cameras. *Disturbia* (2007) shows a young man (Shia LaBeouf) using high-tech surveillance to spy on his neighbors, a motif also taken up in *Mimic 3: Sentenial* (2003).

24   Karl Marx was born in Trier, Germany, so the *New Trier* appears to refer to Marx's former hometown, although it was misspelled by the subtitle writers for the DVD as *Treer*. The film also refers to a Jenny Westphalen, who happens to be the name of Karl Marx's wife. Her father, Baron Westphalen, provides the name in the film for the deranged German who produced the zeppelin and the alternative energy source that has ripped the time-space continuum. Kelly's imaginative vision draws on Philip K. Dick, Thomas Pynchon, and David Lynch, all of whom receive homages in the picture, as does Busby Berkeley for the musical numbers. A *Kiss Me Deadly*-style opening nuclear bomb triggers the fun.

5

The Cinematic Iraq War

In addition to Robert Greenwald's documentaries and Michael Moore's *Fahrenheit 9/11* (see chapters 1 and 3), an important cycle of non-fiction and fiction films have dealt with the US invasion of Iraq and its aftermath. Despite attempts by the US and its allies to control images and information in the Iraq War (see Kellner 2005), the invasion, occupation, insurgency, civil war, and chaos opened a Pandora's Box visible to an expanding global media. The Iraq Horror Show was documented on digital camera and video, film, and military blogs, as well as print news articles and critiques, often distributed throughout the world on the Internet. There were more primary media sources and diversity of images and opinion than in any other previous war, as eight Arab news channels supplemented the European, American, and other major global media, adding new voices and representations to the media mix, often showing much more horrible images and articulating more critical discourses than the Western media. The flourishing of documentary filmmaking helped generate an astonishing number of documentaries on Iraq, and Hollywood too made a series of fictional films on the Iraq War and its aftermath.

In this chapter, I discuss the first wave of Iraq *cinéma vérité* documentaries that used new digital media to capture the experience of US soldiers and the Iraqi people, in some cases to provide preliminary analyses and critiques of the war. A second wave of documentaries then critically analyzed and dissected the war and its momentous consequences, providing analyses of how and why the Iraq intervention and occupation was failing. I then examine some attempts to present fictional film portrayals of the war and its effects on Iraq and US participants, ranging from action films like *The Situation* (2006), to depiction of US soldiers' homecoming in *Land of the Brave* (2006), and other homecoming films in 2007–2008, including *In the Valley of Elah, Badlands, Grace is Gone, Stop-Loss*, and *The Lucky Ones*. Fictional Iraq dramas released in 2007–2008 include Brian de Palma's experimental use of video in *Redacted*, and *War, Inc*, which satirizes US intervention in Iraq and the role of American corporations. The year 2008 also saw the release of outstanding documentaries like Errol Morris's *Standard Operating Procedure*, and excellent fictional films such as Nick Broomfield's docudrama *The Battle for Haditha*. Together, these films illustrate the historical magnitude of the Iraq fiasco in geopolitical, national, and personal terms.

Documenting Iraq

The first wave of documentary films on the war in Iraq made use of new digital technologies and hand-held cameras to capture the immediacy of war, to gain intimate access to the experience of US troops and the Iraqi people. Early *cinéma vérité* documentaries on Iraq were supplemented by more analytical and critical responses to the invasion and its aftermath, such as Robert Greenwald's *Uncovered* (see chapter 1).[1] Together, these documentaries laid bare the origins and destructive unfolding of the Bush-Cheney administration's Iraq invasion and occupation.

As Susan L. Carruthers suggests, a number of the early Iraq documentaries "align sights with the US military" and show the war from its experience and perspective, while another group "strives to convey the texture of everyday life under occupation for ordinary, and extraordinary, Iraqis."[2] Early *cinéma vérité* documentaries on the invasion and occupation itself include Stephen Marshall and the Guerrilla News Network's *Battleground: 21 Days on the Empire's Edge* (2004). These filmmakers sent a documentary crew to Iraq in September 2003, about six months after the US assault. The film shows a variety of Iraqi citizens responding in highly conflicted ways to the US intervention, although the critical views tend to predominate. *Battleground* interviews US soldiers as well, probing into their notions of why the US invaded Iraq. Some soldiers present quite coherent arguments based on desire for the US to control oil and the geopolitics of the region. The documentary shows the Iraqi opposition and insurgency growing and provides prescient previews of the horrors to come.

Other *cinéma vérité* films that take the point of view of US soldiers include Michael Tucker and Petra Epperlein's *Gunner Palace* (2005), which uses humor, insight, and humanity to depict the inappropriateness and dangers of the US occupation. It shows a group of US troops operating out of one of Saddam Hussein's palaces (hence the title). Using ironic juxtapositions, the film takes viewers from watching the troops swimming in an opulent pool to breaking into the houses of suspected insurgents, terrifying their inhabitants, and engaging in fights with anti-American forces.

Garrett Scott and Ian Olds' *Operation Dreamland* (2005) is a product of the filmmakers' embedding within the 82nd Airborne's Alpha Company, stationed in a former resort outside Fallujah, ironically called Dreamland. The film shows US troops' experience of one of the most hostile and violent parts of Iraq, opening with the company arriving in Fallujah in January 2004. At first, soldiers go on patrol, talk about why they joined the military, and describe future job prospects. A variety of soldiers are presented, breaking stereotypes that US troops are monolithically pro-war and militarist. Yet as the soldiers are exposed to more hostility and violence, they become critical of the invasion and occupation, as well as antagonistic toward the Iraqis. As the troops break into houses seeking weapons and insurgents, we see children and women cowering in the background; men are pushed around and sometimes made to lie on the floor, and at other times are handcuffed and taken away from their families, obviously producing a climate of hostility. One scene is shot in a night-vision phosphorescent green that makes everyone's eyes glow like extraterrestrials, poignantly highlighting how the two sides appear as monsters and aliens to each other. The documentary ends on an ambiguous note with titles indicating that Alpha Company was replaced by Marines in March who fought vicious battles and then were forced to abandon Fallujah to insurgents. Further titles recount how the Marines returned in November to retake the city. Glimpses of the wreckage of the city capture the extent of its devastation, raising questions about the destructive effects of the US intervention.

Another cycle of documentaries used the form of personal witness, which itself had become a major documentary genre, to show filmmakers themselves going to Iraq and bearing witness to events in the war zone. Mike Shiley's *Iraq: The Untold Stories* (2004) features the filmmaker getting a press pass and using his own money to travel to Iraq to see what is really going on. Edited in a personal quest and witness style, we hear Shiley explain why he wanted to go to Iraq, watch him take a dangerous cab ride across the desert into an unknown country, and learn episode by episode what he experiences. Arriving in December 2003, we learn that many Iraqis are unhappy with the US occupation and we see many examples of their suffering, such as massively long lines for gasoline, and anger when the pumps are suddenly dry; a technical university without computers, due to looting; a bomb that explodes and kills 294 people, the aftermath of which Shiley is able to film; Christian churches which the filmmaker visits and are then bombed; Kurds killed and injured by landmines; a booming arms market which no doubt fueled insurgents; and other images and voices of Iraqis not shown in the US media at the time.

There are also some unexpected sights in *Iraq: The Untold Stories*, such as a successful Baghdad porno theater, sold out every day, and gangs of Iraqi kids fighting over items that the US military discards in a dump. The last sequences of the film show Shiley embedded with the US military. Here he seems unable to decide whether he wants to fit in and become buddies with the troops or expose their ignorance of Iraqi culture. During a rap session with the troops, one young soldier expresses harrowingly murderous sentiments against Iraqis. A young woman soldier tells of how she and her boyfriend went into a mosque to have sex. After the deed was discovered, two of their officers are shown entering the mosque with the same intention – hardly a way to impress the Arab world about US morality and values.

One rightwing documentary project gave the Iraqi people 1,500 video cameras to record their experience of life in Iraq after Saddam Hussein. *Voices of Iraq* (2004) was edited by three American filmmakers. The resulting film largely provides documentation of the anti-Saddam and pro-intervention response of Iraqis, thus transcoding the conservative and pro-war position. Obviously, in a country as divided as Iraq it is possible to construct a documentary using Iraqi voices to support any number of positions. *Voices of Iraq* dishonestly claims to be an unbiased voice of truth compared to the biases of anti-war voices like Michael Moore or the allegedly pro-war corporate media. Although there are those who claim that life was better under Saddam and who complain about the US invasion and occupation, *Voices of Iraq* overwhelming shows positive views towards Americans and hopes for democracy. One of its ploys is to take US newspaper headlines about negative events and juxtapose them with positive images of happy Iraqis going about their daily lives, thus reproducing the conservative critique of the US media. Long segments deal with the Hussein regime's oppression of Shiites in the South and Kurds in the North, with harrowing footage of men described as Uday Hussein's thugs torturing and murdering Iraqis. Positive segments depict graduation at Baghdad University, preparation for the 2005 election, and Iraq's victories in world soccer competition. The film ends with the mendacious claim that it was "filmed and directed by the Iraqi people." It was actually produced, edited, and assembled by three Americans: Eric Manes and Martin Kunert, who had done MTV "fear" reality shows, and Archie Drury, a TV actor who told reviewers he had served in the military.[3]

A response to the pro-war and rightwing film *Voices of Iraq* was compiled by Iraqi director Hayder Daffar in *The Dreams of Sparrows* (2005). The documentary made by Iraqis examines life in Baghdad and Fallujah under US occupation, showing a great diversity of Iraqi responses to the US invasion and occupation. Interviewing a wide range of Iraqis with strongly conflicting opinions, Daffar and his crew show artists and intellectuals, cab drivers, schoolchildren and ordinary Iraqi citizens candidly telling their opinions about the war and their hopes for their nation. Footage captures the dangers and violence in Iraq as insurgents attack Americans and Iraqis alike and the breakdown in infrastructure makes surviving daily life a challenge. The film unfolds *in media res*, depicting a chaotic situation without any hopes for normality or resolution.

Michael Franti's *I Know I Am Not Alone* (2005) features the singer/peace activist visiting Iraq in summer 2004 to examine what the Iraqi people believe is going on under the US occupation.[4] Taking a small crew to record his visit, the very engaging Franti easily connects with Iraqis, who are surprised to see an American of color complete with dreadlocks and a guitar coming to sing and talk to them. He quickly wins the confidence of crowds with his improvised song "Habibi," an Arab word for dear friend, which he uses as a hook for improvised sing-alongs. Iraqis quickly warm to him and tell him of their woes under the occupation. In a concert for US troops, wary soldiers open up to Franti's infectious personality, embrace him warmly after the concert, and confide how much they would love to go home.

Franti travels next to Israel, where he discovers three generations of Palestinian refugees. He connects both with Israelis and Palestinians, demonstrating that people in the Middle East warm to open diplomacy with Americans and people of good will – exactly what was woefully lacking in the Bush-Cheney era, with disastrous results in December 2008 when war broke out between the Israelis and Hamas in Gaza.

A 2006 documentary nominated for an Academy Award, Laura Poitras's *My Country, My Country*, shows the impact of the US invasion and occupation of Iraq on Iraqi citizens, focusing on the experiences of an Iraqi doctor and his family. The film takes place during the 2005 Iraqi election and raises questions whether a truly democratic election, imposed by outside forces, can really occur in such a divided country. Sunni skepticism toward the process is evident, and the results are left deliberately ambiguous.

Some documentaries focused on specific units of US National Guard soldiers and their Iraq experiences and return to civilian life. Brent and Craig Renaud's *Off to War* (2005) follows a small group of Guardsmen from the Arkansas town of Clarksville to their October 2003 deployment to Fort Hood and then Iraq through their 18 months' tour of duty.[5] The troops are a diverse lot with a bevy of different opinions about the war, some of which change after they arrive in Iraq. Using a reality TV format, but more restrained, probing, and reflective, the series puts a human face on the tremendous sacrifices that US soldiers make in Iraq. The series shows that the Arkansas Guardsmen receive inadequate training and are given Vietnam-era equipment, then suddenly find themselves in violent combat situations for which they are not prepared.

When asked why they were sent to Iraq, the troops at first are hard-pressed to answer. A couple of men claim "they killed a lot of our people," and others agree, referring to false claims that Iraq was involved in 9/11. As the months go by and members of their unit are killed or maimed, as marriages disintegrate, and folks on the home front and some of the Guardsmen are torn with anguish, the series make clear the price paid by ordinary citizens for the Bush-Cheney administration's reckless and costly intervention.

In Deborah Scranton's *The War Tapes* (2006), three New Hampshire National Guardsmen use digital cameras provided by the filmmaker to capture the strangeness of occupying a country they do not understand and confronting hostility they cannot grasp. After declining an invitation to be an embedded journalist with the New Hampshire National Guard, Scranton negotiated a deal whereby a number of Guardsmen volunteered to send footage via the Internet to be compiled and edited.[6] *Fog of War* (2003) producer Robert May and *Hoop Dreams* (1994) creator Steve James joined the project. After a year of editing more than 800 hours of footage, the film was premiered at the Tribeca Film Festival, where it was awarded the prize for best documentary.

Assigned to serve in Fallujah in March 2004, the Guardsmen arrived just before insurgents hung up the burned bodies of several US war contractors. The US responded with extreme military force, providing a follow-up to the documentation of *Operation Dreamland*.[7] Assigned to Camp Anaconda in the Sunni triangle, *The War Tapes* shows Guardsmen escorting Halliburton supply trucks, patrolling local neighborhoods, and hanging out during downtime. The film includes footage of their families and their homecoming, and has the troops reflect throughout on their war experiences.

One of the solders notes that Halliburton is Dick Cheney's old company and the film makes clear that contracts for Bush-Cheney cronies are among the driving forces of the war, along with oil. The anti-war thrust of the film is expressed by the articulate mother of the Lebanese-American soldier Sgt. Zack Bazzi and the girlfriend of Sgt. Steve Pink, who makes clear the senselessness of the incursion and the distress for the soldiers' families. The soldiers themselves are cynical. Steve Pink insists the war is being fought for money and oil; Zack Bazzi basically sees the war as just providing jobs for himself and those who worked for the corporations that profited from it.

Some of the soldiers in *The War Tapes* are shown suffering from post-traumatic stress disorder (PTSD), a topic taken up in Patricia Foulkrod's poignant *The Ground Truth* (2006), which features interviews with US troops. The film contains scenes detailing or describing atrocities and showing the effects on wounded and maimed US troops, who try to understand what happened and come to terms with it.

In a similar genre, HBO's award-winning *Baghdad E.R.* (2006) focuses on emergency hospital treatment of wounded US troops and Iraqis, providing powerful images of the carnage of war on the bodies of young soldiers and Iraqi innocents. Likewise, HBO's *Alive Day Memories: Home From Iraq* (2007), directed by Jon Alpert and Ellen Goosenberg Kent, documents the experience of ten wounded American soldiers who describe the moment after being injured when they realized they were still alive and must carry on with the rest of their lives. Produced for HBO by *Sopranos* star James Gandolfini, who interacts compassionately with the troops, the film provides a very empathetic look at returning US soldiers who have to deal with the stress of injury, rehabilitation, and the after-effects of war.[8]

The Ground Truth (2006) shows the aftermath of US soldiers' experiences in Iraq, including post-traumatic stress syndrome.

Body of War (2008) is about the horrific effects of the war on return-ing vets. The film was co-produced by documentarian and cinematog-rapher Ellen Spiro and talk show host Phil Donahue, who lost his popular MSNBC talk show in 2003 when the network decided it did not want a daily anti-war TV-show on their schedule. *Body of War* takes one Iraq veteran as revelatory of the impact of the war on US troops and the American public, and exposes the infamy of the senators and congressmen who legitimated the rush to war. Focusing on returned paraplegic Tomas Young and his family, *Body of War* traces Young's struggle with medical rehabilitation and personal problems, and his foray into anti-war activism. The 22-year-old Kansas City youth joined the military two days after 9/11, hoping to fight its perpetrators in Afghanistan. Instead, he was sent to Iraq and was shot after less than a week of duty. The bullet penetrated beneath his collar-bone and para-lyzed him. Connecting the story of an average young man who suddenly faces enormous challenges and becomes an articulate activist within congressional debates over the infamous October 2002 war resolution, the film effectively demonstrates the lies and political cowardice that sent the nation to a disastrous war and the terrible effects on young people. Clips throughout the film of senate and congressional debate on the resolution which gave the president extraordinary powers to go to war show how pro-war senators and congressmen echo the mendacious "talking points" of the Bush-Cheney administration about Iraq's alleged possession of WMDs and ties to al Qaeda and terrorism. In the context of the 2008 presidential election, the passionate arguments of John McCain to go to war, echoing the lies of the Bush-Cheney administration, tie the Arizona senator to one of the most catastrophic policies of theRepublican administration, and reflect clearly his poor judgment and incapacity to be president. The litanies of infamy supported by Democrats and Republicans disgraced most of the Senate, and are contrasted with 90-year-old Robert Byrd's (D-W.Va) passionate argument to his fellow senators not to surrender their constitutional powers and to avoid a dangerous war. The film ends with Byrd proudly showing a plaque listing the 23 senators who voted against the war resolution. The old senator and the young vet read the roll of honor, naming one by one the heroic anti-war senators.

Body of War thus contrasts two bodies: that of a young man paralyzed by the war and the body of Congress that enabled the war. The film makes the strong constitutional argument that Congress made a grave error in surrendering its power. It also documents the honorable activities of the anti-war group that Young joined, Veterans Against the Iraq War (VAIW). In one memorable sequence Young meets Robby Mueller, a Vietnam vet who was also paralyzed and became a highly effective anti-war activist. The two trade war stories and discuss how to deal with the effects of a paralyzing wound. This episode suggests how it is youth who pay the price for misguided wars like Vietnam and Iraq. Another striking sequence pits Young's conservative and pro-war stepfather, who repeats Republican pro-war litanies and the vilification of those who oppose the war, with Young's anti-war mother and young wife, both of whom care for Tomas and support his anti-war activism.

Long sequences documenting Young's medical difficulties and painful recovery are harrowing, as is Terry Sander's film *Fighting for Life* (2008), which also focuses on combat injury cases among returning Iraq vets. The film shows traumatically wounded soldiers, and the doctors and nurses who struggle to save and rehabilitate them. *Fighting for Life* celebrates the medical care and rehabilitation of the vets, playing, in Susan L. Carruthers' words, "like an extended promotional ad for the beleaguered West Point of combat medicine."[9]

Interpreting the Iraq Fiasco

Following Robert Greenwald's *Uncovered* (2003, 2004), a number of documentaries took partisan positions on the Iraq War. Jehane Noujaim's *Control Room* (2004) shows the invasion and occupation of Iraq from the point of view of the Al Jazeera television network. Focusing on Al Jazeera reporters and executives, the invasion and occupation receive critical Arab perspectives, as well as footage and viewpoints not seen in Western mainstream media. There are also compelling interviews with a young US military public relations official who at first attempted to defend US pro-war positions, but who begins to question them as the horrors of the occupation proceed. *Control Room* documents the daily news gathering operation of Al Jazeera in Iraq, interspersed with criticisms of the network by Donald Rumsfeld and other US officials. We are forced to evaluate the network and the war from the compilation of news clippings, *cinéma vérité* footage, and interviews with a wide range of people.

Danny Schechter's *WMD: Weapons of Mass Deception* (2004), based on Sheldon Rampton and John Stauber's (2004) book, demonstrates how the US corporate media failed in their democratic responsibilities and were used as an instrument of manipulation and propaganda by the Bush-Cheney administration in selling and promoting the Iraq War.[10] Investigative journalist and self-described "news dissector," Schechter combines Michael Moore-like personal intervention with copious media images that demonstrate a pro-war and propagandistic bias on the part of the US corporate television networks. The film suggests how embedding war correspondents with troops is unlikely to produce critical reporting: MSNBC's Ashleigh Banfield makes a useful distinction between war journalism and war coverage, admitting the US corporate networks did more of the latter, thus providing Pentagon spin.

Michael Samstag and Debbie Etchison's *War and Truth* (2005) uses the topic of war correspondents to critique the mainstream corporate media's performance in Iraq.[11] After an idealized presentation of the heroics of war correspondents in World War II and Vietnam, with extended interviews with Norm Hatch and Joe Galloway and excellent footage and photos, the film switches to Iraq, where inevitable criticisms of the decline of journalism in the US corporate media's devolution from a truth-telling to a propaganda apparatus emerge, especially in the full interviews with Galloway and Helen Thomas on the DVD of the film.

From the right, *Buried in the Sand: The Deception of America* (2004) is a propaganda film that would have made Joseph Goebbels proud. It opens with the claim that it will reveal images not shown by the American media of "the faces of our enemy," ludicrously suggesting that the mainstream media had censored the horrors of Saddam Hussein's regime and the atrocities of radical Islam – surely some of the most reported stories of the contemporary era. Yet the quasi-pornographic images of beheadings, maimed bodies, and brutal torture strung together in the film, much of it available on the Internet, are shocking and grossed out many viewers.[12] Melodramatic narration and rightwing political commentary are provided by Mark Taylor, whose face is buried in blackness for much of the time, making him appear rather sinister. Laughable "factoids" on the DVD put on display the right wing's deep delusions and its proclivities toward a politics of lying, as when it is suggested that since 9/11 under the great leadership of George W. Bush, the US has won two wars, destroyed the Taliban, crippled al Qaeda, and stopped nuclear programs in North Korea, Iran, and Libya. As is now apparent, the leaders of al Qaeda and the Taliban got away in Afghanistan because the Bush-Cheney administration did not put enough troops on the ground to stop them and were distracted by their planned invasion and occupation of Iraq. Indeed, there was evidence by 2005 that both al Qaeda and the Taliban were on the rebound, that the Iraq intervention of choice had turned out to be a disaster, and that stopping nuclear programs by Iran and North Korea will require intelligent diplomacy, of which the Bush-Cheney administration was incapable (Kellner 2005). Yet the right wing seems to believe that by defining reality in its own way it therefore creates it – a practice undertaken by many figures in the Bush-Cheney administration.[13]

James Longley's *Iraq in Fragments*, nominated for an Academy Award in 2006, documents the fragmentation of Iraq into Shiite, Sunni, and Kurdish areas, showing the invasion and occupation from diverse Iraqi perspectives. The remarkable opening segment "Mohammed of Baghdad" focuses on a young Sunni boy, without a father, forced to work for a relative who insults and hits him, and then encourages him to go to school to learn to read and write. A segment shows the young boy idealizing the past and bemoaning a present that is indeed painful for him. The film suggests, without exploring the theme, that the young boy has been traumatized by the war and his country's tragedy and is unable to pass first grade, even after repeating it several times, and is simply not able to learn to read and write.

The second segment focuses on the Shiite South and shows the Islamic followers of Moqtada al Sadr in Najaf and Naseriyah. Shiite rituals of self-flagellation, re-experiencing the suffering of their martyr, are presented, along with militant anti-American speeches, showing the hostility toward the US occupation and united Islamic opposition. A third segment on the Kurdish North shows two young boys and their father attempting to mediate their traditional work-world with the challenges of a new Iraq. The Kurds presented in interviews do not appear to be excited by their "liberation." Footage of a Kurdish rally shows some Kurds are still bitter that they do not have their own flag and country.

Iraq in Fragments uses a stunning variety of documentary compilation techniques and footage to portray life after Saddam, showing moments of hope punctuated with bitter disappointment and tragedy. The fragments capture the variety and diversity of the country and the conflicts between their cultural traditions and the new post-Saddam Iraq. Whereas the film makes clear that many Iraqis were happy to get rid of the Baathist dictatorship, it also reveals the subsequent uncertainty, turmoil, and deep conflicts and contradictions in the country.

Michael Tucker and Petra Epperlei's *The Prisoner, or: How I Planned to Kill Tony Blair* (2007) presents a tragicomedy of the Iraq fiasco in its story of an Iraqi journalist, Yunis Khatayer Abbas, who was arrested, taken to Abu Ghraib, held for months, and then released when it was clear he was innocent. By chance, during the filming of his earlier documentary *Gunner Palace* (see above), Tucker took footage of Yunis's arrest while accompanying a convoy of American soldiers on the night of September 22, 2003 as they raided a house in a residential Baghdad neighborhood. The mission was to catch suspected bomb-making terrorists who allegedly had a plan to assassinate British Prime Minister Tony Blair. Yunis's brothers were soon released, but he was kept in jail and taken to the notorious Abu Ghraib prison, where he was held for months before being released. The film tells his story through photos, videos, animations, comic book graphics, and interviews woven together in a tapestry that attempts to win sympathy for an innocent journalist unjustly imprisoned.[14] The film illustrates in miniature the blundering of the US occupation and how innocent Iraqis were the victims.

Photojournalists Steve Connors and Molly Bingham's *Meeting Resistance* (2007) puts on display the origins of the Iraqi resistance to the US occupation and documents the passion and depth of the opposition. Craig Ferguson's *No End in Sight* (2007) provides a lucid and damning portrait of the blunders made by the architects of the US invasion and occupation. A former member of the Brookings Institute and the Council on Foreign Relations, with a Ph.D. from MIT, Ferguson has the credentials and connections to obtain interviews with high and mid-level members of the Bush-Cheney administration who planned and participated in the Iraq incursion. His portrait of them is devastating.[15] A first-time filmmaker, Ferguson invested $2 million he made from a software company into making the film, which covers the build-up to the war, the war itself, and the growing insurgency, civil war, and chaos in Iraq.

No End in Sight combines interviews (including with Iraqis) and stock and documentary footage shot in Iraq. The calm and authoritative voice-over by Campbell Scott provides context and underscores the critical views voiced in the interviews and contained in the footage. The film is accessible to a large audience, transcending differences between pro- and anti-war, liberal and conservative, in large part because Ferguson mostly interviewed supporters of the war and its architects in the Bush-Cheney administration, although people like Cheney, Rumsfeld, Wolfowitz, and Rice refused to appear.

The portrait it paints of the blunders made after the invasion and during the early months of the occupation is devastating. The major mistakes were lack of planning and the reliance on ideologues and inexperienced Bush-Cheney partisans who had no knowledge of Iraq, little if any military or diplomatic experience, and a thoroughly ideological agenda. Making specific arguments, the film maintains that the first major blunder was excluding the Iraqis from political control of their country, postponing elections for more than a year, and giving crucial authority to Paul Bremer and a small group of American neoconservatives, thus establishing the basis for Iraqis and others to perceive the incursion as a US occupation. While Iraqis had been promised that they would immediately be granted political power, this was withheld for over a year and created a strong impression that the US was stealing Iraq's resources.

The second major blunder involved "de-Baathification" of the ruling Sunni party, in effect firing everyone who had worked for the previous government, depriving Iraq of competent administrators, technocrats, and those who could run a government on a day-to-day basis. This was accompanied by the disbanding of the Iraqi army, which created a large force of angry and unemployed men who naturally gravitated to the Iraqi insurgency. The film interviews Bush-Cheney administration and Pentagon officials who claim they had contacts with the Iraqi military and plans to reconstitute it as a security force, purged of high-level leaders who had committed war crimes. However, these officials suddenly learned that the Iraq military had been completely disbanded. Predictably, outraged former Iraqi soldiers seized weapons from the arms stockpiles they were familiar with and a lethal insurgency began.

These fatal decisions were made by Paul Bremer, closely connected to Rumsfeld and the neoconservatives, whose Coalition Provisionary Authority (CPA) replaced the organization of Recovery and Humanitarian Assistance in Iraq (ORHA). ORHA had been developing plans made by State Department diplomats and included people with diplomatic and military experience. The people who joined Bremer and the CPA were largely ideologues totally lacking in military and diplomatic experience and knowing little about Iraq.

Many of the devastating blunders in the opening days of the occupation were already known and have been the subject of a stack of books. Yet Ferguson manages to get many participants on camera who themselves state how shocked they were by it all. In particular, the head of OHRA, who was believed to have been anointed the major US political czar of Iraq, General Jay Garner, tells how he was not consulted about disbanding the Iraqi government and military and was quickly relieved from his post and replaced by Bremer, who claimed a monopoly of authority. In another painful exchange, Col. Paul Hughes, who was in Iraq at the time of the invasion, describes his shock when he heard the Iraqi government and military were disbanded and how this went against the consensus of the US military and political leaders on the ground. In a revealing montage, Col. Hughes notes how his Pentagon and administration colleagues never discussed the momentous decision with him. Moreover, when the one Bush-Cheney administration architect of the failed occupation plan, neocon Walter Slocombe, speaks on camera, he first claims he discussed the decision with his counterpart Hughes, then goes memory dead, before moving on to defend the decision criticized by Hughes, Richard Armitage, and others.[16]

At one point, Donald Rumsfeld is asked in a press conference to describe what is going on in Iraq and bandies around some words like "guerrilla warfare" and "insurgency," while a reporter suggests "quagmire." Rumsfeld appears ready to go on the attack, but smiles and says with a self-confident smirk: "Quagmire…. That's somebody else's word. I don't do quagmires." The title of the documentary is, of course, *No End in Sight*, and the film demonstrates that Iraq has indeed led to a quagmire without apparent resolution.

Although the film brilliantly documents the incredible mistakes made by the Bush-Cheney administration, it does not question the origins and rationale of the war and presents it instead as a noble cause undercut and rendered disastrous by blundering ideologues and fools. Nor does it critically engage the second wave of disastrous policy choices that include the senseless fighting over and destruction of Fallujah, the horrors of Abu Ghraib and Guantanamo, and failures to produce any viable political settlement (although the film does end with dramatic figures on the cost of the war to the US, which could rise to trillions of dollars). Further, *No End in Sight* hints at but does not explore the more sinister sides of the Iraq fiasco. It pins the major blame for what went wrong on the CPA and its clumsy and blatant incompetence, with the support of Rumsfeld and the Bush-Cheney neoconservatives, but it does not really explore the reasons why Bremer and his associates made such disastrous and seemingly idiotic decisions, and thus does not really clarify why the US went into Iraq in the first place and what went wrong.

While it is still not clear exactly why the Bush-Cheney administration undertook to invade and occupy Iraq, there are a set of reasons quite different than the official ones. Whereas the explicit war aims were to shut down Iraq's alleged WMDs and thus enforce UN resolutions mandating that Iraq eliminate its weapons, there were many hidden agendas behind the offensive. To begin with, there were domestic political reasons why a war against Iraq could benefit the Republicans. When asked in summer 2002 why the Bush-Cheney administration was not more vigorously promoting the need for a war against Iraq, Bush's Chief of Staff Andrew Card proclaimed: "You do not roll out a new product in August." During Fall 2002, by contrast, the administration began hyping the dangers of Iraq – just before the November mid-term elections during which the Republicans asserted they were the firm national security party, ready to protect the country, while the Democrats, who were opposing an Iraq invasion, were said to be weak on defense. This was an argument used again in the 2004 presidential election.

Moreover, ideologues within the administration wanted to legitimate a policy of preemptive strikes and the so-called Bush doctrine. A successful attack on Iraq could inaugurate and normalize this policy that critics would later cite as an illicit preventive war.[17] Some of the same unilateralists in the Bush-Cheney administration envisaged world hegemony (the elder Bush's

New World Order), with the United States as the reigning military power and world police (Kellner 2003a, 2005). Increased control of the world's oil supplies provided a tempting prize for the former oil executives with key roles in the administration. Contracts for corporations like Halliburton and sectors of the military-industrial complex would be an even more highly profitable source of revenue for groups that supported the Bush-Cheney regime, and oil companies have benefited from the chaos in the region through higher prices and profits, ashave US construction and security companies.

Furthermore, key members of the neoconservative clique in the administration were linked to Israel's reactionary Likud party, which wanted to destroy Saddam Hussein's regime because it was seen as a threat to Israel. In addition, one might speculate on an Oedipus Tex drama. Perhaps George W. Bush wished to conclude his father's unfinished business and simultaneously prove himself and defeat evil to constitute himself as good. This might provide a psychological dimension to his thrust toward a war with the fervor of a religious crusade.

Complex events in history often have multiple causes and there were no doubt different agendas at work. To sell the policy to the public the Bush-Cheney regime had to provide reasons that would resonate and generate support. After 9/11, it used fear to win consent for its extreme rightwing policies, evoking images of nuclear attack, chemical and biological weapons, and purported connections between the Hussein regime and al Qaeda to attack the US. Intelligence was "cherry-picked" and "stove-piped" (Hersh 2004). *No End in Sight* does not explore these agendas or ask why the various principals in the administration supported the war. Bremer obviously shared the neoconservative belief that privatization of the Iraq economy and destruction of its state sector would open the door for American and other corporations to come in and take control of assets, including oil. Thus, disbanding the Baath regime and eliminating the Iraqi army would remove obstacles to US control of Iraq's economy. In addition, any disorder caused by an insurgency would produce hefty contracts for Halliburton, Blackwater, and the other US corporations who pocketed billions.

Curiously, *No End in Sight* barely mentions Dick Cheney, who was a major architect of the war and pushed harder for it than anyone else, profiting immensely his old firm Halliburton (which he had almost bankrupted as CEO), other corporate allies in the military-industrial and security sectors, and himself.[18] Both Rumsfeld and Cheney pushed for privatization of the US defense industry on issues ranging from security forces to food provision and toilet cleaning, all of which went disastrously wrong, filching billions from the US Treasury into corporate coffers, as well as enabling blatant corruption and incompetence.

As for Bush himself, *No End in Sight* shows him looking confused and out of his league, even in the infamous "Mission Accomplished" footage and "Bring 'em on" rhetoric. The "Mission Accomplished" footage is followed by a powerful montage of split-screen images of the insurgency and growing chaos in Iraq. Another image captures the "deer-in-the-headlights" stare of a little Bush (a.k.a. Shrub) as he prepares to make an Iraq speech. Thus, Bush is largely shown as a cipher out of the loop on major decisions and largely a figurehead. In fact, he was likely one of the major promoters of the overall policy of invasion and occupation, for many of the reasons suggested above. Consequently, while *No End in Sight* has gained non-partisan audiences and good reviews from all parts of the political spectrum, it leaves some crucial issues unexamined.[19]

Other documentaries explore the incarceration and torture of "enemy non-combatants" in Iraq and other arenas of the Bush-Cheney terror war. *Gitmo: The New Rules of War* (2005), directed by Swedish documentary filmmakers Erik Gandini and Tarik Saleh, investigates the Guantánamo Bay detention facility. Surprisingly, they arrange a trip to the base, which includes a free flight from Puerto Rico, $12 a night lodging, a tour of the base, and interviews with soldiers who spout the talking points of the moment. The filmmakers' intent, however, is serious, as they try to learn of the fate of a Swedish citizen, Mehdi Ghezali, held in the prison without charge, whose father had installed himself in a cage in a Stockholm public square to dramatize the case. The young Swede is released and after a period of silence accuses the Americans of torture, but refuses requests for interviews. When the Abu Ghraib story breaks, the filmmakers pursue the relatively unreported firing of Brigadier General Rick Baccus, who was in charge of interrogation at Gitmo and who allegedly refused harsh interrogation procedures (read torture). They are not able to interview the General, but do get on-camera time with Janice Karpinsky, who was in charge at Abu Ghraib and who is resentful of being scapegoated. She claims Major General Geoffrey Miller, who succeeded General Baccus at Gitmo, instituted more aggressive interrogation procedures, which he imported to Abu Ghraib.

Rory Kennedy's *Ghosts of Abu Ghraib* (2007) examines the mechanisms that produced the scandalous Abu Ghraib prison photos and tapes, which documented the humiliation and torture of Iraqi prisoners. The documentary opens with footage from psychologist Stanley Milgram's early 1960s Yale University "Obedience" experiment, which shows ordinary citizens administering supposedly increasingly severe electric shocks to subjects when ordered to do so by anonymous authorities. While the documentary focuses on the young men and women who produced the dossier of visual horror, it shows how specific policies formulated in the Bush White House and by Donald Rumsfeld in the Pentagon redefined torture and promoted the policies that resulted in Abu Ghraib and other torture scandals.

Alex Gibney's Academy Award winning documentary *Taxi to the Dark Side* (2007) adopts a more hard-hitting style and comprehensive framework in examining how the Bush-Cheney administration embraced torture as a weapon of choice. The documentary sets out the evolution of the justifications for torture, the mechanisms of both physical and psychological torture, and the problematic results of such interrogation. Focusing on an Afghan taxi driver named Dilawar, the film tells the story of his arrest while driving passengers in December 2002, his interrogation as a suspected Taliban, and his death in the notorious Bagram prison in Afghanistan. Tracking down family members who had been told that his death was treated as a homicide because of beatings inflicted in captivity, and five highly upset US soldiers implicated in his death, the film makes clear that the torture policies were the result of high government decisions in the Bush-Cheney administration and the Pentagon. *Taxi* suggests that the origin of the torture policy and practice is Dick Cheney and his associates, who received legal sanction from the US Justice Department and law professor John Woo, who drafted some of the most controversial measures legitimating torture and who continues to defend it. Gibney also demonstrates how the use of torture and its sanction by officials in the administration violates international law, morality, and a tradition of American values. He also questions whether torture really works. A poignant section on the DVD presents an interview with Gibney's father, dying of cancer, who strongly criticizes the use of torture and compares the interrogation procedures he and others used with Japanese prisoners in World War II, which were humane, created bonding with the prisoners, and produced useful results.

With *Standard Operating Procedure* (2008), Errol Morris joined the select group of documentary filmmakers who focused on Abu Ghraib and other torture scandals. Morris's stunning film is utterly original, exhibiting his signature style, thematics, and aesthetic. Combining the infamous Abu Ghraib photos, haunting interviews with those US soldiers who took them, recreations of scenes, and a discordant musical score by Danny Elfman, Morris inexorably reveals some of the truth about Abu Ghraib, while leaving some questions unanswered. The film demonstrates the full magnitude of what was going on in these barbaric events, and how low the US fell during the reign of Bush, Cheney, Rumsfeld, and their hench-people.

Starting off slowly, Morris shows some of the photos and the US soldiers who took them, most of whom were lowly guards in the 372nd MP company at Abu Ghraib and who were scapegoated for the atrocities. We see a startlingly older and broader Lynndie Englund telling how she posed for the pictures at the behest of her military superior and lover, Charles Graner. She blames him for her misdeeds, universalizing the crime by claiming that behind every horrible thing a woman has ever done is a man who goaded her to it. Many other interviewees attempt to justify themselves. General Janet Karpinski, the highest Pentagon official who was initially scapegoated, defends herself, claiming that a general above her put a colonel below her in charge of the interrogations and the "dark side," while she remained totally innocent and "out of the loop" concerning all of the crimes. Morris undercuts this defense, however, with tight framing and headshots that make Karpinski appear like a criminal under interrogation; Morris also shifts her image quickly from one side of the frame to another, subliminally suggesting that she is spinning.

Some of the guards who seemed to be the good guys earlier in their interviews reveal complicity that makes the viewer suspicious. Yet Morris's vision and the situation are so complex that we feel some sympathy for all of the guards (except perhaps Graner and Ivan Frederick, the seniors to the young guards who are still in prison and whom the army would not allow Morris to interview). Morris does his best to contextualize the guards' behavior, allowing them to tell him how all of the heinous practices at Abu Ghraib were already going on when they arrived. Further, the prison was constantly mortared by Iraqi insurgents, so the guards were always on edge. One Iraqi guard smuggled a gun into the prison and a prisoner shot wildly at US troops, wounding one, before he was killed. The accused young underlings insist they were merely guards under orders to "soften up" prisoners for interrogation, while the really rough stuff was going on in the interrogation side of prison, of which we see and learn little in the film. (One interviewee, Tim Dugan, was a contract interrogator from a private firm, CACI – a startling revelation of the extent to which Rumsfeld, Cheney, and Co. privatized the military so that their corporate allies could grab a slice of the Iraqi pie.)

The film builds to a shocking conclusion. Brent Pack, a military analyst who was part of the prosecuting team, states that some of the activities seen in the film were a crime for which the guards were sentenced to various prison terms (revealed in titles at the end of the film). However, many horrific activities were merely judged standard operating procedure (SOP), which raises fundamental questions about the morality of the US military and its political leaders. For instance, the infamous photo of a hooded prisoner, who we now know by his nickname Gilligan, forced to stand on a box for hours with wires affixed to his hand, was deemed SOP.

Morris's unpacking of the context of the Abu Ghraib images is compelling, but he does not really go into the broader context, or inquire into who was really responsible for some of the most monstrous military crimes in US history. We see some pictures of Rumsfeld in the beginning of the film, a quick image of Bush, but not much more. Interrogator Tim Dugan claims he heard that Rumsfeld and top Iraqi US commander Ricardo Sanchez had ordered the humiliation and torture. Dick Cheney is not mentioned, nor is there any attempt to establish the hierarchy and chain of command of responsibility.[20] To be sure, the angry and bitter General Karpinski names military superiors and one subordinate, but Morris does not investigate the military authorities' responsibility, nor the role of the CIA, DIA, FBI, and other government agencies mentioned in the film.[21]

Morris is also concerned to interrogate the photos and the ways they conceal and reveal at the same time. The scandal erupted globally because three guards used digital cameras and one cell phone video device to document the appalling humiliation, torture, and death of Iraqi prisoners. We learn that the guards had a variety of motives for taking the pictures, which were collected on CDs and sent around the world on the Internet. Eventually, some of them were sent to the military police, who were forced to investigate, especially after the military learned that photos had been sent to CBS News and investigative reporter Seymour Hersh (Morris does not recount this part of the story). Morris's achievement is to show how documentary film can help us understand people and events and interrogate important phenomena like digital photographic images.

It is, of course, impossible to gauge the impact of these anti-Iraq documentaries on US and global public opinion. Some of the most acclaimed and critically rewarded Iraq docs did not take in much box office, or even get general release, and many did not appear on television. On the other hand, many were shown on television, were awarded prizes at film festivals, and were promoted nationally by their filmmakers. Moreover, Robert Greenwald and others involved in guerrilla networking and promoting their films on the Internet had a new distribution strategy that enabled film to be an instrument of political education and mobilization. On this model, films become part of political organizing and dialogue, preparing the public for the struggles ahead.

Iraq and Its Aftermath in Fiction Films

In addition to critical documentaries on Iraq, a wave of fiction films appeared during the war itself that portray its consequences for the Iraqi people and US veterans. While during the Vietnam War the sole fiction film to appear was John Wayne's comic book-like and highly conservative *The Green Berets* (1967), a laughable propaganda piece for the war in the mode of World War II combat films, critical films were coming out almost immediately in the 2000s that deal with the horrors of the Iraq fiasco and the emotional effects on soldiers, families, and friends on the home front.

Initial Iraq fiction films included low budget pot-boilers like *American Soldiers* (2005) and the disappointing film by Irwin Winkler, *Home of the Brave* (2006). Starting with *The Situation* in 2006, noteworthy fiction films appeared in 2007 and 2008, including *In the Valley of Elah*, *Redacted*, and *War, Inc.* In 2008 there was the poignant and powerful homecoming film *Stop-Loss*, the highly revealing and graphic HBO miniseries *Generation Kill*, Nick Broomfield's stunning *The Battle for Haditha*, and other Iraq fiction films that cumulatively constitute an astonishing engagement with a highly unpopular war, despite the low box office of most of the films in question.

Philip Haas's *The Situation* (2006) combines the genres of war film, romance, and political thriller to try to capture the complexity and turmoil of the Iraq quagmire. The film opens with US soldiers throwing two young Iraqi boys off a bridge because they do not understand the soldiers' orders to return home. Based on a true incident, one of the Iraqi kids could not swim and was drowned.

The film shows reporter Anna (Connie Nielsen) investigating the story and discovering the complexities of the Iraq incursion. Set mostly in Baghdad and Samarra, the film attempts to portray "the situation," which comprises protracted political conflicts between Iraqi moderates and extremists, insurgents and Iraqi police, and US occupation forces squabbling among themselves as they fight Iraqis, al Qaeda, and indeterminate others. Although a love triangle and melodrama detract somewhat from the politics, the film makes clear that the various factions will probably not be able to come together and resolve their conflicts, and that the US is condemned to make unholy alliances with unsavory forces in an impossibly muddled and violent situation.

Abstracting from the horrors of the war itself, Irwin Winkler's *Home of the Brave* (2006) focuses on the homecoming of four Iraq veterans. Since Iraq was not the uplifting "good war" of World War II, the narrative and tone is bound to be downbeat and muted. Yet *Home of the Brave* turns out to be an ideological vessel that tries to redeem the terrible losses of the destructive invasion and occupation through the heroic struggle for recovery and redemption of the returning US soldiers. The film opens idyllically, with US troops shooting baskets and then getting together a small football game in their Iraq desert base. These activities code them as appealing and typical Americans. During the opening Iraq sequence, we also see an American soldier carrying a dog, and a surgeon helping out Iraqi children, while an Iraqi insurgent rigs a dog with explosives. Thus, the Americans are coded as good and the Iraqi resistance as evil – exactly the way of seeing of the Bush-Cheney administration.

The company is sent on a humanitarian mission, only to be ambushed by the evil insurgents. Predictably, one of the soldiers shown in the opening sequence is killed. Further, a pretty and lively young woman who had been shooting basketball hoops, and who had just called her family to tell of the imminent homecoming of the company, is maimed.

Keeping the narrative gears rolling, the next sequence portrays the homecoming of the unit, focusing first on the surgeon, Will Marsh (Samuel L. Jackson). Marsh returns in a cab to his Spokane home, is greeted by his overjoyed wife, and is eyed suspiciously by his teenage son Tommy, signaling father-son conflict as part of the plot machine. As Marsh hugs his wife, a cut to his eyes shows that not all is well in the land of the free and the home of the brave, and that trauma and melodrama will soon ensue.

A backyard barbeque scene shows Marsh alienated from the trivial concerns of everyday life, existing in his own space of hurt and horror, cut off from others. Struggling with his demons and fueled by excessive alcohol, Marsh embarrasses his family at a Thanksgiving dinner, coming in drunk with bar buddies and making an inappropriate speech. He then explodes with anger and pulls off his son's lip-ring. Marsh pulls himself together in a later scene, and defends his son in a meeting with the principal of the high school who wants to discipline him for wearing a Buck Fush T-shirt. Marsh strongly defends his son's right to protest the Iraq War, bringing the family closer together. The scene elicits the only political discussion of the war in the film, with the son criticizing the "occupation" and conduct of the war that violates fundamental American principles. However, as Jeanine Plant notes:

> As he and his son walk back to the car, Marsh tells him he has no right to criticize a war he hasn't participated in, and therefore knows nothing about. As if to ensure there will be no boycotts of the movie, Marsh later concludes that his son is against the war not merely on principle, but because he's just a typical teenage boy rebelling against his father, and a war his father happened to be in. Depoliticizing a deeply political topic is nothing new for a mainstream Hollywood film. But political aversion at this moment in time is practically spineless. It would not be considered remotely radical to criticize the Iraq War on political grounds during a time when Bush's approval ratings are so low, and there is a resounding, bipartisan consensus that the war in Iraq is a mess.[22]

That's it for the politics. The rest of *Home of the Brave* creaks on to themes of reconciliation and banal sentimentality. Tommy reconciles with his father, who ends up rejoining the military so he can be with his band of brothers and help them out in Iraq, acknowledging that the war may not be popular and right but it's the place for him, a position that would make John Wayne proud.

This largely conservative Iraq homecoming film never really questions the politics of the war, which it generally avoids like the plague. Moreover, it fails to address the fact that one of the reasons so many Iraq veterans return traumatized and deeply disturbed is that the Iraq intervention had no legitimate rationale and was a disaster that greatly harmed the US. None of the returning troops in *Home of the Brave* utters a single anti-war sentiment and no anti-war activity is shown. The political cowardice of the film undercuts its well-meaning intention of showing Iraq war veterans trying to cope with war trauma and adjust to normal life.

In 2007 some big-budget and serious independent fiction films on Iraq and the "war on terror" were released, including *Rendition*, *Lions for Lambs*, *In the Valley of Elah*, *Grace is Gone*, and *Redacted*.[23] While none was successful financially, the cycle testified to disillusionment with Iraq policy and helped compensate for mainstream corporate media neglect of the consequences of the war.

Brian De Palma's *Redacted* takes the shocking story of the rape and murder of a young Iraqi girl by a US troop unit to explore the horrors of the war. The film is also an avant-garde interrogation of media technology and the politics of representation. Shot completely in video, the film uses documentary video footage, Vblogs and YouTube entries, websites, video surveillance, courtroom testimony, and television to tell the story of one of the most disgraceful atrocities of the war. Set in Samarra, the film reproduces the real-life rape, murder, and burning of Abeer Qasim Hamza al-Janabi, a 14-year-old Iraqi girl, in March 2006 by US soldiers, who also killed her family and burned their bodies. The story replicates the rape and murder portrayed in De Palma's 1989 Vietnam film *Casualties of War*, but is rougher and rawer.

Redacted opens with Pvt. Angel Sakazar (Izzy Diaz) beginning a digital video documentary that he thinks will help him get into film school at the University of Southern California after his Iraq tour of duty. Footage goes back and forth from Angel's video diary to a French documentary replete with bombastic classical music, in a witty satire of French art documentary, and the other forms of video mentioned. De Palma's point is that the various media, ranging from an Al-Jazeeresque Arab TV channel, Jihadist websites, and the video produced by the American participants and their families all construct a very different version of the Iraq situation, which has all been edited or redacted to provide a very partial, biased, and one-sided version of a complex reality. De Palma's own redaction, however, provides a strongly anti-war statement by choosing a US atrocity as its topic.

An opening episode has the unit shooting at a car full of Iraqi civilians at a road-block and killing a pregnant woman. While this upsets some of the unit, others are unconcerned with the civilian deaths and begin having rape fantasies, an idea nurtured by their physical harassment of young Iraqi girls going through the checkpoint. When their sergeant in killed by insurgents, they go into a rage and plan and execute the rape, which Angel videos. Others in the unit try to restrain them but end up fleeing in disgust.

The film premiered at the 2007 Venice Film Festival, where De Palma won a Silver Lion best director award for the film. De Palma effectively references and appropriates some of the themes and cinematic techniques of the Iraq documentaries discussed in this chapter. *Redacted* shows the US troops shooting Iraqis and breaking into houses and terrorizing families, while they are themselves subject to attacks, roadside bombs, and mines, all explored in previous Iraq docs. In a very effective technical move, De Palma deploys the green nighttime camera images used in *Operation Dreamland* and *The War Tapes* to portray the unit at they move through the dark to attack the house of the young girl where they plan the rape, coding them visually as monsters with green alien eyes. The rape scene is harsh and nightmarish, leading some of the platoon to withdraw and later expose the incident.

A series of other fictional films deals with the plight of veterans returning from Iraq or relatives dealing with the trauma of a missing or killed sibling. Paul Haggis's *In the Valley of Elah* (2007) uses a quest drama and police thriller for the story of a father seeking to find out what happened when he is told that his son has gone AWOL after returning from a tour of duty in Iraq. Vietnam veteran Hank Deerfield (Tommy Lee Jones) sets out for the military base in New Mexico where his son had been stationed. In pursuit of the truth, he learns that his son and other Iraq vets had been brutalized by their war experiences and returned highly traumatized, driving them into drugs and heavy drinking and periodically exploding into violent rage. Deerfield learns that his all-American good kid son has been terribly altered by these experiences, as have his young platoon squad, who at first appear polite and professional when Hank questions them about his son's last days. As the story unfolds, however, it turns out that they were lying. More shocking, it is revealed that one of his son's military buddies brutally stabbed him in an inexplicable drunken rage, and the rest of the guys cut him up into pieces and deposited the remains in the desert to make it appear that it was Mexican drug dealers who had done the dirty deed.

Based on a true story, the plot slowly unfolds how the Iraq experience has turned typical good-natured young Americans into highly traumatized individuals who are dangerous to themselves and others. While the film follows the conventions of a police thriller, the father's quest is really to find out what happened to his son in Iraq and what Iraq has done to

Americans. Deerfield steals his son's cell phone from the military base and gets a hacker to send him reconstructed images from his son's tour in Iraq. In fragmented and fractured form, the images capture the chaotic reality of the US troops' experiences, including revelations that his son regularly tortured Iraqi prisoners, winning him the nick name "Doc," and suggesting that the son was especially traumatized by the accidental killing of a young Iraqi boy by his platoon's vehicle.[24]

The narrative is organized around two major metaphors that illuminate the characters and plot development. "In the Valley of Elah" refers to the biblical site where David fought and defeated Goliath, and the metaphor highlights Deerfield's fight to uncover the truth against the military criminal justice system and a malignant state apparatus. Deerfield is assisted by a police investigator (Charlize Theron) who fights against an incompetent police bureaucracy and highly sexist colleagues.

The other major metaphor is the American flag as a symbol of the ship of state. Deerfield sees a flag on a public building being flown upside down and puts it the right way up, explaining to a Salvadorean worker that flying the flag upside down symbolized SOS, that people are suffering dire crisis and need help. At the end of the movie, Deerfield goes back to the building and turns the flag upside down, telling the Salvadorean that this is now how the flag should be flown, signifying that the crusty veteran has come to understand the immense crisis his country is in.

Francesco Lucente's *Badland* (2007) documents with brutal realism how the Iraq War has traumatized its veterans and shows the human

In the Valley of Elah depicts Tommy Lee Jones' ex-military man turning the flag upside down to denote crisis in the country.

costs of the war. It opens with a voice-over during which we learn that Jerry (Jamie Draven) has been dishonorably discharged from the Marines after being court-martialed. We see him at work in a filling station, falsely accused of stealing and selling propane and docked $60 from his meager paycheck. Returning home, he is henpecked relentlessly by his pregnant wife Nora (Vinessa Shaw), who is pilfering his wages and not paying bills. When he discovers that his wife is hoarding his wages he shoots her and their two boys. A jammed gun and his daughter Celina's (Grace Fulton) pleading eyes stop him from shooting her and himself. The rest of the film deals with their flight from their trashy Montana trailer across a desolate landscape to a small town where they seek to create a new life.

Newspapers and television reports make it clear that national law enforcement are searching for the soldier who killed his family. His daughter retreats into a fantasy world in which God speaks to her and promises the return of her mother and brothers. Wandering into a local diner, Jerry is offered a job by the comely owner Oli (Chandra West), who makes clear the possibilities that he has lost because of his actions, which are bound to catch up with him. Oli introduces Jerry to Max (Joe Morton), a Gulf War reserve veteran who had been drafted and sent to Iraq, where he served 18 months in Najaf, and is seriously traumatized. Max is also police chief and as he bonds with Jerry it is clear that he will discover his crime. Before the inevitable confrontation, the two open up to each other. Jerry tells of the brutal crimes his unit perpetrated in Fallujah and how they were scapegoated and dismissed in disgrace, while Max is wracked with guilt and shame and is not able to fathom why they were sent to Iraq.

Badland's concluding scenes are extremely shocking. The images and narratives transcode a bleak existential vision of the meaninglessness of life and how individuals become brutalized by their circumstances. The daughter's constant religious utterances provide a pendant to the father's growing disbelief and experience of utter abandonment in a harsh and unforgiving universe where American life has become a "badland" for its victims.

James C. Strouse's *Grace is Gone* (2007) shows the impact of Iraq on family and loved ones in its tale about a husband, Stanley (John Cusack), whose wife Grace is serving with the military in Iraq. He receives notification that Grace has been killed in action and the rest of the film shows how Stanley deals with the loss. He cannot summon up the courage to tell his daughters and instead takes off on a trip to a Florida amusement park. A visit with his brother reveals that Stanley cheated on an eye test to get into the military, but when his poor eye-sight was uncovered he was dismissed. The encounter with the brother, who is still living with their mother in the family home and questions the war aims, also reveals that Stanley is incapable of questioning his conservative beliefs. He does not allow his daughters to think for themselves, but imposes upon them his rigid conservatism.

This sad, muted, and tender movie, with a delicate Clint Eastwood score, attempts to portray the bonding and love of a father and two daughters in a time of adversity. However, perhaps inadvertently, it puts on display the rigidity of a blinkered conservatism that is unable to see its limitations and complicity in a failed war. The film also shows the problematic nature of conservative socialization, as the father gently but firmly imposes his views on his daughters. Conservatives in George W. Bush's America are shown in a state of willful denial, unable to see the catastrophe brought about by their president and his policies. Further, although the film's sympathy ultimately lies with the bereaved Stanley, he fails to display the least insight or self-reflection. His brother's anti-war views are barely articulated and are counterposed by a vigorous background speech on television by Donald Rumsfeld, thus allowing conservatives to continue to believe that it is their duty to support the Bush-Cheney administration, whatever the costs.

A low-budget political thriller, *Conspiracy* (2008) features an Iraq veteran suffering from PTSD returning to the US, seeking his missing Marine buddy, and uncovering astonishing corruption in a New Mexico town. Learning that crooked cops killed his buddy, he goes after the evil doers and blows the town apart. Set in the same thematic universe as *Bad Day at Black Rock* (1955) and *Rambo: First Blood*, which also show returning veterans uncovering corruption and rot in the land, *Conspiracy* takes on the very forces that got us into the Iraq War and who profited by it. The film opens in Iraq in 2005 with a Marine Sergeant Special Operations officer, MacPherson (Val Kilmer), and his company entering an urban compound to take out terrorist snipers. MacPherson summarily executes an Iraqi general, who is presumably guilty of aiding terrorists. As the company leaves the city it encounters a young girl with a teddy bear who is booby-trapped with a suicide bomb that explodes. MacPherson saves a comrade, Mexican Corporal Miguel Silva (Greg Serano), but both are seriously wounded, with MacPherson losing a leg. Flashbacks recreate the carnage that severely injured them and evidently traumatized MacPherson.

The two men bond during their months of rehab. Miguel tells MacPherson how he learned English and joined the Marines to take his family to New Mexico to become citizens and start a new life. Out of the hospital and retired, MacPherson tries to escape from his trauma with drink and whores, but Miguel constantly calls to ask him to come to New Mexico, and eventually MacPherson relents. Arriving in New Lago, near the border with Mexico, MacPherson finds that nobody knows of his buddy. The townspeople are generally sinister and threatening, bullying MacPherson. Eventually, he learns that the CEO of Halicorp (an obvious Halliburton reference) is buying land, constructing a simulated Western town and community, exploiting cheap Mexican workers and then sending them packing, while employing a vigilante border patrol to keep out unwelcome immigrants.

MacPherson discovers that the CEO, Rhodes (Gary Cole), killed Miguel and his family. He vows vengeance, blowing up the town and killing the villains with knives, assault weapons, his prosthetic leg, and his bare hands. Before doing so, MacPherson verbally assaults Halicorp that drives the US war against Iraq, makes money off of rebuilding the country, and uses the profits to buy up land and political patronage in the US. This is a surprisingly acute political message for a low-budget action film. Likewise, it provides a critique of vigilante border patrols who seek to keep out undocumented workers.[25] In fact, as the action and carnage unfold, it's the "good Americans" versus the corrupt and vicious henchmen of the CEO and his corporation, anticipating the political battles to come against Bush-Cheney-McCain.[26]

John Cusack's *War, Inc.* (2008) carries out a full-scale attack on the military-industrial complex, American culture and society, and popular and commodity culture as a defining export. *War, Inc.* captures the insanity and surreal chaos of the Bush-Cheney administration's Iraq War and mania for privatization. Inspired by Naomi Klein's conception of the "shock doctrine,"[27] and based on a script by Cusack, novelist Mark Leyner, and *Bullworth* author Jeremy Pikser, the film engages in a biting satire of the invasion and occupation of Iraq, and the privatization and commercialization of its economy. Directed by Joshua Seftel, the film stars Cusack as corporate assassin Brand Hauser, sent to the Middle Eastern country of Turaqistan (read Iraq), where he works for a Halliburton-like corporation, Tamerlane. Hauser is sent to assassinate the Iraqi oil minister, who is planning to build his own oil pipe-line and is thus an obstacle to the take-over of Iraq by US corporations. Hauser says the venture is

"the first war ever to be 100-percent outsourced to private enterprise."
He receives his instructions from the Tamerlane CEO (Dan Aykroyd),
who is an "ex-vice president," and, in a great imitation of Dick Cheney,
orders the hit via live video-phone while sitting on the toilet.

The satire suggests there are profits to be made on rebuilding a country
that the US destroyed, a theme embellished in Hauser's assignment to a
trade show where corporations sell their products to the Iraqis. We see a
trade show dance routine by war-amputee Rockettes, who show off their
prosthetic legs. The political critique is offered through the eyes of journalist Natalie Hegalhuzen (Marisa Tomei), who writes for liberal maga-
zines like *The Nation* and who Hauser falls for. A subplot follows the
marriage at the trade show of Hilary Duff as a Central European singer
named Yonica Babyyeah. She at first comes off as a pop slut who belts
out repeated double (actually triple) entendres such as "I want to *blow*
you ... *up.*" She tries to seduce Hauser, but it turns out she is really a nice,
sensitive girl, exploited by managers and commercial pop culture.
Journalists also get savaged in the film, as the international media are
shown "experiencing the war" via Combat-O-Rama, a virtual "Implanted
Journalist Experience" in which they experience war by means of a video
game. Reporters gladly accept implanted chips from Tamerlane which
intensify the experience. They shout with glee "I've been hit!" as they
enter virtual war and no doubt do their reporting to promote the war
aims of the corporation giving them a good time.

However, an extremely harrowing battle scene unfolds when Hauser
and Hegalhuzen investigate affairs in an off-limit town named Felafel –
obviously a stand-in for Fallujah, where stories about four murdered
American contractors hung on a bridge by insurgents led Cusack to look
into the role of US corporations in Iraq. In the film's satire, the war is
fought solely by private corporations like Tamerlane. The surreal war
scene is genuinely frightening and evokes those in films like *Full Metal
Jacket.*

Satirizing puppet government, the American viceroy of Turaqistan,
Walken (Ben Kingsley), turns out to be Hauser's CIA trainer who runs
affairs within the Emerald City in a bunker fronted by a Popeye's Chicken.
He gives his directives by means of electronic billboards that emit messages from faces that morph every few seconds from one American pop
icon to another – Ronald Reagan, Pamela Anderson, John Wayne, the
Fonz, and so on. Hauser unveils the diminutive figure running the country who, like himself, has transformed from CIA thug to corporate tool.

War, Inc. is thematically connected to the 1997 cult film *Grosse Pointe Blank* in which Cusack (who co-wrote the script and helped produce the film) plays a military/CIA assassin who has gone freelance. He reconsiders his trade when he attends his tenth high school reunion, is reunited with the love of his life, and comes under attack from rival assassins. This low-key satire captures the cynicism of the Reagan-Bush I era, when state assassination was part of US policy and Gen-X yuppies were led to believe that business and making money, no matter what the cost, were the be all and end all of the American Dream. Thus, *Grosse Pointe Blank* effectively satirized the values and amorality of an era whose crass capitalism and aggressive imperialism expanded to the point of insanity in *War, Inc.*, signaling the continuities between the two conservative eras.

Nick Broomfield's *Battle for Haditha* (2008) uses the form of docudrama and fictional re-creation to depict the November 19, 2005 bombing of a Marine convoy and the resulting rampage by the Marines in an Iraqi village, killing 24 civilians. A documentary filmmaker renowned for exposés in which he himself plays a major narrative and interventionist role (*Kurt and Courtney, Biggie and Tupac*, and *Aileen: Life and Death of a Serial Killer*, among others), Bloomfield uses former Marines and Iraqi refugees to play the participants. Using a nervous, hand-held camera, Broomfield attempts to capture the gritty reality and violence involved in the US occupation's fight against the Iraqi insurgency, with innocent Iraqis caught in the middle.

The action takes place in Haditha, a city in the hotly contested "Sunni triangle" of Al Anbar province west of Baghdad, controlled periodically by insurgents and a major battleground. The story opens with US Marines buying DVDs in an Iraqi shop. A young boy leaves, joining an older man, Ahmad (Falah Flayeh), to meet with al Qaeda representatives who pay them to set a roadside bomb to kill Americans patrolling the area. Ahmad makes it clear that he was formerly a member of the Iraqi army and is desperately trying to feed his family. For him, it was a great mistake that the Americans disbanded the army, throwing so many armed Iraqis onto the street and into the hands of the insurgency.

Focus then switches to Marines patrolling convoys on the road leading to Haditha, where 60 Marines had been killed recently in the aftermath of the Fallujah battles. A Marine platoon is led by Cpl. Ramirez (Elliot Ruiz), a competent and articulate young man suffering from sleep disorder. The third group of major characters comprises an extended Iraqi family next to the roadside where the bomb will explode and who are seen celebrating the circumcision of a young baby and going about their daily lives. In particular, a love story between an ordinary couple dramatizes the humanity of the people and their conversations, and that ordinary people are caught in the cross-fire.

The fatal bomb explodes, killing one Marine and injuring several, and Ramirez is given orders to go after the perpetrators. Filled with anger, he shoots five young Iraqis in a roadside car near the bombing and leads his platoon into the village, shooting up innocent families, including women and children. While the action is brutal and shocking, the film makes the major villains the al Qaeda operatives who smugly proclaim that pictures of Americans killing civilians will constitute a victory for the insurgency. The other heavies are the Marine officers who congratulate Ramirez after the massacre, awarding him a medal, and then cover-up the killing of civilians in a totally mendacious report when the facts of the day's events become known.

Battle for Haditha's construction of events on a fatal day in the war was both attacked and praised,[28] but it emerges as one of the most provocative films dealing with the war. *Stop-Loss* (2008), writer-director Kimberly Peirce's first feature since *Boys Don't Cry* (1999), combines powerful Iraq battle footage with intense scrutiny of the problems and injustices US soldiers face on their return home. The film opens with a troop of young soldiers horsing around and making their own videos in Iraq, but their high-spirited absurdism is followed by a cut to a battle in Tikrit, Iraq, Saddam Hussein's hometown and a hotbed of Sunni insurgency. A young staff sergeant, Brandon King (Ryan Phillippe), directs his squadron into an alleyway to pursue Iraqi assailants when the soldiers themselves come under attack. Several are killed and others are seriously wounded. The long battle sequence shows the brutality of urban warfare, as the squadron is assaulted by snipers and groups of well-armed insurgents, while the soldiers kill innocent civilian women and children.

The soldiers are given leave and three longtime friends return to their hometown in Texas, where they participate in a boisterous parade, are awarded medals, and party until they drop. Behind the fun of the homecoming, however, lurk demons, with excessive drinking, flashbacks to the brutal war, and explosions of violence. Just as *Boys Don't Cry* captured the brutality that could explode at any moment from hypermasculinity out of control, so too does *Stop-Loss* explore how traumatized men socialized into a violent hypermasculinity can be a danger to themselves and others.

Troops who thought they were coming home from Iraq learn they will be sent back in *Stop-Loss*.

Brandon, a highly decorated war hero and leader of the pack, decides not to re-enlist. While helping his childhood buddies deal with the stress of post-Iraq traumatic stress disorders, he learns he is not going to be discharged after all. Instead, he will be sent back to Iraq thanks to a policy – Stop-Loss – that lets the military redeploy soldiers to battlefields even after they've completed their military service. The highly patriotic young soldier explodes in anger, telling his military superior to "Fuck the president," and then escapes and goes AWOL .

The rest of *Stop-Loss* pursues Brandon's fruitless and hopeless road trip to see a senator who had promised him at the homecoming parade that if he ever needed anything to just ask. Brandon is accompanied by his best friend Steve's fiancée, Michele (Abbie Cornish), who Steve had punched in a drunken stupor on his homecoming night and who he later informed that they will not be getting married because he has re-enlisted. The road trip provides a harrowing look at small-town America, as Brandon and Michele meet other US troops on the run from Stop-Loss recalls. One African-American soldier who has been on the move for 14 months and is leaving the country tells of a New York lawyer who will help them escape to Canada.

The trip also includes a visit to the family of a fallen soldier from Brandon's unit. He explains how their son died: "following standard operating procedure," the unit had gone into a civilian neighborhood to pursue assailants. The bitter brother asks Brandon if it was standard operating procedure to lead troops into an ambush and a suicidal mission, and he grimaces with remorse. Upon leaving the family's house, Brandon discovers his car has been broken into, and explodes with rage when he comes across the young perpetrators who stole his luggage, as if he were still in the war in Iraq and facing insurgents.

In another poignant visit with a maimed, burned, and blinded amputee buddy at a military hospital, Brandon helps the young man put on his artificial arm, a scene recalling William Wyler's coming-home film from World War II, *The Best Years of Our Lives* (1946). *Stop-Loss* makes it clear that these are the worst years of their lives for the returning Iraq vets, with no end of the war in sight. Brandon learns that there are no easy answers to his dilemma. He meets a lawyer in New York to see about assuming a new identity and moving to Canada, and also considers crossing the Texas border into Mexico. The film's last scenes reveal that Brandon has signed up again, rejoined Steve, and is off to Iraq.

Neil Burger's *The Lucky Ones* (2008) depicts the homecoming of three soldiers on leave from tours of duty in Iraq, but it is more of a bonding and friendship film than Iraqi homecoming film (the three protagonists end up going back to Iraq after assorted problems on the home front). The HBO movie *Taking Chance* (2009), by contrast, demonstrates the pain and cost of lost lives in its story, based on his book, about how Marine Lt. Col. Michael Strobl (Kevin Bacon) chose to take the body of 19-year-old Chance Phelps, killed in 2004 in Anbar province, back to his family in Wyoming. While Kevin Bacon's eyes and demeanor poignantly portray the sacrifice and loss of the young soldier's life, the narrative provides a highly conservative redemptive vision in an Iraq homecoming film, as ordinary citizens exhibit reverence and respect for the dead soldier. This deeply conservative film attempts to provide a redemptive gloss on the Iraq tragedy by making it appear that the tragic loss of a young soldier's life has meaning. His family is supposed to be consoled by how all the people whom Strobl encountered on his cross-country journey were touched by Chance and how he supposedly made an impact on their lives.

The year 2008 marked the fifth anniversary of the seemingly endless Iraq War, which had taken over 100,000 Iraqi and over 4,000 US lives, and cost $863,744,580,496 as of June 2, 2009.[29] It has also left countless veterans traumatized, often without adequate medical care. Over 81,000 troops have been recalled via Stop-Loss, when they thought they had escaped from the nightmare. While the box office failure of many Iraq films shows that the experience is too painful for audiences to confront, Hollywood should be congratulated for attempting to show the horrors of one of the defining events of the era.

Yet the best of the Iraq homecoming films, like *In the Valley of Elah*, *Badland*, and *Stop-Loss*, run the risk of demonizing US soldiers rather than those who sent them to a senseless war, who deployed Stop-Loss to send them back, and failed to provide adequate care afterwards. Still, the Hollywood Iraq cycle has helped break through the indifference and failure to confront what the Iraq disaster is doing to both Iraqis and US soldiers and their loved ones. Hence, on the whole, it is laudatory that Hollywood has engaged with the issues in the Iraq War while it was still ongoing and a festering sore in the body politic that the corporate media and many politicians and citizens chose to ignore.

Notes

1   On *cinéma vérité*, see Mamber (1974).
2   Susan L. Carruthers, "Say cheese! Operation Iraqi Freedom on film," *Cinéaste* (Winter 2006): 31. Pat Aufderheide distinguishes between Why-We-Are-in-Iraq Docs, Grunt Docs (from the standpoint of US soldiers), and Learning from Iraqis Docs (that are made by or focus on the experience of Iraqis), and then takes on the issue of "impact and reach," categories and issues I will also discuss here. See "Your country, my country: How films about the Iraq War construct publics," *Framework* 48, 2 (Fall 2007): 56–65. On the role of new digital media representations of Iraq that elude conventional documentary categories, see Patricia R. Zimmermann, "Public domains: Engaging Iraq through experimental digitalities," *Framework* 48, 2 (Fall 2007): 66–83.
3   Archie Drury told a reviewer he had actually shot some of the footage in *Voices of War* and that the US-financed Iraq Foundation gave him footage of Saddam-era crimes. Those involved with the film would not say who financed it. See Eartha Melzer, "A dubious doc," *In These Times*, December 13, 2004 at www.inthesetimes.comarticle/1744/ (accessed December 21, 2007). The Wikipedia page on *Voices of Iraq*, probably assembled in part by the filmmakers or their public relations firm, presents the film as an answer to the Noam Chomsky and Michael Moore view of the Iraq War, while Archie Drury admits the film "makes Bush look good." The site also indicates that the film was released in 2004 to attempt to

influence that year's election and that it was promoted by the same public relations firm used by the US Army and big corporations like General Motors and Proctor and Gamble; see www.en.wikipedia.org/wiki/Voices_of_Iraq (accessed December 21, 2007). The film's home page seems to have disappeared.

4   Franti was a major force in the the Disposable Heroes of Hiphoprisy from 1991 to 1993, the rock/reggae group Spearhead, and a committed peace activist who also participated in the anti-globalization film *This is What Democracy Looks Like*; see the Michael Franti entry at www.en.wikipedia. org/wiki/Michael_Franti (accessed December 29, 2007).

5   The initial release to film festivals in 2005 of *Off to War* portrayed the first month of the National Guard troop's deployment, while a multi-episode Discovery Channel series showed the entire 18 months, now available on DVD on four disks. User comments on the Internet Movie Database from families of troops are generally positive, claiming that the documentary "allows a non-biased, first-person account, of what's happening to these men... *Off to War* is the closest you're going to get to experiencing a tour of duty in Iraq without actually serving." Others state, however, that the soldiers complain too much and that the series has an anti-war bias, arguments contested by viewers who claim that soldiers always gripe and that the series captures the reality of their Iraq experiences and the anguish of relatives at home. See www.imdb.com/title/tt0455986/usercomments (accessed January 11, 2008).

6   See Gina Piccalo, "War, as seen through these soldiers' eyes," *Los Angeles Times*, October 11, 2006: E4. Piccalo notes that ten of the 180 soldiers in the regiment agreed to take the cameras and shot the footage, although just three were chosen for the film.

7   Another documentary, Iraqi journalist Ali Fadhil's *Fallujah: The Real Story* (2005), documents the incredible level of destruction of the city. On the film, see the *Democracy Now!* interview with the filmmaker and other information available at www.democracynow.org/article.pl?sid=06/01/25/155226 (accessed December 21, 2007).

8   Susan L. Carruthers' third article on Iraq documentaries, "Bodies of evidence: New documentaries on Iraq War veterans," covers a series of films that deal with returning vets' medical issues. See *Cinéaste* (Winter 2008): 26–31.

9   Carruthers, "Bodies of evidence," p. 29.

10   For information on Schechter's documentary, see the website www.wmdthe-film.com/mambo/index.php. See also Loretta Alpert and Jeremy Earp's documentary *War Made Easy: How Presidents and Pundits Keep Spinning Us to Death* (2007). Based on Norman Solomon's analysis of war and media and narrated by Sean Penn, this contains an astonishing montage of US

corporate media broadcast journalists parroting Bush-Cheney adminis-tration propaganda, including a bevy of erroneous claims about Iraqi WMDs, Iraq and al Qaeda connections, and other assertions revealed to be utterly mendacious. The film also shows members of the corporate media attacking critics of the Iraq War. *War Made Easy* is produced and distributed by the Media Education Foundation and is available at www.mediaed.org/videos/CommercialismPoliticsAndMedia/WarMadeEasy (accessed January 11, 2008).

11 For more information, see www.warandtruththemovie.com/ (accessed January 11, 2008).

12 See viewers' comments at www.imdb.com/title/tt0436149/ (accessed December 21, 2007).

13 A high official in the Bush administration told journalist Ron Suskind that "guys like me were 'in what we call the reality based community,' which he defined as people who 'believe that solutions emerge from your judicious study of discernible reality.' I nodded and murmured something about Enlightenment principles and empiricism. He cut me off. 'That's not the way the world really works anymore,' he continued. 'We're an empire now, and when we act, we create our own reality. And while you're studying that reality – judiciously, as you will – we'll act again, creating other new realities, which you can study too, and that's how things will sort out. We're history's actors ... and you, all of you, will be left to just study what we do.' " Ron Suskind, "Without a doubt," *New York Times*, October 17, 2004 at www.cs.umass.edu/~immerman/play/opinion05/WithoutADoubt.html.

14 For an excellent analysis of the inventive aesthetic of Tucker's film, see Brian Gibson, "The War on Film. Reanimating the Post-9/11 Viewer in The Prisoner, or: How I planned to Kill Tony Blair," *CineAction*, Issue 77 (2009): 18–24.

15 Ferguson is a highly informed and competent interviewer, as his revealing interview with Richard Armitage on the DVD version of the film demon-strates. Ferguson fires one intelligent and difficult question after another at Armitage, rattling the grizzled old warrior and diplomat, and eliciting some compelling answers that explain why Armitage and his boss Colin Powell did not resign in protest against the catastrophic blunders of Bush-Cheney administration ideologues.

16 The excellent DVD of *No End in Sight* contains interviews with Col. Hughes, Walter Slocombe, and Richard Armitage. Hughes is obviously tremendously pained by the experience and sharply critical of the Bush-Cheney ideologues and incompetents who managed the debacle, while Armitage is more dis-tanced, claiming history will judge, and refuses to criticize his own and Colin Powell's failure to speak up more forcefully and articulate their criticisms of the momentous policy mistakes being made. But Armitage makes clear in the

documentary his and Powell's criticisms of the specific policies that led to such disaster.

17 As critics of the Iraq policy have indicated, the invasion was really a preventive war in that there was no imminent threat or clear and present danger to the United States. Whereas preemptive war is grounded in international law, preventive war would be a departure from previous US military doctrine and is akin to the Japanese attack on Pearl Harbor. On preventive war, see Keller and Mitchell (2006), Suskind (2006), and Kellner (2007b).

18 On Cheney, see Nichols (2004) and Gellman (2008).

19 Reviews from audience members on Netflix and user comments on the Internet Movie Database from many viewers who label themselves as conservative are very positive. See www.imdb.com/title/tt0912593/usercomments (accessed February 10, 2008). Thus, the price of reaching a larger audience appears to be truncating the political scope and critical thrust of a film. *No End in Sight* has a respectable, if not spectacular, box office gross of $1,433,319. See www.boxofficemojo.com/movies/?id=noendinsight.htm (accessed December 31, 2008).

20 Alex Gibney's *Taxi to the Dark Side* points to Dick Cheney, who said on camera in famous news footage that fighting terrorism will take us into the "dark side." Gibney's film provides documentation that Cheney and his office were strongly involved in establishing torture as a legitimate means of interrogation, as do Hersh (2004) and Mayer (2008).

21 Some reviewers criticized Morris for not establishing the context and chain of responsibility for Abu Ghraib and other US torture centers. See Michael Atkinson, "Errol Morris' myopia," *In These Times*, May 13, 2008 at www.inthesetimes.com/article/3680/errol_morris_myopia/ (accessed January 7, 2009). My response would be that while other films I have analyzed were better at establishing the context of Abu Ghraib, Morris provides a unique vision which illuminates aspects of the scandal that other filmmakers and investigative reporters were not able to access. Deleted scenes on the DVD of *Standard Operating Procedure* and Morris's commentary provide a richer sense of the political context and invaluable insight into the whole affair.

22 Jeanine Plant, "Home of the Brave: The psychic toll of the Iraq War," *Alternet*, March 19, 2007 at www.alternet.org/story/45856/ (accessed December 21, 2007).

23 I discuss *Rendition* and *Lions for Lambs* in the conclusion.

24 Some critics claim that Haggis's film is anti-war and not anti-Iraq War. Roger Ebert says those who see the film as anti-Iraq War "will not have been paying attention. It doesn't give a damn where the war is being fought." See www.rogerebert.suntimes.com/apps/pbcs.dll/article?AID=/20070913/REVIEWS/709130304/1023. In fact, *In the Valley of Elah*'s use of Iraq footage and its plot and characters make it clear it is very specifically dealing

with Iraq, as does the aural montage of speeches on Iraq by George W. Bush as background throughout the film. James Berardinelli makes the same problematic claim and attacks the film's "ridiculously ham-fisted symbolism" at www.reelviews.net/movies/i/in_valley.html. Against these critiques, I would agree with David Denby, who argues: "Haggis, the writer-director of 'Crash,' has done something shrewd: he has mounted a devastating critique of the Iraq War by indirection. Rather than dramatizing, say, the disillusion of a young soldier as he experiences the chaos of the occupation, he has moved disillusion into the soul of a military father." See www.newyorker. com/arts/critics/cinema/2007/09/24/070924crci_cinema_denby.

25 Directed by Adam Marcus – of *Jason Goes to Hell: The Final Friday* (2003) fame – and co-written by Debra Sullivan, who had no other film credits on her Internet Movie Database site, *Conspiracy* suggests there were folks out there so fed up with eight years of Bush-Cheney that they were willing to use any means necessary to chuck an incendiary cinematic bomb at them. The movie was filmed on Val Kilmer's ranch in New Mexico and was part of his efforts to bolster the New Mexican Film Investment Program. The story was too leftwing for average action-adventure fans, went straight to DVD, and was attacked by many conservative viewers on the user comment message board at the Internet Movie Database site. Of the 15 reviews posted as of May 31, 2008, 11 were critical on political and cinematic grounds (see www. imdb.com/title/tt1043838/usercomments).

26 One viewer commented: "I think this film represents the hope that 'We the people' can regain our freedoms from the corrupt corporations and governments that hide behind a false cloak of democracy." Another viewer said: "The director should be slapped around, kicked in the balls, and dumped south of the border without his passport this movie is so terrible." See www.imdb.com/title/tt1043838/usercomments (accessed May 31, 2008). Obviously, typical Val Kilmer action-adventure film buffs don't appreciate critique of the Bush-Cheney administration thrown in with their escapist fare.

27 In interviews, Cusack said he was inspired to write a film about US corporations in Iraq and the privatization of the Iraqi economy after reading an article by Naomi Klein, "Baghdad year zero: Pillaging Iraq in pursuit of a neocon utopia," *Harper's*, September 2004, at www.harpers.org/ archive/2004/09/0080197 (accessed January 1, 2009). Klein (2007) expanded on this with her conception of the shock doctrine and disaster capitalism, whereby US corporations benefit and profit from disasters like Iraq or Katrina – an analysis also applicable to the winter 2008 financial meltdown.

28 Member reviews on www.netflix.com/Movie/Battle_for_Haditha/70081082? trkid=188469 (accessed December 31, 2008) contain negative comments such

as "I gave this movie 0 Stars, because it simply did not warrant them. First off, Marines dont 'REVENGE KILL' and to suggest it is simply an ignorance of the values of the US Military and the USMC in general. Second, every Marine, with the exception of one, has been vindicated in this shabbily politically stilted pseudo representation of the FACTS. Spending two tours in Iraq and witnessing COUNTLESS acts of heroism, I am dissapointed [*sic*] to see that all Hollywood can do is sanction this kind of garbage all the while neglecting the real stories of our service men and women who are indeed winning this war and winning it by being brave and compassionate." There are also positive comments: "Anyone who defends the American military in Iraq is dangerously deluded. They are defending the foreign policies of George Bush and NOT OUR FREEDOM. You people don't think American soldiers commit atrocities. Where on Earth have you been? They are volunteers for an army of occupation and only deal with collaborators and do not deserve our praise or support." Response to the film thus reveals the division in the country over Iraq. The negative comment is correct that only one Marine so far was found guilty and imprisoned because of the massacre, although the Haditha event has been well documented and discussed and there is no question but that scores of civilians were massacred.

29   See the total at the National Priorities Project at www.nationalpriorities.org/ costofwar_home (accessed June 2, 2009).

Conclusion
Hollywood Cinema Wars in the 2000s

The Bush-Cheney era was one of the most turbulent and contested in history. While Washington and Wall Street disgraced themselves, and the economy entered the most frightening period since the Great Depression of the 1930s, as the standing of the US in the world declined to an all-time low, Hollywood could stand relatively tall and proud. Its cinematic visions in the 2000s included a large number of films critical of the Republican administration and its policies and ideologies, among them some high quality films and a cycle of some of the most impressive documentaries ever made. The right wing has long excoriated Hollywood as a hotbed of liberalism, but in opposition to Bush-Cheney extremism and the collapse of contemporary conservatism, this criticism became a badge of honor.[1]

The 2000s have been comparable to the so-called Hollywood Renaissance of the late 1960s and 1970s described by Kellner and Ryan (1988), Wood (1995), and others. Of course, at the same time, there have been the usual failed blockbusters, dreary sequels, and very bad films, but Hollywood's production as a whole does not deserve some of the polemics against it, such as David Thomson's trashing of contemporary US cinema in *The Whole Equation: A History of Hollywood* (2004). It is easy to critique mindless and overhyped blockbusters and a predominance of mediocre films, but there are also surprisingly many critical films that engage with the key issues of the day. Critics like Thomson have not kept up with the trajectory of Hollywood, or for that matter world cinema, and instead nostalgically celebrate earlier Hollywood film history, against which present offerings are found wanting.[2] Thus, while Thomson attempts to provide an overview of "the whole equation" of Hollywood film (i.e., business, stars, successes, art, audiences, social and cultural resonance), he fails to contextualize his studies in the sociopolitical history of cinema in the United States and is uninterested in the ways that critical and oppositional cinematic visions can oppose dominant ideologies and political hegemony.[3] In fact, Thomson generally fails to see film within the framework of US politics at all, except for a discussion of the McCarthy era blacklist, when politics entered film from outside. He fails completely to see that film is bound up with social struggle by articulating opposing positions within society or transmitting social and political ideas. While there is minimal recognition of gender and race in his book, there is almost no discussion of class, sexuality, or the clash of political ideologies in film. Contemporary Hollywood film seems to have left someone with Thomson's aesthetic-literary interests behind, and in particular he appears to have lost interest in critical engagement with it.

Critical Representations

I have argued throughout this book that Hollywood's cinema wars provide critical representations of key events, struggles, crises, and challenges of our time. Certain films captured the crux of the economic, political, and social crises and scandals of the era. Tony Gilroy's *Michael Clayton* (2007) portrays the greed, corruption, viciousness, and immorality embedded in the US corporate sector that has contributed so much to the economic crisis that exploded in Fall 2008. Drawing on the 1970s genre of the corporate conspiracy thriller, it shows individuals who have devoted their lives to serving corporations and performing highly unethical acts thrown into moral and personal crisis.

George Clooney plays Michael Clayton, a corporate lawyer who is the firm's "fixer," a person who cleans up the biggest messes and often is forced to go beyond the law and morality to resolve corporate crises. The plot involves the moral and psychological breakdown of one of the firm's top litigators, Arthur Edens (Tom Wilkinson), who has been representing for years a sinister agrochemical corporation, U/North. The corporation is being sued for the harmful effects of a pesticide that it markets, which is accused of poisoning farmland and water supplies, as well as people. After investigating the case for years and trying to construct a defense for the corporation, Edens realizes that he is on the wrong side, defending the indefensible. In the opening scenes, Edens, who has gone off his medications, reveals that he has had a sudden illumination into the evil that the law firm Kenner, Bach, & Ledeen and their corporate clients have been immersed in. When he learns that his longtime friend Michael Clayton is seeking to find him and bring him in after he has taken off his clothes and babbled incoherently at a meeting with U/North executives, and then disappeared, Edens leaves a startling message on Clayton's answering machine:

> Michael. Dear Michael. Of course it's you, who else could they send, who else could be trusted? I realized Michael, that I had emerged not from the doors of Kenner, Bach, & Ledeen, not through the portals of our vast and powerful law firm, but from the asshole of an organism whose sole function is to excrete the ... the-the-the poison, the ammo, the defoliant necessary for other, larger, more powerful organisms to destroy the miracle of humanity. And that I had been coated in this patina of shit for the best part of my life. The stench of it and the stain of it would in all likelihood take the rest of my life to undo.

Accompanying images to this monologue show the cold halls, empty office spaces, sterile boardrooms, and unappealing interiors of the corporate environment, using muted color and gauzy filters to denote the barrenness and moral ambiguity of the place. One shot features a janitor at the end of the hall, a symbol for Michael Clayton, who describes himself as the (metaphorical) janitor of the firm who cleans up the messes.

The scene changes to morning as the office quickly fills up and Marty Bach, one of the main corporate sharks (brilliantly played by the late Sidney Pollack in one of his last roles), learns of the firm's predicament

Michael Clayton opens with soulless images of corporate office space.

and assembles his troops for battle. A quick cut to another corporate or hotel suite focuses on the sweaty armpits of Karen Crowder (Tilda Swinton), carefully rehearsing speeches to defend its client U/North that is being sued for the environmental and lethal qualities of its product, a "cancer-delivery machine," as Arthur Edens put it.

Michael Clayton himself is in deep moral crisis, and not only because of the ethically dubious work he does. Divorced, addicted to gambling, and in debt to the mob for his wayward brother's destructive behavior, he faces losing the bar and restaurant that he and his brother had long dreamed of running and that Clayton saw as a way out of his current morass. In a mysterious sequence, Clayton drives through the country-side, stops his car to gaze at wondrous horses, noble and innocent, and turns around to see his car being blown up. A flashback to several days earlier combines the corporate conspiracy genre with film noir, depicting a completely amoral corporate universe. Off his medications, Arthur Edens is ecstatically happy, freed from the moral corruption of the law firm, but since he possesses crucial information that could cost U/North billions and is calling the plaintives in the case to help them sue the cor-poration, U/North thugs murder him and then go after Michael Clayton. Karen Crowder coldly guides U/North through its conniving and murder. Her character represents a crisis in corporate femininity, where a woman is forced to be as cold and ruthless as men, and as a result is totally alone and alienated. Michael, meanwhile, muddles through his personal prob-lems, connects with his family and at the end does the right thing, expos-ing U/North's corruption and criminality, and positioning himself to get out of the whole stinking corporate mess.

In retrospect, the film captures the ethos of corporate corruption which in the first Bush-Cheney term included the crimes of Enron, Worldcom, and other corporations who were acting far outside the bounds of moral-ity and legality. This corruption empowered by the Bush-Cheney policies of deregulation, led later in the second term to the near-collapse of the financial and banking sector and the worst economic crisis since the Depression.

Economic hard times and their challenges were anticipated and docu-mented in several Hollywood films of the era. Using the mode of com-edy, Dean Parisot's *Fun with Dick and Jane* (2005), a remake of Ted Kotcheff's 1977 film with Jane Fonda and George Segal, features Téa Leoni and Jim Carrey as a yuppie couple who turn to bank robbery after the corporate executive husband has his company wrecked by a greedy

CEO (Alec Baldwin), who loots the corporation for personal gain. Concluding credits of the film cite Enron, WorldComm, and other financial scandals of the era, and the film anticipates the financial sector crash which emerged in late 2008. In Callie Khouri's satirical comedy *Mad Money* (2007), Diane Keaton plays an upper-middle-class housewife whose husband loses his job and goes into massive debt. After the husband gives up trying to find a job, the wife takes a minimal wage job at the Federal Reserve and conspires with underpaid co-workers to rob piles of the money stored there.

Ron Howard's *Cinderella Man* (2005) uses the 1930s Depression as backdrop for its story of boxer James J. Braddock's (Russell Crowe) ascent from washed-up fighter reduced to working on the docks and taking local fights to becoming world heavyweight champion. The film immerses the viewer in a world of oppressive poverty, but transmits the can-do message that with hard work, will, and talent one can overcome the limitations of one's situation. Similarly, *Kitt Kittredge: An American Girl* (2008) uses the 1930s Depression as the setting for its feel-good teen adventure story. The auto-salesman father of a 9-year-old middle-class girl loses his job and goes to Chicago to seek work, and her mother takes in borders and sells eggs to survive and save their home. Young Kitt struggles throughout to pursue her dream of becoming a reporter. The film strongly supports a liberal political agenda to fight the depression, attacking conservatives who show no sympathy for those out of work and out of luck, and who vilify President Roosevelt and his policies.

Kevin Smith's *Zack and Miri Make a Porno* (2008) show a couple of slacker friends played by Josh Rogin and Elizabeth Banks as platonic roommates unable to pay their bills. As their financial situation becomes impossible, Zack sees that there are quick bucks to be made from producing and self-distributing a porno film. Almost pulling it off, their porno spoof of *Star Wars* is shut down when it turns out an unscrupulous real estate agent sold the team an old building to serve as their film studio scheduled for demolition. Struggling to succeed facing financial collapse, the couple make a porno in the coffee shop they work in and escape their economic woes.

Michel Gondry's *Be Kind Rewind* (2007) shows two young would-be filmmakers who save a local video rental store from bankruptcy when hard economic times set in. Jerry (Jack Black) is a mechanic who lives in a trailer next to a power plant. When he attempts to sabotage the power plant, he becomes magnetized and inadvertently erases the videotape inventory in a local store, Be Kind Rewind, where his buddy Mike (Mos Def) works. To provide tapes for the remaining customers, Jerry and Mike begin remaking such popular classics as *Ghost Busters* with their own low-tech equipment. Telling customers that the films are imported from Sweden, they begin "sweding" classical films and their business prospers, showing creative uses of technology and a self-organizing community trying to survive in an environment of hostile economic forces.

In a more serious dramatic vein, writer-director Courtney Hunt's debut feature *Frozen River* (2008) portrays the struggles of a working-class family to survive economic bad times. Ray Eddy (Melissa Leo) has been abandoned by her husband and struggles to provide for her children. Living in the small town of Massena, New York, close to the US-Canadian border, Ray works part time at a retail store. She is barely able to put meager food on her family's table. Living in a dilapidated mobile home, she dreams of purchasing a double-wide trailer for which she needs to make the full deposit in order to avoid losing her down-payment. Desperately searching for her gambler husband, Ray meets Lila (Misty Upham) on a nearby Mohawk Indian reservation, and circumstances throw her into helping Misty in the dangerous activity of transporting immigrants across the border, in the hopes of securing the new home for her family, and showing the degree to which people will go to survive in a downturn economy.

As for Bush-Cheney administration foreign policy, discussed throughout this book, an astonishing number of documentaries and fiction films have engaged the catastrophe of Iraq and depicted torture, "extraordinary rendition," and the violation of international law and human rights, which have cumulatively empowered the terrorist enemies of the US in terms of fundraising and recruitment and alienated the US from its allies and people of the world.[4]

Robert Redford's *Lions for Lambs* (2007) uses three overlapping plotlines to explore the quandaries and impasses of US foreign policy under the Bush-Cheney administration. The film opens with Redford playing a liberal political science professor at a California university in an early morning meeting with a once-promising student, Todd (Andrew Garfield), who has been cutting class. The scene moves to an apparently one-time liberal TV journalist, Janine Roth (Meryl Streep), preparing for an interview in the office of hawkish and ambitious Republican Senator Jasper Irving (Tom Cruise). The office scenes unfold long discussions of university life and the responsibility of students and the failures of US policy, while the scenes with the reporter and senator discuss how to get back on the right track in the "war on terror." The highly didactic and discursive style is atypical of Hollywood film, as is the extent to which there is serious discussion of contemporary issues.

The senator's plan to take the initiative in Afghanistan and turn the corner on the war on terror involves sending small patrol units into Afghan mountain areas to fight guerrillas. In Afghanistan we see that a military crew plans exactly this strategy, involving sending troops to occupy a strategic mountain top. The troops include two special forces soldiers, Ernest (Michael Peña) and Arian (Derek Luke), who, later flashbacks reveal, were students of the California professor and who had volunteered for the military to prove their political seriousness and commitment. The two young soldiers are the victims of guerrilla fire: one is shot and falls out of the helicopter and the other jumps out to try to save him. They are surrounded by enemy troops and eventually are killed. Their senseless deaths dramatize the successive blunders that have caused the deaths of so many US troops in Afghanistan and Iraq (see Kellner 2005). They also illustrate the words of a German military commentator in World War I, who noted of British troops: "Nowhere else have I seen such lions led by such lambs." A subtext of the film involves the contrast between the white student, totally cynical of politics, and the young African-American student and his Latino buddy who prove their commitment and help generate career possibilities by joining the military. Their deaths highlight the fact that it is the poor and people of color who are sacrificed in the political ambitions and blunders of politicians and military leaders.

A clash between the reporter and her producer reveals that a critical exposé of the new military plan cannot be broadcast. The scene suggests that conservatism, corporate control of media, and fear of the government have killed broadcast news. Near the end of the film, news crawl headlines tout the new military plan as an important turning point in the phony war on terror, whereas the audience knows it's only another failed policy packaged and sold as something new. Another telling scene depicts breaking news of a celebrity scandal, reported by an attractive woman with big hair who breathlessly puts it over as a big deal. This sequence shows how entertainment and infotainment have replaced hard news, reducing it to a feeble crawl along the bottom of the screen, without context or interpretation.

Lions for Lambs depicts two young soldiers of color who volunteer for duty in Afghanistan and meet a tragic end.

Lions for Lambs evokes the failures of US military policy, the gutlessness and ineptitude of the corporate media, and how young people are sacrificed for political ambitions and failed policies. It suggests as well how a public drowned in entertainment is made apathetic about the realities of war and questionable decisions. However, the limitations of the film reveal the failure of nerve of contemporary liberalism. It would be easy to imagine another turn in the plot where the media discover the fraudulent and failed nature of the "new" US strategy and even to envisage the exposure and destruction of the rightwing senator. In the 1970s *All the President's Men* – a film that also starred Redford – showed not only a dogged and heroic press, but one that overthrows a presidency. It is as if in the Bush-Cheney hegemony of the 2000s, there was no hope for exposure of flawed policies, let alone the overthrow of corrupt politicians and a corporate media by a defanged liberalism.

Lions for Lambs does not explore the harmful consequences of US Middle East policy for the region, or the nature of the terrorist enemy produced there. Gavin Hood's political thriller *Rendition* (2007), while itself limited by its liberal humanism, does take on these tasks by dramatizing the US outsourcing of terror interrogations (a.k.a. torture), and by putting a human face on the seizure, detention, and brutal treatment of terror suspects. Its story revolves around the abduction of an Egyptian-American chemical engineer, Anwar El-Ibrahimi (Omar Metwally), at a US airport and the diligent efforts of his wife (Reese Witherspoon) to find out what happened to him and have him released. The complex multi-character plot, similar to the narrative structure of *Syriana* and *Babel*, explores the conflicted relations between the CIA official in charge of the "rendition," Corrine Whitman (Meryl Streep), a young CIA case officer, Douglas Freeman (Jake Gyllenhaal), who finds himself representing the US at the actual torture site in North Africa, and a US senator's ambitious aide, who the wife enlists to help her (Peter Sarsgaard).

A parallel plot shows the daughter of the head of the North African country's secret police (Israeli actor Igal Naor) becoming involved with a young man whom she and the audience learn is an Islamicist militant, planning a suicide bombing that will kill the girl's father in revenge for the killing of his beloved brother. The movie clearly displays the monstrousness of terrorist bombings that kill innocent civilians, the fanaticism of the terrorists, and the brutality of the US strategic response.

Rendition opens with beautiful images of Cape Town, South Africa (Gavin Hood's home country), where Anwar has delivered a paper to an academic conference and is respectfully escorted onto an airplane by his colleagues. There is a quick cut to his pregnant wife playing with their son in the DC suburbs, while Anwar's mother sits on the porch – an idyllic scene of an assimilated Arab-American family. The scene changes to North Africa, where CIA agent Douglas Freeman gets out of bed and greets an attractive Arab woman who we learn is his girlfriend and colleague at work, followed by a quick cut to a young Arab girl, Fatima, meeting her boyfriend Halid in a market square where there will soon be an explosion intended to kill Fatima's father, the North African secret police official. The explosion, however, instead kills the new CIA case officer who Freeman had just met and whose death will propel him from a "pencil pushing desk job" to CIA field operative.

As Gavin Hood emphasizes in his excellent commentary on the DVD, we have been introduced to three generations: a younger generation that has been largely acted upon, represented by Halid and Fatima (who Hood characterizes as the Romeo and Juliet characters); a middle generation that is beginning to act in the world and must make important choices in the narrative; and an older cynical and amoral generation that includes the North African police chief and his Washington CIA colleague, who orders interrogation of Anwar and who in the course of the film will make the case for "extraordinary rendition."

The torture scenes are graphic and brutal, showing beatings and electric shocks applied to the naked Anwar, as well as water-boarding, which lead Anwar to make up a story of his complicity with a terrorist

Rendition depicts the kidnapping and torture of suspected terrorists, including innocent suspects.

operative. On the DVD commentary, director Gavin Hood notes that Anwar is a composite of several young Arab men thus tortured who turned out to be completely innocent. *Outlawed*, a documentary on the DVD, is about several cases that influenced Hood during the making of the film. The film clearly shows terrorists as a danger and allows conservative voices to make a strong case for rendition. However, the illegal and immoral dimensions of rendition and torture are also shown, forcing characters to make genuine moral choices and the audience to reflect on US policy.

Eventually, Freeman comes to believe that Anwar is innocent and smuggles him out of prison, while the senator's aide tries to assist Anwar's wife by getting the senator to put pressure on the CIA to release him, an effort that fails. The film concludes with a replay of the opening sequence in which the Muslim terrorist, who we now see is Halid, explodes a suicide bomb in the square that kills the police chief's daughter. Terror war is thus shown as a tragic consequence of out-of-control forces in the Muslim and Western world, both of which have descended into barbarism. Yet the film also depicts the emergence of a few, good, young men and women ready to break with the failed policies of the past.

Ridley Scott's epic *Body of Lies* (2008) deploys the same tropes of older, more seasoned CIA operatives cynically pursuing torture, lies, and dirty tricks in the so-called war on terror, while younger operatives question the morality and efficacy of old school tactics. Russell Crowe plays Ed Hoffman, a disillusioned and overweight veteran operative who runs Middle East operations via earphone while multitasking at his office, at home, and doing chores. A younger agent, Roger Ferris (Leonardo DiCaprio), by contrast, is operating on the ground, interacting with people and trying to discover terrorist threats. Ferris attempts to bond with a smooth Jordanian intelligence chief to capture an emerging terrorist suspect, but in the confused jumble of Middle Eastern politics, lies and deceit and the cold indifference of bureaucratic operatives undermine his morale and he ends up resigning. *Body of Lies* thus suggests that the US needs to rethink its strategy and requires a new kind of agency and operative.

By 2008 it was possible to laugh at the follies of the US government and "intelligence" apparatus. The Coen brothers' *Burn After Reading* (2008) continues their exploration of an utterly chaotic universe where violence and death can emerge at any moment. In an absurdist satire of the spy drama that takes the form of a screwball comedy with all its narrative screws loose, the film captures the absurdity of intelligence agencies in contemporary Washington, but without any specific political references to the Bush-Cheney administration. Opening shots pan into the CIA office in Langley, Virginia, where a longtime operative, Osbourne Cox (John Malkovich), is told that he is being retired because he drinks too much. A party that night makes clear that the operative's wife Katie (Tilda Swinton) is having an affair with an ex-Treasury agent Harry (George Clooney), who still carries a gun, and whose affair will trigger a cascade of unexpected episodes and complications. Meanwhile, in the working-class milieu of the Hardbody gym, an aging gym worker, Linda Litske (Frances McDormand), seeks plastic surgery to make her more appealing to men, but her insurance company refuses to pay for the operations. Desperate for money, when an associate finds a CD full of what appears to be spy intelligence information, she and her high-energy but low-brain power co-worker Chad (Brad Pitt) concoct a blackmail scheme. The bumbling amateurs first try to shake down the CIA operative from whose computer the data appear to come. It turns out that the disk and files contain the operative's feeble attempt at a memoir and his wife's scanning of their financial data to aid her in a divorce case.

When Cox refuses blackmail, the hapless gym workers go to the Russians to try to sell the data. Meanwhile, top CIA officials who have been monitoring Cox have discovered his wife's affair with the Treasury dude, who in turn is having an affair with Linda. There are also divorce detectives monitoring the scene and although there is copious surveillance of the major characters, no one can make heads or tails out of what is happening, pointing to the disfunctionality of government and more generally American life. As one character after another is killed by pure mischance or misidentification, the senseless violence of the contemporary moment is evoked with absurdist humor. The Coens' nihilistic comedy thus provides a fitting end to the Bush-Cheney era and a sense of relief that we can now laugh at the error and blunders that characterized the US government during the first eight years of the millennium.

History Lessons

Near the end of 2008, when the country could breathe freely in the belief that a new era was dawning, it was appropriate to look back at historical landmarks. Rather than celebrating American history in the mode of ideological spectacles that denote American exceptionalism, virtue, and triumphalism, a series of films engaged with the turmoil of recent US and global history. Some presented critical visions of major US presidents like Richard Nixon (Ron Howard's *Nixon-Frost*) and George W. Bush (Oliver Stone's *W.*). Gus Van Sant's *Milk* celebrated an important leader of an oppositional gay and lesbian movement who was tragically assassinated, while Steven Soderbergh's *Che* presents an epic biopic of revolutionary icon Che Guevera. All of these films were marked by critical examination of recent history, the rupture of conservative ideological consensus concerning American triumphalism, and controversial presentation of major figures and events that opened up discussion and debate rather than comforting ideological closure.[5] This cycle of political films points to the maturity of Hollywood filmmakers able to use film as an instrument of historical inquiry, representation, and critique.

While Oliver Stone's tragicomedic *W.* (2008) did not satisfy Bush's fervent critics, it opened up serious questions about the Bush-Cheney legacy and provided a unique historical interrogation of a sitting president during the last days of his failed administration. Stone has obviously digested stacks of books about the Bush-Cheney administration and the fickle and fateful life of George W. Bush, and he provides an illuminating and highly entertaining overview in *W.* The first two chapters of Stone's story tell in flashbacks and flash-forwards the rise to the presidency of the improbable George W. Bush, while the last chapter tells of the tragedy of Iraq, presented as the collapse of the Bush presidency and Bush family fortunes.

An opening sequence has George W. Bush alone in an outfield imagining a baseball stadium with a crowd cheering him on as he races to catch a fly ball headed to the stands. W. then segues into a series of vignettes of his early life and rise to the presidency, told in comedic, satirical, and even sympathetic tones. We see George W. initiated into his Yale Skull and Bones fraternity. Saturated with booze and immersed in homoerotic sadomasochism, young Bush turns out to be the pledge best able to recite the names of all the other future and present "masters of the universe" in the secret society pledge class, presaging his later political skills.

After bouts with boozing and card-playing with his Texas buddies, womanizing, and failing at job after job, Bush decides he is going to run for Congress, but is whipped by Democrat Kent Hance, who presents Bush as a Yankee carpetbagger coming in from elite east coast schools to seize a West Texas congressional seat. As election results pour in showing him losing, Bush vows never again to be out-Texanized and out-Christianized, presaging his purchasing of the Crawford, Texas "ranch" and cowboy duds and becoming a born-again Christian after his excessive drinking takes him to near-collapse (Stone spares us the drugs).

Along the way, George meets Laura, who is presented as his rock-solid and supportive helpmate. Such maintenance is especially needed in the Bush family, where Jeb is the favorite son and the successful and priggishly proper father, George H. W. Bush, disapproves of his wayward son George's excesses and failures. Somehow Bushie (Laura's term of endearment for George W.) gets it together and successfully runs a baseball team. Seeing his ambition to be baseball commissioner foiled, however, he decides to run for governor of Texas, entering the family business. His barb-tounged mother Barbara is highly skeptical, believing that Junior can never beat the popular Ann Richards. George's plan to run for Texas governor also meets with the disapproval of his father, who wants Jeb to become governor of Florida first, setting him up on a fast track to national politics.

Stone's biopic also shows George W.'s effective role in Poppy Bush's 1988 election victory and the heartbreak of his participation in his father's 1992 loss to Bill Clinton. Vowing he's learned from his father's mistakes, W. goes on, in Stone's family centered drama, to prove to daddy that he's got the right stuff. With the help of Karl Rove he goes on to become governor of Texas and then the 43rd president of the United States.

Once Bush becomes president, the comic and sympathetic satirical tone shifts to darker, more biting drama, as Stone sketches Bush's interactions with Dick Cheney, Karl Rove, Colin Powell, Donald Rumsfeld, Condoleeza Rice, and CIA head George Tenet. A brief scene shows Bush and Cheney at lunch, with Cheney pushing a three-page memo authorizing torture and the violation of human rights that Bush resists signing without reading, showing that he is not just a puppet of Cheney, but fully complicit in the crimes of his administration. Yet in the debate leading up to Iraq, Bush seems to be on the sidelines, with Cheney pushing the case for war, while Rumsfeld eggs him on and Rice nods her head in approval. Stone's Colin Powell makes extremely strong arguments for not going into Iraq, but Bush appears to go along with the majority. The macho Powell cannot help getting on board, even selling the Iraq intervention to the world in his infamous United Nations speech, filled with lies about Iraq's alleged weapons of mass destruction and ties to al Qaeda.

The last section of *W.* shows that after apparent victory in Iraq and triumph for Bush and his "war cabinet," the adventure unravels: no weapons of mass destruction are found, civil war breaks out, US casualties mount, and the world turns against the war and the administration. To some extent, the structure of *W.* parallels Michael Moore's *Fahrenheit 9/11*, with opening episodes taking a satiric and comic tone, while the build-up to Iraq shows the Bush-Cheney administration leading the US to a tragic replay of Vietnam. Stone, a Vietnam veteran, takes up the last theme and presents Iraq as an almost fateful inevitability, given the militarist proclivities of key administration figures, and Karl Rove, who insisted on the need for a military triumph in order to win the 2004 election. Stone also sees Bush held in the prison of his family, with a powerful need to prove himself and finish his father's business by taking on Saddam Hussein.

Like Michael Moore, Stone makes exceptionally clever and effective use of music, using Freddie Fender's "Help me make it through the night" to punctuate Bush's destructive partying; portraying the war cabinet swaggering on the Crawford, Texas ranch to the tune of "The adventures of Robin Hood" as they embark on their Iraq adventure; and satirically using "The yellow rose of Texas" when the caper misfires. Like Michael

Moore in *Fahrenheit 9/11*, Stone deploys "What a wonderful world" to show that it really isn't, and effectively uses Bob Dylan's "With God on his side" over the closing credits to dramatize the role of Bush's born-again religious fanaticism and his absolutist sense of certainty, ending the film with a cross morphing into the title W.

While critics generally found Josh Brolin to be an uncannily effective George W. Bush, they were divided on the portrayal of members of Bush's cabinet and close advisers like Cheney, Rove, Rumsfeld, and Rice, complaining of *Saturday Night Live*-type caricature. No doubt Dick Cheney is much more cunning, Machiavellian, and downright evil than the caricature played by Richard Dreyfus, and Karl Rove likewise is much more vile and destructive than the buffoon played by Toby Jones, but these and other caricatures capture the comic-book villainy of the Bush-Cheney-Rove Gang and will establish their images forever as part of an "Axis of Evil." Thandy Newton's Condi Rice sneered, smiled, and assented to all of the macho guys' war-mongering, kicking in with a pro-war aside only when Colin Powell needed to get on board with the plan. It is certainly likely, however, that she played a much more significant role in assuring and nurturing Bush, while Laura was presented by Stone in far too sympathetic a light, as she too enabled him to carry through his highly destructive presidency.[6]

Stone's presentation of George W. Bush's collapse was uncharacteristically restrained and stuck carefully to the known historical record, although he allowed himself two cinematic flourishes to bring the film to a conclusion. In a stunning dream sequence, George H. W. Bush confronts Junior about the enormity of the collapse of the Iraq misadventure and chides him on ruining the family brand, as W. wakes up bathed in sweat. The concluding image returns to the opening fantasy of Bush alone in a baseball stadium, racing to make a game-saving catch. The frame freezes and Stone's brutal camera tightly focuses on his face with the familiar deer-in-the-headlight gaze and with his plaintive eyes asking, "What Happened? What Went Wrong? And Why?"

Thus Stone's opus presents George W. Bush's story as a personal and family tragedy, with no sense of the Bush-Cheney regime wrecking the economy, carrying through a hard-right agenda on everything from the environment to human rights, and seriously tarnishing Brand America, and not just Brand Bush. Yet Stone makes clear for later generations at least part of the tragedy of the Bush-Cheney years, aspects of the villainy of the Republican administration, as well as its buffoonish elements, the problematical aspects

In Oliver Stone's *W.*, Bush breaks down at a press conference when it becomes clear his presidency is a failure.

of the Bush family, and the utter unfitness of George W. Bush to serve as president. For my taste, Stone was too sympathetic to George W. Bush and George H. W. Bush, but to circulate critical perceptions of the Bush-Cheney-Rove Gang and Bush family to a popular national and global audience he probably went as far as he could.[7]

Based on Peter Morgan's play *Nixon-Frost*, Ron Howard directed a compelling cinematic version of how Richard M. Nixon negotiated a series of TV interviews with David Frost, seen at the time as a lightweight celebrity interviewer.[8] The film opens with Nixon resigning in disgrace after the Watergate hearings and returning to California, trying to rehabilitate himself and choosing to do so by means of a set of four televised interviews with Frost. The film focuses on Frost's difficulties in getting financing for his project, his many personal distractions, and how Nixon was manipulating him to control the interviews. Frank Langella brilliantly captures Nixon's mannerisms and the film generously presents Nixon's virtues and command of geopolitics, while also revealing his paranoia, deceitfulness, and human frailties. In a December 11, 2008 preview of the film at the Arclight Cinema in Los Angeles, playwright and scriptwriter Peter Morgan admitted that he took liberties with the facts. Morgan confessed he made up a story about a drunken Nixon calling Frost on the night before the final debate, trying to bond with him as a victim of establishment snobbery and prejudice (both are from the lower middle class). Morgan defended his artistic license by claiming he drew on the fact of Nixon's class resentment and propensity to call people late at night while intoxicated. At the same event, Ron Howard noted how he attempted to present Nixon as a human being and fairly present his virtues as well as his glaring failures, and suggested that in comparison with George W. Bush, Nixon looks presidential. Indeed, it would be hard to disagree with Nixon's lawyer and the key witness at the Watergate hearings, John Dean, who concluded that the Bush-Cheney regime was "worse than Watergate" (Dean 2004).

Near the end of the interviews, Frost confronts Nixon with a recently unearthed document that indicates Nixon had lied about what he knew about the Watergate break-in. Nixon breaks down and confesses that since he was president, he thought he was above the law and was not bound by legal restrictions (a concept of the imperial presidency that Bush and Cheney had also aggressively and publicly advocated). Nixon's quasi-confession of his personal involvement in Watergate and his lying to cover it up provided Frost with the sensational sound-bite he needed to publicize his series and make it a success.

Appearing at the same time in December 2008, Gus Van Sant's *Milk* tells the story of Harvey Milk, a San Francisco city supervisor and the country's first elected aggressively "out" gay politician. Opening with somber black and white archival images of gays being arrested in police bar busts and beaten up in protests, the film cuts to Sean Penn playing Harvey Milk in 1978, audio-taping his story with the expectation that he would be assassinated and should get his version of his life down in his own words. Next, *Milk* cuts to New York in 1970 where, approaching his fortieth birthday, Milk is shown as a closeted gay who works on Wall Street. He meets a charming free-spirited gay man, Scott (James Franco), on the subway, who he picks up to help celebrate his birthday, telling him that so far he has done nothing that he is proud of and needs to radically change his life. In a tender montage sequence, the two men make love and the film exuberantly cuts to San Francisco, where Milk and his new partner Scott set up a camera shop in the Castro district and immediately become deeply involved in gay politics, making Castro a Mecca for gays and lesbians and winning Milk renown as "King of Castro Street." Much of the film concerns Milk's own political education as he learns to speak to crowds, organize campaigns, find and articulate issues, make alliances, and eventually win elections. Defeated three times in runs for a seat on the San Francisco Board of Supervisors – the equivalent of a powerful city council – Milk eventually wins in 1977 and uses his position as a platform to push gay issues.

As backdrop to Milk's political ascendancy, Van Sant intersperses documentary footage of Anita Bryant campaigning nationally against gays and lesbians, events central to Rob Epstein's 1984 Oscar-winning documentary *The Times of Harvey Milk* that Van Sant heavily draws upon. A major challenge to gay rights emerges in a 1978 ballot initiative, Proposition 6, sponsored by a California assemblyman, John Briggs, influenced by Anita Bryant, which would fire gay and lesbian schoolteachers. Polls indicate a 2 to 1 lead for the conservatives going into the election, but Milk debates its defenders, organizes against the proposition, and in a surprise upset, it is defeated handily on election night.[9]

A subplot of *Milk* involves Harvey's relations with conservative supervisor Dan White (Josh Brolin), who represented a highly Catholic ethnic neighborhood in the city. Initially antagonistic, Milk tries to charm White, who invites him to his child's christening, and they attempt to forge alliances on issues important to them. White is portrayed as deeply disturbed, a heavy drinker, and possibly a closeted gay who snaps when at the last minute Milk does not back him on a measure important to his district. White resigns in anger and when he tries to retract his resignation the mayor, George Moscone, portrayed as a strong ally of Milk, refuses to take White back. In premeditated anger, White coldly stalks and assassinates Moscone and then walks to Milk's office to kill him. Closing titles indicate that Dan White was arrested, tried, and found guilty, but was charged with manslaughter and released after five years. He then committed suicide. In a wonderful closing montage, titles describe the activities of those associated with Milk, juxtaposing the actors' faces with photographs of the real characters, all of whom had highly productive and successful lives devoted to progressive political causes.

We conclude our Hollywood political film history lessons by going back to the revolutionary era of the 1960s, and examining Steven Soderbergh's four hour-plus two-part epic *Che* (2008) that deals with Cuban revolutionary Che Guevera. The first part, "The Argentine," shows Che meeting Fidel Castro in Mexico in the mid-1950s and joining his rebel group set on igniting a Cuban revolutionary war to drive the dictator Batista from power. In a highly fragmented and almost clinical fashion, we see the small group land on Cuban soil, march up country gathering recruits and arms on the way, interacting with peasants, and finally moving on to seize the Villas province. After triumph in the battle for Santa Clara that opened the way to power in Havana when Batista fled and his army surrendered their arms, the film concludes with the victorious rebels on their way to a new political era for Cuba.

The Cuban revolutionary war sequences, based on Che's *Reflections on the Cuban Revolution* and diverse sources, tell the story from Che's point of view, showing him first as a doctor and eventually rising to the position of commandante, who wins the respect of the fighters and comes to be seen as a major representative of the Cuban revolution.[10] We see Che administering medical aid to peasants, teaching illiterates to read and write, helping strategize the fighting, participating in the armed struggle, and becoming a revered hero of the revolution.

"The Argentine" segment uses many wide shots that contextualize the action and do not especially monumentalize Che, who is often a small figure in the proceedings without close-ups. The Cuban revolutionary war segment also intersperses footage in black and white of Che's 1964 trip to New York and the United Nations. He is received as a revolutionary superstar in the US and his speeches and interviews reproduced in the flash-forward sequences provide some explanatory insight into his revolutionary ideology and allude to events of the revolution and their great significance for Latin American and world revolution. Soderbergh's presentation of the Cuban revolution is highly structuralist, showing us events and episodes, dynamics and challenges, and the eventual victory without explaining the story of Che and the revolution in any straightforward fashion. "The Argentine" segment is thus rigorously modernist and demands that the audience piece together events that are often shown in fragments and without explanation.

The second part of *Che*, "The Guerrilla," shows Guevera entering Bolivia in disguise in an effort to incite a revolution there. This would eventually fail and lead to his death. This second part is much more slowly paced than the first and follows the lines of Che's *Diary of the Bolivian Revolution*, tracing his year in Bolivia from 1966 to 1967. From the beginning, Che learns that the Bolivian communist party does not support his efforts and the Bolivians are suspicious of the foreigners in their midst. Che tries to win converts through his medical talents and his explanations of exploitation to the peasants. His efforts, however, produce little success and everything seems to go wrong: the small revolutionary band's radio and cache of weapons and books have been harmed by the weather, Che does not have the medicine for his asthma, and US counterinsurgency forces from Vietnam come to Bolivia to train the army once word is out that Che Guevera and a group of Cuban revolutionaries are trying to foment revolution.

The last half of "The Guerrilla" shows Che's forces increasingly under fire and surrounded, leading to his eventual capture and execution. Soderbergh's dyptich of revolution thus shows the dynamics, mechanics, and events of one successful and one failed revolution and the major role of Che Guevera in both. Together, the two *Che* films provide a remarkable tapestry of the revolution and counterrevolution of the 1960s and 1970s and Che Guevera's heroic and often enigmatic participation. The filmmakers make no effort to provide a well-rounded and easily accessible Hollywood biopic of Che. Indeed, Soderbergh's highly didactic narrative focuses instead on historical reconstructions of events, how they impacted on Che, how he influenced and was moved by events, and how Che Guevara became a revolutionary hero and martyr for some and a villain for others.

Final Reflections

The intersection of film and politics during the Bush-Cheney era documents the end of an era of American unilateralism and imperialism and the collapse of the Republican Party administration and its rightwing supporters' imperial dreams. As I argue in chapter 5, the invasion and occupation of Iraq were conceived in part as helping to establish an American empire. This would enable the US to control Middle Eastern oil and position its military to remove opponents and achieve regime change in order to promote American imperial interests. This fantasy collapsed in the morass of Iraq when US troops found themselves immersed in horrors with no end in sight. The golden age of documentary in the 2000s depicted this catastrophe, while fiction films showed the nightmare for the people of Iraq and its impact on US soldiers, as well as the reasons why the intervention went so terribly wrong.

The period also saw the collapse of market fundamentalism and neoliberalism amid the great economic meltdown of 2008, a fitting end to the eight years of misrule of the Bush-Cheney administration. Hollywood has a tradition of documenting (as well as exhibiting) economic greed and corruption. Documentary and fiction films put on display the problems with the corporate economy, corruption and stupidity, and the misdeeds and utter incompetence of the Bush-Cheney regime. In addition to films discussed above, Paul Thomas Anderson's *There Will Be Blood* demonstrated the destructive rapacity of the capitalist-patriarchal desire for power and domination, while Alex Gibney's *Enron: The Smartest Guys in the Room* revealed the hype and criminal deception that had entered the financial markets and would lead to ruin.

Furthermore, an entire cycle of social apocalypse films anticipated the feared collapse of the socioeconomic system discussed in chapter 1 and elsewhere throughout the book. One hopes, of course, that the spiral into severe crisis of the first eight years of the millennium will be reversed and that the many visions of systematic breakdown and collapse in Hollywood films of the era will not be fully realized.

The other great event of the contemporary era was the fierce primary contest between Barack Obama and Hillary Clinton for the Democratic nomination for presidency and then the battle for president between Obama and Senator John McCain. In the introduction, I noted how Hollywood films and TV series anticipated the election of a president of color and how uncannily the TV series *The West Wing* anticipated the Obama/McCain face-off and the election of Obama.

As this book has documented, Hollywood films sharply critiqued salient aspects of the Bush-Cheney administration in entertainment and documentary cinema. They presented different and more critical visions of 9/11 and the so-called war on terror than either the Republican administration or the mainstream corporate media. Hollywood film attacked the Iraq misadventure in an unprecedented number of documentaries and fiction films; assailed the Republican neglect of the environment in documentaries and fiction films portraying environmental disaster; presented critical allegories of out-of-control and corrupt corporations and the state in a variety of documentary and fiction films; took frequent shots at the Bush-Cheney administration in a large number of documentaries, dramas, political thrillers, allegories, and satires; and presented very different views on class, race, gender, and sexuality than the conservative regime.

The first eight years of the new millennium exhibited intense political struggle and infamy, and Hollywood film was right at the center of the action, offering cinematic visions that provided contemporary viewers and future audiences insight into the nightmares of the period. As we enter a new era, there will no doubt be further crises, struggles, and dramatic events, and it will be fascinating to see how Hollywood film develops in the emerging historical moment.

Notes

1   For rightwing attacks on the purported liberalism of Hollywood films, see Medved (1993).

2   See the critique of Thomson's *Dictionary of Film* by Adrian Martin, "Chronicle of a backsliding cinephile, or The two Daves," *Cineaste* 28, 3 (Summer 2003): 11ff.

3   In a review of Thomson's book *The Whole Equation*, Richard Schickel (2008: 15ff) attributes the shortcomings of Thomson's attempts to capture the whole equation of Hollywood film to his primarily literary orientation toward film and focus on certain Hollywood studios, directors, and films to the exclusion of others.

4   A book anonymously published by a U.S. intelligence agent who was involved in torture and observed its limitations systematically critiques the failures of Bush/Cheney administration policies that legitimated torture and presents more humane and effective methods of interrogation; see Alexander and Bruning 2008.

5   McCrisken and Pepper (2005) distinguish between films that present an ideological version of American exceptionalism and/or dominant ideologies of the US as a force of universal progress and goodness, compared to films that question, oppose, and perhaps subvert an idealized view of US history.

6   On the enabling role of "Bush women," see Flanders (2004).

7   For reasons why George H. W. Bush Senior should not receive sympathy or respect, see the appendix to my book *Television and the Crisis of Democracy* (Kellner 1990). I document how the corporate media failed to probe into a lifetime of scandal for George H. W. Bush, the former CIA director, vice-president, and president, including his connections as CIA director with Panamanian dictator Manuel Noriega and other scoundrels; his possible role in the so-called October Surprise, in which there were serious allegations that it was George H. W. Bush who negotiated with the Iranians before the 1980 election to hold Americans hostage in Iran until after the election; his role as Reagan administration point man for Saddam Hussein during the 1980s, helping to secure loans and covert information for Iraq while it was fighting a vicious war with Iran (1980–1988); and Bush senior's key role in the Iran-contra scandal, in which illegal arms were sold to Iran while profits were given to the Nicaraguan contras fighting an illegal war condemned by Congress and the United Nations. The US corporate media's failure to expose these many scandals and crimes involving Bush senior enabled the rise of the wayward son and the horrors of the Bush-Cheney administration.

8   Members of the Nixon administration planned a break-in to the Democratic Party headquarters in the Watergate apartment complex in Washington

before the 1972 election. Senate hearings into the scandal led Richard Nixon to resign the presidency. The story is recounted in Carl Bernstein and Bob Woodward's 1974 book *All the President's Men*, made into a popular film in 1976.

9   Reviewers of *Milk* noted the uncanny resonance of Proposition 6 with the Proposition 8 initiative on the 2008 California ballot that would ban gay marriage, previously approved by the courts, and would thus take away hard-won gay and lesbian rights. This time, despite fierce opposition, strong financial support for the initiative by the Mormon church and evangelical Christians pushed the ballot through, producing protests that I observed shortly after the election in both San Francisco and Los Angeles, which had strong echoes of the earlier gay rights struggles that Harvey Milk was involved in. The power and success of the film *Milk* provides hope that gay marriage rights will be restored and nasty and bigoted homophobes will be forced back into the closet.

10 At the Landmark Cinema in Los Angeles on December 13, 2008, during a Q&A session following the screening, scriptwriter Peter Buchman said that while he had been researching the film for about seven years, during the last four years he had intensively read everything he could on Che. Benicio Del Toro recounted that he had been actively researching Che for about seven years. During at least six trips to Cuba Del Toro had interviewed individuals who had fought with Che and knew him, as well as researching Che's hometown and upbringing in Argentina. Che's early life does not come up in Soderbergh's film, but is presented in Walter Salle's *The Motorcycle Diaries* (2005), while Che's time as a functionary in the Cuban revolution is portrayed harshly in Andy Garcia's *The Lost City* (2005).

References

Books cited here are those that most influenced my work on cinema and contemporary politics. For film reviews, articles, websites, and other sources used in interpretation of a specific film or topic, see the notes to individual chapters.

Alexander, Matthew and Bruning, John (2008) *How to Break a Terrorist: The US Interrogators Who Used Brains, Not Brutality, to Take Down the Deadliest Man in Iraq.* New York: Free Press.

Baxter, John (1999) *Mythmaker: The Life and Work of George Lucas.* New York: Spike.

Benjamin, Walter (1969) [1934] "The Work of Art in the Age of Mechanical Reproduction" in *Illuminations.* New York: Shocken.

Berman, Marshall (1981) *All That is Solid Melts in Air.* New York: Simon and Schuster.

Best, Steven and Kellner, Douglas (1997) *The Postmodern Turn.* New York and London: Guilford Press and Routledge.

Best, Steven and Kellner, Douglas (2001) *The Postmodern Adventure: Science, Technology, and Cultural Studies at the Third Millennium.* New York and London: Guilford Press and Routledge.

Biskind, Peter (2004) *Down and Dirty Pictures: Miramax, Sundance and the Rise of Independent Film.* New York: Simon and Schuster.

Boggs, Carl and Pollard, Tom (2006) *The Hollywood War Machine: US Militarism and Popular Culture.* Boulder, CO: Paradigm.

Bordwell, David (2006) *The Way Hollywood Tells It: Story and Style in Modern Movies.* Berkeley: University of California Press.

Bordwell, David, Staiger, Janet, and Thompson, Kristin (1985) *The Classical Hollywood Cinema: Film Style and Mode of Production to 1960.* New York: Columbia University Press.

Brock, David (2004) *The Republican Noise Machine: Right-Wing Media and How It Corrupts Democracy.* New York: Crown.

Buck-Morss, Susan (1977) *The Origins of Negative Dialectics*. New York: Free Press.

Bugliosi, Vincent (2001) *The Betrayal of America: How the Supreme Court Undermined the Constitution and Chose Our President*. New York: Thunder's Mouth Press/Nation Books.

Cavell, Stanley (1971) *The World Viewed: Reflections on the Ontology of Film*. Cambridge, MA: Harvard University Press.

Centre for Contemporary Cultural Studies (1980) *On Ideology*. London: Hutchinson.

Clarke, Richard A. (2004) *Against All Enemies*. New York: Free Press.

Cooley, John (2002) *Unholy Wars: Afghanistan, America, and International Terrorism*. London: Pluto Press.

Coyne, Michael (2008) *Hollywood Goes to Washington: American Politics on Screen*. London: Reaktion Books.

Cubitt, Sean (2005) *Eco-Media*. New York: Rodopi.

Dean, John (2004) *Worse Than Watergate: The Secret Presidency of George W. Bush*. Boston: Little, Brown.

Dean, John (2006) *Conservatives Without Conscience*. New York: Viking.

Dean, John (2007) *Broken Government: How Republican Rule Destroyed the Legislative, Executive, and Judicial Branches*. New York: Viking.

Debord, Guy (1967) *Society of the Spectacle*. Detroit: Black and Red.

Deming, Barbara (1969) *Running Away from Myself*. New York: Grossman.

Dershowitz, Alan (2001) *Supreme Injustice: How the High Court Hijacked Election 2000*. New York: Oxford University Press.

Dick, Philip K. (1987) *The Collected Stories of Philip K. Dick*, Vol. 4. New York: Citadel Twilight.

Durham, Meenakshi Gigi and Kellner, Douglas M. (eds) (2006) *Media and Cultural Studies: Key Works*, 2nd edn. Oxford: Blackwell.

Final Report of the National Commission on Terrorist Attacks upon the United States (2004) *The 9/11 Commission Report*. New York: Norton.

Fitrakis, Bob and Wasserman, Harvey (2005) *How the GOP Stole America's 2004 Election and Is Rigging 2008*. Columbus, OH: CICJ Books.

Flanders, Laura (2004) *Bushwomen: How They Won the White House for Their Man*. London: Verso.

Foucault, Michel (1989) "Film and Popular Memory." In Sylvere Lotringer (ed.) *Foucault Live*. New York: Semiotext(e).

Gellman, Barton (2008) *Angler: The Cheney Vice-Presidency*. Baltimore: Penguin.

Greenwald, Glenn (2007) *A Tragic Legacy: How a Good Vs. Evil Mentality Destroyed the Bush Presidency*. New York: Crown.

Gumball, Andrew (2005) *Steal This Vote: Dirty Elections and the Rotten History of Democracy in America*. New York: Nation Books.

Hammer, Rhonda and Kellner, Douglas (eds) (2009a) *Media/Cultural Studies: Critical Approaches*. New York: Peter Lang.

Hammer, Rhonda and Kellner, Douglas (2009b) "The Gospel According to Mel Gibson: Critical Reflections on *The Passion of the Christ.*" In Joe L. Kincheloe and Shirley R. Steinberg (eds) *Christotainment: Selling Jesus through Popular Culture.* Bouldner: Westview Press, pp. 83–116.

Hardy, David T. and Clarke, Jason (2004) *Michael Moore is a Big Fat Stupid White Man.* New York: Regan.

Hatfield, J. H. (2000) *Fortunate Son: George W. Bush and the Making of an American President.* New York: Soft Skull Press.

Heath, Stephen (1981) *Questions of Cinema.* Bloomington: Indiana University Press.

Hersh, Seymour (2004) *Chain of Command: The Road from 9/11 to Abu Ghraib.* New York: Harper Collins.

Hilliard, Robert L. (2009) *Hollywood Speaks Out: Pictures that Dared to Protest Real World Issues.* Oxford: Wiley-Blackwell.

Horkheimer, Max and Adorno, T. W. (1972) *Dialectic of Enlightenment.* New York: Seabury Press.

Hunter, James Davison (1991) *Culture Wars: The Struggle to Define America.* New York: Basic Books.

Jameson, Fredric (1981) *The Political Unconscious.* Ithaca, NY: Cornell University Press.

Jameson, Fredric (1992) *The Geopolitical Aesthetic.* Bloomington: Indiana University Press.

Jeffords, Susan (1994) *Hard Bodies: Hollywood Masculinity in the Reagan Era.* New Brunswick, NJ: Rutgers University Press.

Jensen, Richard (1995) "The Culture Wars, 1965–1995: A Historian's Map," *Journal of Social History* 29: 17–37.

Jewett, Robert and Lawrence, John Shelton (2002) *The Myth of the American Superhero.* Grand Rapids, MI: Eerdmans.

Johnson, Chalmers (2000) *Blowback: The Costs and Consequences of American Empire.* New York: Henry Holt.

Johnson, Chalmers (2004) *The Sorrows of Empire: Militarism, Secrecy, and the End of the Republic.* New York: Henry Holt.

Johnson, Merri Lisa (ed.) (2007) *Third Wave Feminism and Television: Jane Puts It In A Box.* London: I. B. Taurus.

Jones, Stephen (2001) *Others Unknown.* New York: Public Affairs.

Kapell, Matthew Wilhelm and Lawrence, John Shelton (eds) (2006) *Finding the Force of the Star Wars Franchise: Fans, Merchants and Critics.* New York: Peter Lang.

Katz, Jackson (2006) *The Macho Paradox.* Naperville, IL: Sourcebook.

Keller, William and Mitchell, Gordon (eds) (2006) *Hitting First.* Pittsburgh: University of Pittsburgh Press.

Kellner, Douglas (1978) "Ideology, Marxism, and Advanced Capitalism," *Socialist Review* 42: 37–65.

Kellner, Douglas (1979) "TV, Ideology and Emancipatory Popular Culture," *Socialist Review* 45: 13–53.

Kellner, Douglas (1989) *Critical Theory, Marxism, and Modernity*. Cambridge, UK and Baltimore: Polity Press and Johns Hopkins University Press.

Kellner, Douglas (1990). *Television and the Crisis of Democracy*. Boulder, CO: Westview.

Kellner, Douglas (1995) *Media Culture: Cultural Studies, Identity and Politics between the Modern and the Postmodern*. London: Routledge.

Kellner, Douglas (1997) "Brecht's Marxist Aesthetic." In Siegfried Mews (ed.) *A Bertolt Brecht Reference Companion*. Westport, CT: Greenwood Press, pp. 281–95.

Kellner, Douglas (2001) *Grand Theft 2000*. Lanham, MD: Rowman and Littlefield.

Kellner, Douglas (2003a) *From 9/11 to Terror War: Dangers of the Bush Legacy*. Lanham, MD: Rowman and Littlefield.

Kellner, Douglas (2003b) *Media Spectacle*. London: Routledge.

Kellner, Douglas (2005) *Media Spectacle and the Crisis of Democracy*. Boulder, CO: Paradigm Press.

Kellner, Douglas (ed.) (2007a) *Art and Liberation*, Vol. 4 of *The Collected Writings of Herbert Marcuse*. London: Routledge.

Kellner, Douglas (2007b) "Bushspeak and the Politics of Lying: Presidential Rhetoric in the 'War On Terror,'" *Presidential Studies Quarterly* 37 (4): 622–45.

Kellner, Douglas (2008) *Guys and Guns Amok: Domestic Terrorism and School Shootings from the Oklahoma City Bombings to the Virginia Tech Massacre*. Boulder, CO: Paradigm Press.

Kellner, Douglas (2009) "Barack Obama and Celebrity Spectacle in the 2008 US Presidential Election," *International Journal of Communications* 3: 715–41.

Kellner, Douglas and Ryan, Michael (1988) *Camera Politica: The Politics and Ideology of Contemporary Hollywood Film*. Bloomington: Indiana University Press.

Kellner, Douglas and Streible, Dan (eds) (2000) *Film, Art and Politics: An Emile de Antonio Reader*. Minneapolis: University of Minnesota Press.

Kelley, Kitty (2004) *The Family: The Real Story of the Bush Dynasty*. New York: Doubleday.

Klein, Naomi (2007) *The Shock Doctrine: The Rise of Disaster Capitalism*. New York: Metropolitan Books.

Kracauer, Siegfried (1947) *From Caligari to Hitler: A Psychological History of the German Film*. Princeton: Princeton University Press.

Kuhn, Annette (1982) *Women's Pictures*. London: Routledge & Kegan Paul.

Larner, Jesse (2005) *Moore and Us*. London: Sanctuary Publishers.

Larner, Jesse (2006) *Forgive Us Our Spins: Michael Moore and the Future of the Left*. New York: Wiley.

Lawrence, John Shelton (2006) "Introduction: Spectacle, Merchandise, and Influence." In Matthew Wilhelm Kapell and John Shelton Lawrence (eds) *Finding the Force of the Star Wars Franchise: Fans, Merchants and Critics*. New York: Peter Lang, pp. 1–20.

Lawrence, Ken (2004) *The World According to Michael Moore*. Kansas City: Andrews McMeel Publishing.

Light, Andrew Ronald (2003) *Reel Arguments: Film, Philosophy and Social Criticism*. Boulder, CO: Westview Press.

McChesney, Robert (2000) *Rich Media, Poor Democracy: Communications Politics in Dubious Times*. New York: New Press.

McChesney, Robert (2007) *Communication Revolution: Critical Junctures and the Future of Media*. New York: New Press.

McCrisken, Trevor and Pepper, Andrew (2005) *American History and Contemporary Hollywood Film*. New Brunswick, NJ: Rutgers University Press.

McVeigh, Stephen P. (2006) "The Galactic Way of Warfare." In Matthew Wilhelm Kapell and John Shelton Lawrence (eds) *Finding the Force of the Star Wars Franchise: Fans, Merchants and Critics*. New York: Peter Lang, pp. 35–58.

Mamber, Stephen (1974) *Cinéma Vérité in America: Studies in Uncontrolled Documentary*. Cambridge, MA: MIT Press.

Mann, Michael (2003) *Incoherent Empire*. London: Verso.

Marcuse, Herbert (1979) *The Aesthetic Dimension*. Boston: Beacon Press.

Mayer, Jane (2008) *The Dark Side: The Inside Story of How The War on Terror Turned into a War on American Ideals*. New York: Doubleday.

Medved, Michael (1993) *Hollywood vs. America*. New York: Harper.

Metz, Christian (1974) *Language and Cinema*. The Hague: Mouton.

Miller, Mark Crispin (2004) *Cruel and Unusual: Bush/Cheney's New World Order*. New York: Norton.

Miller, Mark Crispin (2005) *Fooled Again: The Real Case for Electoral Reform (Unless We Stop Them)*. New York: Basic Books.

Mitchell, Elizabeth (2000) *Revenge of the Bush Dynasty*. New York: Hyperion.

Moore, James and Slater, Wayne (2003) *Bush's Brain: How Karl Rove Made George W. Bush Presidential*. New York: John Wiley.

Moore, Michael (2003) *Stupid White Man ... and Other Sorry Excuses for the State of the Nation*. New York: Regan Books.

Moore, Michael (2004) *The Official Fahrenheit 9/11 Reader*. New York: Simon and Schuster.

Nichols, John (2004) *Dick: The Man Who Is President (Dick Cheney)*. New York: New Press.

Orwell, George (1961) [1948] *1984*. New York: Signet.

Palast, Greg (2003) *The Best Democracy Money Can Buy: The Truth about Corporate Cons, Globalization, and High-Finance Fraudsters*. New York: Plume.

Parry, Robert (2004) *Secrecy and Privilege: The Rise of the Bush Dynasty from Watergate to Iraq*. Arlington, VA: Media Consortium.

Phillips, Kevin (2004) *American Dynasty: Aristocracy, Fortune, and the Politics of Deceit in the House of Bush*. New York: Viking.

Phillips, Kevin (2006) *American Theocracy: The Peril and Politics of Radical Religion, Oil, and Borrowed Money in the 21st Century*. New York: Viking.

Pierson, John (1995) *Spike, Mike, Slackers and Dykes. A Guided Tour Across a Decade of American Independent Cinema*. New York: Hyperion.

Powdermaker, Hortense (1950) *Hollywood: The Dream Factory*. Boston: Little, Brown.

Robb, David L. (2004) *Operation Hollywood*. Amherst, NY: Prometheus Books.

Schechter, Danny (2008) *Plunder: Investigating Our Economic Calamity and the Subprime Scandal*. New York: Cosimo Books.

Schickel, Richard (2008) *Film on Paper: The Inner Life of Movies*. Chicago: Ivan R. Dee.

Schulz, Emily (2005) *Michael Moore: A Biography*. Toronto: ECW Press.

Semmerling, Tim Jon (2006) *"Evil" Arabs in American Popular Film: Orientalist Fear*. Austin: University of Texas Press.

Shaheen, Jack G. (2001) *Reel Bad Arabs: How Hollywood Villifies a People*. New York: Olive Branch Press.

Sharrett, Chris (ed.) (1993) *Crisis Cinema: The Apocalyptic Idea in Postmodern Narrative Film*. Washington, DC: Maisonneuve Press.

Sklar, Robert (1975) *Movie-Made America: A Social History of American Film*. New York: Random House.

Staiger, Janet (1991) *Interpreting Films: Studies in the Historical Reception of American Cinema*. Princeton: Princeton University Press.

Stroup, John M. and Glenn W. Shuck (2007) *Escape into the Future. Cultural Pessimism and its Religious Dimension in Contemporary American Popular Culture*. Waco, TX: Baylor University Press.

Suskind, Ron (2006) *The One-Percent Doctrine*. New York: Simon and Schuster.

Thompson, John (1990) *Ideology and Modern Culture*. Cambridge, UK and Stanford, CA: Polity Press and Stanford University Press.

Thompson, Kirsten Moana (2007) *Apocalyptic Dread: American Film at the Turn of the Millennium*. Albany: State University of New York Press.

Thomson, David (2004) *The Whole Equation: A History of Hollywood*. New York: Vintage Books.

Toplin, Robert Brent (2006) *Michael Moore's Fahrenheit 9/11: How One Film Divided a Nation*. Lawrence: University of Kansas Press.

Tyler, Parker (1944) *The Hollywood Hallucination*. New York: Simon and Schuster.

Tyler, Parker (1947) *Myth and Magic of the Movies*. New York: Simon and Schuster.

Tzioumakis, Yannis (2006) *American Independent Cinema*. New Brunswick, NJ: Rutgers University Press.

Vidal, Gore (2002) *Perpetual War for Perpetual Peace: How We Got To Be So Hated*. New York: Thunder Mouth Press/Nation Books.

Vidal, Gore (2003) *Dreaming War: Blood for Oil and the Cheney-Bush Junta*. New York: Thunder Mouth Press/Nation Books.

Wilson, Joseph (2004) *The Politics of Truth: A Diplomat's Memoir: Inside the Lies that Led to War and Betrayed My Wife's CIA Identity*. New York: Carroll and Graf.

Wolfenstein, Martha and Leites, Nathan (1950) *Movies: A Psychological Study*. Glencoe, IL: Free Press.

Wood, Robin (1986) *Hollywood from Vietnam to Reagan*. New York: Columbia University Press.

Woodward, Bob (2003) *Bush at War*. New York: Simon and Schuster.

Woodward, Bob (2004) *Plan of Attack*. New York: Simon and Schuster.

Woodward, Bob (2006) *State of Denial*. New York: Simon and Schuster.

Wright, Lawrence (2006) *The Looming Tower: Al Qaeda and the Road to 9/11*. New York: Knopf.

Index